New Library of ?
GENERAL EDITOR

Derek Blows is a psychother
Hospital, a Professional M
Analytical Psychology and
Westminster Pastoral Foundation. He is also an honorary
canon of Southwark Cathedral.

Listen to the Voice Within

Titles in this series include:

New Library of Pastoral Care
GENERAL EDITOR: DEREK BLOWS

———

LISTEN TO
THE VOICE WITHIN

A Jungian Approach to Pastoral Care

———

Christopher Perry

First published in Great Britain 1991
SPCK
Holy Trinity Church
Marylebone Road
London NW1 4DU

Second impression 1992

British Library Cataloguing in Publication Data

Perry, Christopher
Listen to the voice within: a Jungian approach to
pastoral care.
1. Christian church. Pastoral work. Psychological aspects
I. Title   II. Series
253.52

ISBN 0-281-04497-X

Filmset by Pioneer, Perthshire
Printed in Great Britain by
The Longdunn Press Ltd, Bristol

To Roland, Clement and Margot

The meaning and purpose of a problem seem to lie not in its solution but in working at it incessantly. C. G. Jung, CW8 para 771

Contents

Acknowledgements

I would like to express my thanks to Routledge for permission to quote from *The Collected Works* of C. G. Jung (abbreviated to CW, plus volume and paragraph number), and to Faber and Faber Ltd and Harcourt Brace Jovanovich, Orlando, Florida, for permission to quote extracts from *Four Quartets* by T. S. Eliot.

I am very grateful to Victoria Graham Fuller, Roderick Peters, Richard Rusbridger, Malcolm Rushton, Jean Thomson, Jan Wiener and Nicholas Zinovieff. Their critical comments on the first draft of the book nudged me into greater efforts to regain a focus when my vision was becoming blurred. Their helpful suggestions in no way detract from my taking full responsibility for what I have written.

Out of the many people who have helped, influenced, taught and encouraged me along the way, I wish to mention Richard Crocket, Sally Hornby, Pat de Maré, Norah Moore, Joseph Redfearn, Ronald St Blaise-Molony, Mannie Sher and Mary Williams. I am truly thankful for all that each from their different roles and unique perspectives gave me.

I owe a special debt to Catherine Clancy for providing a stringent critique of the final draft, for drawing the three diagrams, but most particularly for her unfailing support.

Mrs Pamela Edwards has been unstinting in her commitment to seeing the manuscript through to its end, and amazingly thorough in her secretarial assistance; my thanks to her.

I have been greatly helped by Derek Blows, the Series Editor, who, with his feet in the camps of the ministry and analytical psychology, has needled me into enough irritation to attempt repeatedly to clarify my thinking a little further.

Judith Longman has been a steady and constant presence throughout this venture. She has nursed it along from its chaotic embryonic beginnings into its present form with a faith that has been encouraging in times of doubt.

Finally, this book could not have been written without the goodwill, support and tolerance of my family.

Christopher Perry
Chiswick, London
June 1990

Introduction

As a young and newly trained psychiatric social worker, I obtained my first job in what was in those days called an approved school, a school approved by the Home Office for the care, control and education of senior adolescent boys deemed by the courts as unruly and antisocial. The school was in the process of being transformed into a therapeutic community, and had as its headmaster a man who was shrewd and politically astute, the son of a prison governor. From his early professional life as a worker with the delinquent and disadvantaged youth of his time, he had spotted the need for an establishment that catered for boys of high intelligence, a sort of grammar school of approved schools, and had persuaded the Home Office of this need.

I was appointed initially as the full-time, and later the part-time, representative of a psychiatric team, consisting of a social psychiatrist, who was the director of a therapeutic community, and a psychoanalyst, who was the director of a child-guidance clinic. My job was to assess each boy admitted in terms of his psychological, developmental and social needs; to conduct therapeutic groups for the boys, and, at a later stage, a community meeting for the entire establishment; and to participate in a weekly staff group, in which the concerns of the staff could be aired, explored and, in some cases, resolved. Other aspects of the job included dealing with some of the families of these adolescents, who were often mystified and deeply hurt by their offspring's delinquency, and liaising with a diversity of social and psychiatric provision throughout the country.

Shortly after I arrived at this establishment, I was sent the referral notes of a sixteen-year-old arsonist. He and a friend had burned down their entire school in the suburbs of a large city. This boy, Rufus, had an almost immeasurably high IQ.

1

Nothing wayward, unusual or fascinating had been noted about him by those who had educated or cared for him, including his parents. Why, then, this extraordinary act of destruction, anger and excitement? What could be the purpose of such an act? This question took on a new meaning when his housemaster pleaded with me to come over on Christmas Day and stop him from laboriously and compulsively freezing himself. What he had been doing all day was to go up and down the playing fields as if he were mowing the lawn. In fact, he had started at one corner with a handful of snow and had rolled this into a snowball so large that he could no longer move it. Then, like Sisyphus, he would start again. By the time I arrived, I was seething with resentment at being called out on Christmas Day (although officially 'on-call'), but also in the grip of a heroic rescue fantasy. As I came along the drive, I beheld this forlorn figure in shirtsleeves surveying his collection of giant snowballs, apparently oblivious of the elements. To what inner voice was he listening? We spoke for a while, and he told me of his fantasy—namely, that he wanted to bury the school in an avalanche of snow. He had declined from going home for Christmas—in the circumstances a healthily angry gesture—but was re-experiencing an upsurge of murderous hatred displaced on to those *in loco parentis*.

I had done some basic studying of human development; I thought I understood something about transference, defences, anxiety about change, group processes, etc. But I quickly discovered that I was out of my depth. At the suggestion of the psychoanalyst I saw Rufus individually every week for almost two years. I also had him in a small group, in community meetings and in family sessions. I found myself colluding with the school in the role of rescuer, and was sometimes the only person who could truncate his violence, and grope, however inadequately, towards an understanding of what at that moment was disturbing him. When he was caught between the opposites of fire and ice, I was caught between the opposites of inflated know-how and terrifying ignorance. The teaching staff found him unteachable, and so closeted him in a room where he was allowed to get on with his own learning, very successfully. He was masterly in the arts of painting and music, as well as being an enthusiastic sportsman. Socially, he remained rather aloof, while at the same time appearing to be uncannily in touch with unconscious anxieties in other people. When his housemaster and a member of the female staff had an affair, he managed to persuade all the boys in his house to reverse their seats in the weekly house meeting so that all the chairs were turned away from the centre of the group, a sort of 'turning a blind eye'. This was one of the clues to the complicated sexual relationships that were taking place inside and outside the family.

I was faced with his internal pathology, the pathology in the family, its transposition to the community in which he now lived, and the denial, yet awareness, in the staff group that the affair was taking place. Furthermore, in the course of my work with him, I was faced every week with the extraordinary and disquieting phenomenon of being related to as if I were someone else. I felt as if I was flying by the seat of my pants and that my inner voice was buried under layers of confusion. Essentially, I found it hard to think for myself in the space of craziness, and felt buffeted by powerful institutional processes.

All this took place in the context of three major developments in the field of mental health — the growth of the therapeutic community movement; the influence of R. D. Laing and the Existentialists in understanding 'madness' and in envisioning traditional psychiatry as a form of social control; and the burgeoning of family therapy. What all these had in common was the belief that an individual became disturbed as a result of being in a disturbed and disturbing network of relationships.

During and after the Second World War, there sprang up all over Europe and the United States a new approach to the understanding and treatment of the so-called mentally ill. What was of interest was that the pioneers of this movement were for some time working independently and in ignorance of each other's ventures. The movement was, then, in Jung's terms, a 'synchronistic event':

a meaningful coincidence of two or more events, where something other than the probability of chance is involved. (CW8 para 969)

Names such as Wilfred Bion, Richard Crocket, Maxwell Jones, Tom Main and Pat de Maré come to mind. What these and others had in common was the conviction that psychological stress arose not only from intra-personal conflict, but also from difficulties in inter-personal relationships. The aim of the therapeutic community was to create a structure in which dyadic (therapist and patient, patient and therapist, therapist and therapist, etc.) group, community and family processes could be used to enhance the social and psychological functioning of the individual. Gone were the white coats, the ECT, the indiscriminate use of drug prescription, the pathologising of the 'named' patient in the family. What was here to stay was the notion that psychological disturbance arose from difficulties in inter-personal communication.

In the early 1960s, R. D. Laing and his colleagues in England and the Palo Alto group in the United States were working on issues of communication and communicative behaviour. The notion of the 'double-bind' ('If you speak, I will hit you; if you don't speak, I will hit you') was explored extensively as a major contributory factor to the genesis of mental illness. Relationships were classified as symmetrical (where the participants exchange the same type of behaviour in a competitive way) and complementary (where the participants exchange different types of behaviour that complement one another). This sort of classification enabled workers in the field to reach a fairly rapid understanding of the processes that were taking place within families and marriages, the sequences of communications, and the shifts between the types of relationships that individual members were required to make or prevented from making.

By 1970 there were something like 2,000 books and papers on family therapy, the development of which I will not go into here. There was also a growing literature on therapeutic communities, and the vast literature produced by analytical psychologists and psychoanalysts. What I felt I needed at that time was an introductory text that would act as a sort of Ariadne's thread to help me find my way through the labyrinth of the human psyche and its manifestation in relationships and in group and organisational settings.

This need jumped out at me from the recesses of time when, some years later, I had the opportunity to work as a consultant with the London Diocese Pastoral Support Group Scheme. It quickly became apparent that the members of those groups were faced almost daily with Rufus-like characters and situations, beavering away at trying to understand them and at discharging their pastoral role conscientiously and beneficially to the people involved. They, like me, seemed to be searching for a framework within which their everyday work experiences could be conceptualised and understood — in other words, that what seemed mystifying or meaningless could be transformed into something comprehensible and meaningful. Similarly, counsellors and other professionals working in a multitude of agencies, all of which could be seen as pastoral in the original sense of the word (i.e. nourishing), seemed engaged in a similar search.

To put it another way, we all seemed to notice from time to time that the inner voice was drowned out by hectic schedules, an eclectic conglomeration of ideas and techniques, normal and everyday personal difficulties, agency pressures and dynamics. We needed a form through which the in-form-ation could be received and processed.

Then Derek Blows asked me one day if I would be interested in writing a book on Jung and religion. I wasn't very enthusiastic, but went away and produced an extremely crazy document of a couple of pages called 'A Journey into the Square Root of Minus 1' — an extremely unpromising beginning, looked at objectively in the light of my poor mathematical ability! The title had appeared in a dream along with much of the content. It was a sort of free association around some of Jung's central concepts. My anxiety about producing something had taken the form of an abstract, fragmented synopsis. Once this was metabolised, the true form could emerge, and I then had space to play. But I did not know why or for whom I was writing; nor, in the subsequent months, did I understand from where the material came. As a dream has us, rather than the other way round, so this book had me, generated by my own clinical work, supervision and teaching throughout my professional life.

The aim of the book is to offer to all those working in pastoral settings, be they parishes, schools, hospitals, community agencies etc., a way of understanding the intricacies of relationships between and within people. I am writing as an analytical psychologist, someone who subscribes to the ideas of C. G. Jung, and not as a theologian. But the reader will see that I also draw quite extensively on psychoanalysis since I believe that Jung's emphasis on spirituality and later life needs the counter-balance of the psychoanalytic understanding of early development and the meaning this has throughout our lives.

A note on terminology: because of the range of professional situations discussed in the text, I have found it impossible to be consistent about the use of words such as 'pastor', 'parishioner', 'counsellor', 'client', 'therapist', 'patient'. I hope the context will make the meaning clear, but wish to emphasise that the roles of pastor, on the one hand, and psychodynamic counsellor/therapist/analyst on the other are very different, the latter being trained to work with unconscious processes and, through interpretation, bring these into consciousness.

The book has a basic structure consisting of numerous quotes from Jung, case examples and explanatory text. Jung is quoted in the hope that he will speak to the reader directly, and the case examples are offered in the hope that some of them at least will resonate in the reader at both a personal and professional level. Details and characteristics of the case examples have been disguised to preserve confidentiality.

In Chapter 1, I engage with the thorny issue of the inner voice that draws us into one of the so-called 'helping professions', tease out the positive and negative aspects of such a calling, and suggest a possible structure of support for those engaged in pastoral work. The notion of support leads into Chapter 2, where I outline some of the main developmental tasks that confront the individual on his journey through life. These are seen as a series of opposites that need to be transcended. The very transcendence of them generates anxiety about change, the containment of and resistance to which is the subject of Chapter 3. The universal anxiety and anger that is evoked by change leads into Chapter 4, where I catalogue some of the ways and means by which we defend ourselves from excessive anxiety provoked by threats from the inner and outer world, ranging from the infant's threat of annihilation to the adult's threat of being overwhelmed by internal imagery, feeling or impulse or, indeed, nuclear disaster.

Just as defences can disguise the inner world, so the phenomenon of transference can distort our perception of the outer world, and intertwine the two in a plait of confusion so that figures in the present are experienced in terms of significant others of the past. Thus, in Chapter 5 various types of this distortion are outlined and described along with the counterpoint of transference, which is counter-transference. What is confusing enough in a dyadic relationship becomes even more confusing in group and institutional settings, which form the subject matter of Chapter 6, in which space is given to groups, the detailed examination of an organisation, and the contentious issue of women's role in the Church, an issue that is amplified in a classically Jungian way.

While Chapters 5 and 6 are addressed to relating to the Other outside oneself, Chapter 7 is devoted to relating to the Other within. I try to distinguish areas of difference between theology and psychology. There follows an exploration of some of the manifestations of the Other within, along with three modes of relating to the Other—befriending dreams, meditation, and active imagination.

In Chapter 8 impediments to healthy separation are viewed from within the opposites of clinging and severing, both of which arise from anxious attachments early on in life. An attempt is made to understand suicidal behaviour as a special form of severing. A section on dying leads full circle back to the problems of pastor–parishioner, counsellor–client separating from one another.

Those readers not well acquainted with Jungian terminology will find a glossary of the main concepts used in this book.

ONE

Discerning the Pastoral Calling

As psyche cannot replace soul, professionalism cannot substitute for vocation. (James Hillman, *Insearch: Psychology and Religion*)

The words 'profession' and 'vocation' tend to stand in a shadow position to each other. Profession is often seen as the darker (shadow) side of vocation. This creates a polarity whereby to side with one is to lose the strengths and weaknesses of the other. The professional (in origin, he who is bound by a religious vow) is paid to perform a task to the best of his ability within a society of colleagues, usually hierarchically structured, and, by implication, oriented to achievement in the outer world. This is recognised by achieved and ascribed status and power. To perform the task, the professional has to train in order to learn the necessary skills. Many professionals feel 'called' by an inner voice, parental expectation, aptitude, or any combination of these factors. The professional sometimes sees the vocational (s/he who is divinely guided towards a special work in life) as a wishy-washy figure, undermining professional standards, and possessing only vague boundaries between a work and a private self; self-sacrifice and the eschewing of material rewards are his or her hallmarks; s/he is engrossed in an esoteric inner journey of little value in contemporary life. The vocational's picture of the professional is also imaginable.

These stereotypes are understandable at a time that is witnessing a drift from the sanctuary to the counselling room, instilling in the pastor a feeling of inadequacy about his vocation and urging him towards the acquisition of professional counselling skills. What is lost in the drift is the awareness that pastor and counsellor both rely in a most profound way on an inner relation with their souls.

Hillman helps us with the idea of soul: 'Soul is a symbol . . .

[that] we take to refer to that unknown human factor which makes meaning possible, which turns events into experiences, which is communicated in love and has a religious concern' (Hillman, 1964). This relation with the soul, with the spacious depths of the interior, unconscious life that is common to us all, makes human communication possible and comprehensible. The more idiosyncratic I am in my behaviour, thought and language, the less accessible I am to comprehension by someone else. This is not to say that my images, my feelings, my experiences, my ideas are not existentially mine. Of course, in one sense they are. In another, they are not. They are borne out of the collective, inherited, culturally determined, and yet shared, basis of all human life. We are at once confronted with the thesis of individuality and the antithesis of collectivity, out of which the task of synthesis through individuation (becoming what I am) in the personal, vocational and professional sense arises. Once the relation with the soul is established, even in barely embryonic form, then there is room to turn to the relation with the Other, which can also be informed by the understandings of depth psychology. In developmental terms, we are groping towards the first I–Thou relationship, that between child and mother, which is the prototype of the relationship between I as the centre of consciousness, and Thou as a supraordinate being, known variously as soul, self, God-image or *unus mundus* (one world). In some Eastern traditions, this is the relationship hinted at in the saying, 'The moment the wave realises that it is part of the ocean.'

The pastor in contemporary society sometimes feels torn between upholding a tradition of stillness in being and contemplation, and a more recent push into busy-ness in doing and social action. The former is often vocationally based; the latter professionally motivated. The care of souls collides with the cure of problems. The space in between, that which allows for healing, for becoming whole, gets filled in with dogma not based on experience or with techniques, which blinds the spontaneous, intuitive, human response.

I was once consulted by a pastor who had been approached by a man for help. This man, Tony, was middle-aged and single. The pastor was experienced and of a similar age to his client, but he had been on a training course at a revered institution and had been taught about depression. Tony was a bit late for his appointment. He looked bedraggled, was dressed in grey; his face was drawn, his posture limp. He spoke slowly, very quietly. The pastor ran through a list of symptoms, systematically checking them out, and came to the 'scientific' conclusion that Tony was depressed. I casually asked the pastor what he had felt immediately on encountering Tony. His reply was: 'My God, this man is depressed.' Within seconds of their meeting, the pastor knew. His life experience, his relation with his own soul, his intuition and his capacity to reflect on it had been beclouded by a more professional approach embodied in a symptom check. The question I pose throughout this book is: How can we reconcile relation with the soul to the purposeful use of skill?

Elizabeth:

Elizabeth was in her late thirties. She had lost an arm in a farming accident when she was fourteen. Two years later her mother died, leaving Elizabeth, the eldest of seven children, as the surrogate mother. Handicapped by her artificial arm she struggled heroically to bring up the children, battling against poverty brought on by her grief-stricken father's heavy drinking. Her maternal duties discharged, she was accepted by an order of nuns and was soon noticed for her managerial competence and efficiency.

After a while, she felt over-burdened by the cares of others, and applied to live as a religious in a lay community. At the same time, she was given the job in the Province of counselling those wishing to leave the order. She had her first sexual relationship with a man, which confirmed her in her belief that for her it was marriage or celibacy, nothing in between. Otherwise, she remained friendless. She obtained a place on a counselling course and went into personal therapy, with a therapist who 'tried to replace my mother'. This failed, and she went into intensive therapy, which nearly broke down when her therapist developed cancer, happily treatable.

There came a time when she wished to further her counselling training. For the first time in her life, she failed to get what she wanted. Among several difficult questions she had been asked was one that inquired into her reasons for wanting to do counselling. She had fallen into a long and tense silence, which she had broken by 'confessing' to her distress at losing two of her clients. She was advised to continue with her therapy and to gain more experience.

This may sound like a harsh judgement on someone who had so effectively cared for others for most of her life. But what Elizabeth's interviewer and her supervisors and teachers had all noticed was a one-sidedness in her towards professionalism at the expense of what beckoned from within — the loss of her arm affecting her changing body image during adolescence and her perception of herself as a whole woman; the loss of her mother at a time when the need to depend on her and to rebel against her would have been tossing her about; the loss of her adolescence in the sense of relating to a peer group; the premature thrust into parenthood; the loss of her father to the stupefying effect of excess alcohol; the threatened loss of her second therapist, which the interviewer rightly or wrongly linked with the loss of her mother, a link Elizabeth had not managed to make.

All these considerations led her trainers to feel that the interior relation with her soul was not sufficiently well established to enable her to create a space into which an Other could unfold, explore and develop.

It was in 1921, in his paper 'The Therapeutic Value of Abreaction', that Jung made the first of his many and insistent pleas that anyone proposing to embark on the profession of psychotherapy should first of all experience the dialectical relationship into which they would enter with their future clients. He goes so far as to say:

> The doctor who has no wish for [analysis] . . . will be found wanting, cling as he may to his petty conceit of authority. . . . How can the patient learn to abandon his neurotic subterfuges when he sees the doctor playing hide-and-seek with his own personality, as though unable, for fear of being thought inferior, to drop the professional mask of authority, competence, superior knowledge, etc.? (CW16 para 287–8)

Freud was hard on the heels of Jung when, in 1926, he outlined the requirements of preparation for analytic activity which 'is by no means so easy and simple'. It included a course of instruction, a personal analysis, the acquisition of knowledge and the learning of a technique. A little later in the same paper, 'The Question of Lay Analysis', he states categorically: 'no one should practise analysis who has not acquired the right to do so by a particular training' (Freud, 1926, p. 336).

The two founding fathers were approaching the question of personal therapy for those in the helping professions from very different perspectives; but enough evidence can be adduced from various passages in their extensive writings to convince us that they were both concerned about the possibility of interference in the therapeutic relationship by unconscious elements in the personality of the helper that might create blind spots in his work, which, at worst, could damage the client. A response to such concerns has become enshrined in almost all psychotherapy training through the pride of place given to personal therapy.

The question can be stated simply: How can you possibly give help if you have no experience of having received it? In Chapter 3, I allude to the feelings of loss of independence and drop in self-image commonly experienced at the moment the client acknowledges his need for someone else. Then there are the barriers to trust to be negotiated; the testing of trustworthiness; the emergence of dependence; the guilt and embarrassment of talking about painful feelings and experiences; the fears of being overwhelmed by emotion and unsavoury impulses; the feeling of being intruded upon by someone supposed to be helping; the frustrations imposed by the limited availability of the person in the helping role; the fear of burdening that person; the agonising conflict over how to express negative feelings to the person upon whom the client is dependent; the dawning awareness that the feelings and images attached to the helper seem awkwardly disproportionate to the situation; the delight or horror at experiencing and wanting to act upon sexual feelings that emerge between the two people; worries about confidentiality; anxiety about change and growth; the loss of old ways of being and doing and the acclimatisation to new-found aspects of the self, new self-awareness, new skills; the grief, gratitude and possible disappointment at the end of the encounter; the relief and joy at the restoration of independence. To read about these feelings in a book is to know *about* them, but not to know them; it is like reading a map rather than travelling through the territory.

We are already at a level different from that which Freud mentions:

> Our friends among the protestant clergy, and more recently amongst the catholic clergy as well, are often able to relieve their parishioners of the inhibitions of their daily life by confirming their faith—after having first offered them a little analytic information about the nature of their conflicts. (Freud, 1926, p. 360)

Such analytic information is based partly on life experience, partly on commonsense, and partly on knowledge. The more it is based on knowledge, the more likely will it be experienced by the parishioner as the spoutings from books of an Old Wise Man, who lacks authenticity and is unaware, too unaware, of aspects of himself.

One such potential blind spot is the multi-faceted motivation that both fuels the urge to help others and creates the profile of the so-called 'helping personality'. The 'helping personality' is a term that embraces those engaged in the ministry, in social work, health visiting, medicine, teaching, psychotherapy, clinical psychology, etc. Before we examine the constituents of the helping personality, here is an example of someone so driven by the urge to help that he ended up in a state of breakdown.

Jim:

Jim was twenty-eight, bright, well-regarded by his social-work colleagues in the psychiatric hospital in which he worked. After the Easter festivities, he went off for a week's climbing in the Lake District. On the second day, he lost his footing and had to be carried by his companions down to the hotel, where the local doctor diagnosed a leg broken in two places. Jim returned home and insisted on getting back to work as soon as possible, fearing that his patients at the hospital would be collapsing without him.

His appearance in the staff room on his first morning back was met with a mixture of welcome and resentment over his absence. He went to his office, and was immediately telephoned by a neighbour of one of his most long-standing clients, a single mother, prone to battering her children. The neighbour had heard screaming during the night and was concerned for the children. Jim and his senior did a home visit, examined the children, and found them bruised; they later obtained a Place of Safety order on the children and removed them amid a hail of abuse from the mother. Later in the day, Jim was approached by a boy from the adolescent unit about a hostel application Jim had made on the boy's behalf. Jim explained that he had not had time to look through his mail to see if there was a reply to the application. The boy went off in a rage and returned with a broken milk bottle, threatening to attack himself or Jim unless immediate action was taken. Jim was paralysed. He was rescued by another patient, who had heard the sound of broken glass, investigated, and called the security staff. They removed the boy, who was subsequently discharged.

Jim returned home that evening, had a quick snack, and hobbled off to a meeting of his political party. After that, he called in on an ex-girlfriend, who had left a message on his answering machine, saying she was depressed and needed to talk to someone. The next day, Jim dragged himself off to work. He had never felt so unwilling. He tramped his way through the day like a robot, frustrated by his restricted mobility but alarmingly disconnected from his work. The evening was punctuated by a PCC meeting, during which he uncharacteristically exploded at the organist, who had put in for the annual rise of his choristers. The committee sat spellbound, uncomfortably silent, its members all looking down embarrassedly at their papers and impotent to intervene.

The meeting ended and the pastor invited Jim round for coffee, guaranteeing him a lift home afterwards, despite Jim's protestations that he would enjoy the walk! The pastor noticed the tautness of the skin across Jim's face, the agitated tapping of his fingers on the armchair, the distractedness in his presence. They got talking, and it was not long before the pastor had pieced together a grim mosaic of Jim's week. The days were spent with disturbed and sometimes violent people; evenings and weekends were a series of committees, political meetings, duty rotas for a voluntary organisation, all interspersed with 'social' engagements with a collection of lame ducks and drakes. The pastor diagnosed a very serious gap between emotional income and expenditure, made a joke about Jim's broken leg being a symbol of his need to get something back from someone, and suggested they meet again to see what changes could be made.

At their second meeting, the pastor poured out some coffee and casually remarked that Jim looked exhausted. This produced an angry confirmation from Jim, who suddenly burst into tears and confessed his secret fear that he was cracking up and burnt out as a social worker. When Jim was calmer, the pastor offered his view of the situation and confirmed Jim's self-diagnosis. He suggested two courses of action: first, that Jim should approach his line manager to discuss his workload and the possibility of some time off; second, he firmly pushed him towards seeking personal therapy, where he would get the opportunity of feeling looked after himself and be able to explore the reasons for his compulsive helping of others.

This example illustrates several points. Jung envisaged the psyche as a self-regulatory system, in which the elements of psychic life strive constantly for balance through the 'regulative function of opposites'. From Heraclitus, Jung borrowed the term enantiodromia, a process in which everything extreme eventually runs into its opposite. Thus, if an extreme one-sided view is held in consciousness, an equally powerful counter-position will build up in the unconscious, and the one will eventually swing into the other. The law of enantiodromia underlies Jung's principle of compensation:

> . . . every process that goes too far immediately and inevitably calls forth compensations. (CW16 para 330)

The counter-position in the unconscious builds up until it

finally bursts through into consciousness like a volcano in the form of symptoms, dreams or images.

Jim was someone who spent his life giving out to others, whom he encouraged to become dependent on him. There was little mutuality in his life and he received little or no nurturing from the love and hate of everyday human contact with a partner, friends or colleagues. The needy side of him, which he despised, had been repressed into his unconscious, where, like a dog locked in a cellar, it became hungrier and fiercer by the day, until it finally broke forth on the mountain, forcing Jim into dependence and hospital. His habitual attitude to life quickly reasserted itself, and he returned prematurely to work, having failed to get the message. Very soon he encountered his needy self projected on to the threatening adolescent, and again the next day in the form of the organist's request for a rise for his choristers. On that second occasion, the hatred and anger he had denied and not expressed to the adolescent flared up inappropriately in a meeting, where it shocked both himself and the committee members. At work, he had related mechanically, feeling empty within himself of anything to give out to others.

We can speculate on some of the reasons for Jim's behaviour. Perhaps his childhood had been so deprived that he was driven into compulsive reparative activity, feeling constantly guilty and trying hard to restore the internal parents he felt he had damaged; alternatively, his ego, the executive part of his personality, had become a victim to inflation (feeling grandiose and behaving accordingly) and identified with an archetypal image (e.g. a Messianic figure). Jung explained that such an image

> seizes hold of the psyche with a kind of primeval force and compels it to transgress the bounds of humanity. The consequence is a puffed-up attitude, loss of free will, delusion and enthusiasm for good or evil alike. (CW7 para 110)

Another form of identification may have taken place, an identification with his persona. In Jungian psychology this is a term that describes the mask, dress, expectations and behaviours that are attached to any social role, such as clergyman, social worker, doctor, etc. When a person identifies with the persona, he loses contact with his inner world and tends to focus entirely on external reality and events. His presentation of himself will tend to feel hollow to the onlooker, like an eggshell devoid of its contents. This pathological identification with the persona links us back to the profile of the 'helping personality'.

This profile was analysed rigorously by Hugh Eadie (Eadie, 1975, pp.2–22), who identified quite distinctive characteristics, and drew on the work of the psychoanalyst Karen Horney to underpin his observations. The profile breaks down into eight components:

(1) idealised self-image: the appeal of love;
(2) guilt: self-hate and self-criticism;
(3) compulsive–obsessive characteristics;
(4) affective controls on sexuality and aggression;
(5) passivity, compliance and conformity;
(6) attempts to resolve the conflicts;
(7) intro-punitive hostility and self-hate;
(8) stress symptoms.

Eadie suggests that it is an idealised self-image that acts as the 'springboard' for the helping personality. The pastor is beleaguered by internal moral injunctions, which make his life patterned by 'shoulds' and 'should nots' congregating respectively round positive and negative feelings. The primary conflict lies in a conviction that self-denial subsumes love of others. Feeding the pressure to love others is the fear of isolation, which his vocation and role can easily impose upon him. To reduce isolation, the pastor exudes love and warmth, at the same time neutralising any aggressive impulses.

Several studies are cited by Eadie to support his claim that pastors are more prone than any other professional group to feelings of guilt, self-criticism and self-denigration. This guilt arises in the gulf between the ideal ('I should be . . .') and the reality ('I am . . .'). The ideal has no truck with the capacity to compete, to be assertive appropriately, to refuse to go a third or even a fourth mile. The ideal is also forcefully shored up by the vocational expectations of pastors. Chronic feelings of failure and inadequacy are then a perpetual source of anxiety.

In the section on compulsive–obsessive characteristics, Eadie maintains that a way out of this persecuting guilt is for the pastor to throw himself into work, being available all the time to his parishioners, pulled between family and parish, depriving himself of recreation and omnipotently refusing to delegate. A potential helper is shrouded in persecutory anxiety and turned into a potential rival.

With so much denial and repression active, it is not surprising to find that sexual fantasies and impulses are not congruent with the ideal image of the pastor, who then becomes asexual. Eadie suggests that the pastor retreats to the safety of pulpit and study, and engages in a wide range of pastoral relationships, all of which avoid intimacy. Thus impoverished, the pastor attempts to meet this basic human need through a rich fantasy world (in which, I would add, he is in total control).

This feeling of safety is enhanced by belonging to an institution, in which roles, rules and expectations are established and relatively clear. There the pastor can comply and continue to reap an abundant harvest of approval, which sustains his ideal self-image. Eadie found, though, that the pastor was sorely taxed by fierce attacks from the laity, a principal source of anxiety and stress, because the pastor felt it wrong to confront his aggressor or to defend himself; rather, he would placate, only to pay the price of a loss of self-respect. He identifies with the negative aspects of the 'martyr complex', in which passive compliance is countered by resentment, hurt and bitterness. No doubt the family suffers too.

To cope with this array of conflicts, pastors tend either to withdraw into an excess of 'being', symbolised through meditation, study and fantasy; or else, they become rebellious and impulsive and enact aggressive or sexual impulses in a destructive and self-destructive way, quite often inviting condemnation from parishioners and ecclesiastical authorities alike. The latter is simply a massive reinforcement of the pastor's tendency to punish himself and to turn his anger against himself.

Depression follows, often masked by a variety of psychosomatic complaints, such as skin problems, ulcerative colitis, digestive complications, migraine, rheumatic and arthritic complaints and heart disease. The inner relation with the soul breaks down, and what belongs to psyche is forced into being expressed by soma. Sometimes, a bodily illness seems to be the one and only way of actually being cared for and looked after without guilt. To retire to bed and be fed is preferable to allowing closeness and emotional feeding. On the other hand, depression can often masquerade as physical illness. Bad feelings about oneself can travel round the body and attack various organs (the heart) or sub-systems (the nervous system), and in some cases produce a fairly intractable clinical picture.

Eadie's profile is still highly relevant to pastors and repays reflective study. In Jungian terms, it is a study of one-sided development, leaving a breach in the person, a split between the light and dark sides of the person, who ends up feeling constantly at war with himself. This dark side was called by Jung the shadow, by which he quite bluntly meant

the thing a person has no wish to be. (CW16 para 470)

This 'thing' contains not only negative aspects of ourselves, but also capacities and functions lying dormant and unused. Much of the important work of therapy, certainly in the early stages as well as later, is involved in integrating the shadow, which often contains elements that are not only useful but sometimes vital to normal adult functioning. By integrating the shadow, consciousness is extended, moral responsibility is developed, and the energy that has been used in keeping the contents repressed is freed. The shadow is invariably met in projection, usually on to a member of the same sex: for example, a pastor may exclaim, 'That man in the next-door parish is a workaholic.'

Just as everyone has their own personal shadow, so it is possible to envisage each profession with its own specific shadow, which

. . . at all counts . . . forms an unconscious snag, thwarting our most well-meant intentions. (CW11 para 131)

as the following example shows.

Justin:

A prosperous suburban parish had been enjoying the fruits of experience of an old-fashioned rector for some years. It was only a select few of the parishioners that were privy to the rector's growing dependence on alcohol, and his discreet but flirtatious behaviour with the parish secretary. These afflictions, as the rector was later to describe his aberrations, had not really interfered with worship, threshold ceremonies or pastoral care. They were most apparent in committee meetings, where he had become irritable, and in areas of parochial administration, where many felt that he had delegated beyond the competence of the secretary and certainly outside her role.

On the Sunday before Ash Wednesday, an astonished congregation was told by the area dean that the rector had resigned, almost overnight. He had left job, house and parish for 'reasons of health'. It was only after the service that gossip buzzed around, indicating that he had left his wife as well. The parish was stunned, and never really recovered despite enormous support from the area dean, who managed to contain some of the feelings of anger, betrayal, guilt and sadness that were prevalent in various cliques in the congregation.

Out of the applicants for the job, it was finally Justin who was appointed. He was young, enthusiastic, keen on counselling, had done some group-relations training, and was immensely eager to get his teeth into his first incumbency. He moved in with his vivacious wife, who had her own career as a solicitor in a law centre, and embarked on 'Justin's mission', as the parish historians later named the period of his stay.

It was generally agreed that his intellect, his physical presence and a holiness unusual in someone so young made him a rather charismatic figure both in the parish and in the deanery. It was not long before he had attracted to himself a band of followers, mainly younger people, including newcomers to the church, whom he was going to lead into a new Christianity inspired by the vision of a democratic Church within the traditional and hierarchical structure of the establishment. Using his skills in group relations, he manipulated the fragmentation he found in the parish, and was soon hailed as a heroic rescuer by his followers and as a diabolical figure by his enemies. An 'in' and an 'out' group formed. Justin took pleasure in ministering to the former and engaging in intimate social intercourse with its members. As this cosy group situation developed, the 'out' group came to be experienced and thought of as enemies, who wanted to attack the chosen few. Not only did they *want* to attack, but they did, calling in senior members of the diocesan structure to sort out rumours of sexual misdemeanours and mal-administration of funds.

Noticing signs of strain in the 'in' group, Justin offered to run a sensitivity group for some of the members. Discussions lasted one and a half hours. Everyone agreed that a lot of hard and painful work was done, as people confronted each other and explored feelings of rivalry, inferiority, as well as issues to do with members' roles in the parish and the perennial dilemma of authoritarian/democratic rule. But things continued to go awry. Essential repair work to the church was given a blind eye, with the result that an unexpected gale ripped off sections of the roof, making the interior unsafe for some months. The church began to take over the lives of the 'in' group, who rushed from one sort of group to another, ignoring their marriages and partnerships. One or two people actually broke down and were hospitalised. Their departure was greeted with relief because their 'illness' was seen as weakness, and because the group was in constant need of a scapegoat. This need became more compulsive as Justin's own health began to decline and he became aware of the destruction of the parish. Just before it was too late, he applied for an academic post, and went into therapy himself.

It is clear from this example that a particular mixture of personality, social pathology in the parish, and an external hierarchical structure can wreak havoc. The pastor can do harm and can unconsciously become a wolf in sheep's clothing, eschewing his role and responsibility and becoming as tyrannical in his democracy as he imagines his authoritarian counterpart to be.

The process I outlined in 'Justin's mission' is known to

some pastors and social psychiatrists, and has hounded the therapeutic community movement in this country. The Jungian analyst Robert Hobson calls it the 'therapeutic community disease' (Hobson, 1979, p. 232). He outlines three phases:

(1) the coming of the Messiah;
(2) the Enlightenment;
(3) the Catastrophe.

In the first phase, an idealist takes up a revolutionary posture within a traditional setting, creating opposition in the establishment. He attracts a group to himself and is experienced by himself and others as magical. He incarnates an archetypal figure, often the Saviour Hero. Attack and counter-attack rage between inner and outer groups. The inner group feels cohesive, but individual differences are denied, giving a feeling of pseudo-mutuality.

Enlightenment is hallmarked by intellectual awareness of the processes under way. Failure to come to terms in depth with the destructive power game leads into the third phase of Catastrophe. Here, illness, breakdown and disillusionment occur as the destructive components of the process force themselves into consciousness. By that time, the process has often been halted by external intervention from the establishment.

Another Jungian who has elucidated the shadow of those in the helping professions is Adolf Guggenbühl-Craig (1971). His thesis is that members of the helping professions can do serious damage, 'caused directly by their very desire to help' (Guggenbühl-Craig, 1971). On the face of it, this is rather a serious claim, potentially undermining for idealists and for those who wish to dedicate their lives to the service of others. It, therefore, deserves some consideration.

Guggenbühl-Craig surveys the models that influence the psychotherapist, and picks out two for special attention: that of the doctor and that of the priest, both of which have their shadow side. The priest in the Judeo-Christian culture is seen as an instrument of God's will, as a mediator. There are always those in the congregation who attempt to constellate doubt in the pastor—in other words, to contact his shadow.

The pastor lives with the dark side of himself as a 'lying hypocrite'; sometimes he is forced to deny his own doubts and 'to mask a momentary inner emptiness with high-flown words'. Secondly, the pastor is yoked to the burdensome expectation of practising what he preaches, and this 'opens the door to another of the clergyman's dark brothers—the one who wishes to present himself to the world (and to himself) as better than he really is'. Thirdly, the pastor is prone to projections of omniscience; he is looked to for answers, for dogma, for advice, for moral pronouncements. It is all too easy for him to identify with this projection, thereby behaving as though he were omniscient or ought to be, and to use his position to exert power and influence the vulnerable. Lastly, Guggenbühl-Craig asserts that pastors work with their souls, with their selves; 'methods, techniques and apparatus are secondary . . . honesty and genuineness are [their] tools . . . there is great pressure to represent these tools as better than they really are, and thus to become victim of [the] shadow'.

He develops his thesis by drawing on the archetypal image of the wounded healer, that of Chiron, the Centaur, who taught Aesculapius the art of medicine, as well as music. While Heracles was fighting the Centaurs, he accidentally shot one of his poisoned arrows into Chiron's knee. Heracles administered one of Chiron's remedies, but it was in vain. The venom was indestructible and Chiron was cursed or blessed with immortality. He eventually gave his immortality to Prometheus, and was placed among the stars as Sagittarius.

The archetypal image of Chiron contains the opposites of healing and being wounded. It is, like all archetypal imagery, bi-polar, both positive and negative, and either pole can swing into its opposite. Jung puts it like this:

> It is an essential characteristic of psychic figures that they are duplex or at least capable of duplification; at all events they are bi-polar and oscillate between their positive and negative meanings. (CW9(i) para 183)

Guggenbühl-Craig asserts that the physician can split this image so that he experiences himself as full of health, strength and activity. The other half of the image gets projected on to the patient, who becomes the sick, weak and passive person in the relationship. As such, he is kept in a passive, dependent position and coerced into a clinging relationship, making separation almost impossible, as we shall see in Chapter 8. A parallel for the pastor would be the split between confessor and penitent. As soon as this split has occurred, the two participants are alienated from an aspect of themselves. Differences become exaggerated and the person occupying the positive pole of the image (healer, confessor, guru, etc.) can be idealised and felt to be affecting the relationship from a position of remoteness.

Philippa:

Philippa worked part-time in a hospital chaplaincy. The sister on the endocrinology ward had asked her to visit Bill, who had expressed a wish to see someone from the chaplaincy. The sister had felt that Philippa's outgoing personality would prove a match in more senses than one for Bill's torrential outpourings, which were humorous, repetitive, aggressive, compassionate and critical—each engendered by an unpredictable mood brought about by the fluctuations of his illness.

Bill was a widower in his late sixties and had a married daughter and grandchildren. He had formed a very positive attachment during his long stay in hospital to the female senior registrar, who had, so Philippa told her pastoral support group, been seduced and frightened into giving Bill special privileges—like his own side room—although his condition had not warranted it.

The sister's intuition had proved fairly accurate; Philippa and Bill had hit it off, and Bill spent quite a lot of time up in the chapel and involved in the life of the chaplaincy, when he was not being whisked round the hospital for tests.

One day Philippa was bleeped by the sister, who was clearly both very anxious and very angry. The registrar, new to the rotation, had asked Bill to vacate his room for a dying patient who had been admitted to the ward, because of the unavailability of beds in a more appropriate ward. Bill had refused and had threatened suicide if he were to be moved back to the open ward. Philippa arrived on the scene. The sister, a junior nurse and the registrar were huddled in the nursing station looking sullen and belligerent. They tossed the problem over to Philippa, who went into the side room and was greeted warmly by Bill, who seemed to have assumed that Philippa would support him. In the exchange that followed, immense moral pressure was brought to bear on Philippa to back Bill. Of her feelings, she said:

'I was an ambassador from God, an angel of mercy, who could, at a stroke, put an end to the cruelty and inconsiderateness of the nurses and doctors. For quite some time, I found myself excited by the feeling of power that had entered into me — power to effect change — but a more sinister power, like that of an executioner over a condemned man. I was an angel, a magician, an executioner. He was an ignorant sinner, and a helpless victim. Almost simultaneously, I felt utterly powerless and helpless, and could not think of how I might alleviate the situation for Bill, for the dying patient and for the staff.'

Philippa explained that she had no doubt in her own mind of the wrongfulness of Bill's stance. She was mindful of Bill's history, which he had recounted endlessly, and of intense rivalrous feelings with younger brothers. But it was not the moment, she felt, to make those sorts of connections. She did feel, however, that it was imperative not to act on this invisible injection of power, but to attempt to hold the split within Bill between the power he was exerting and the powerlessness he was experiencing. Her strategy did not work, and inflamed Bill's feelings of being misunderstood and pushed around. Later, everyone realised that his intense feelings of persecution seemed to have been triggered by the events of that day. The dying patient was shunted off to another ward.

The reader can imagine that Philippa's pastoral support group discussed this episode for some time because it raised so many issues to do with institutional dynamics, multi-disciplinary roles, perceptions by the medical and nursing staff of the chaplaincy, ethical questions, the 'rights' of patients in an NHS setting, etc.

The point I want to emphasise is that this example illustrates Guggenbühl-Craig's thesis that the archetypal image becomes split not only between two people (groups,

institutions or countries, I would add) but also within each of
the two people. Philippa's training and self-awareness helped
her to be in touch with feelings of power and powerlessness
within her role. To have been in touch solely with the power
might have led her into coercive action on behalf of Bill or the
hospital staff or the dying patient; equally, to have been in
touch only with her powerlessness would have rendered her
participation inane and futile. It could be legitimately argued
(and was so by the group) that Philippa hastily accepted a
projection from the hospital staff of an 'angel of mercy', an
idealised rescuer. On reflection, Philippa thought that that
was the case, and that she had become dissociated from her
own helplessness for a time. She considered that it might
have been more effective to hold the projection for a while
and to discuss the dilemma with the staff, rather than let
them be overwhelmed by a mixture of resentment and
powerlessness.

So far, we have concentrated on the shadow aspects of the
carer's motivation. These are important to know since
familiarity with them leads into greater consciousness and
helps to keep the space between pastor and client reasonably
free of intrusions from the pastor's inner world. It is now time
to redress the balance and to tease out some of the many
positive reasons for entering the helping professions and
attitudes that sustain the helper in his work. Jung's personal
struggle to discover what he wanted to do in life is recounted
in *Memories, Dreams and Reflections* (abbreviated to *MD & R*;
see chapter 3, 'Student Years'). Jung recalls that his father
had said, 'The boy is interested in everything imaginable, but
he does not know what he wants.' Inside himself, Jung was
being pulled about by what he called his no. 1 and no. 2
personalities. His no. 1 personality was the one he presented
to the world. His no. 2 was the one that worried over the
meaning of life, religious questions, etc., and the one that
caused him to get depressed. It was secret. This conflict
expressed itself in his uncertainty about whether to study
natural science or philosophy and the humanities. At all
major transition points in his life, Jung relied on his dreams,
and this period of confusion was no exception. He had two
dreams, which left him in no doubt. In the second dream,

Jung found himself in the darkest part of a wood, where there was a circular pool. Half immersed in the water was a round creature, shimmering in opalescent hues, and made up of an infinite number of very small cells, like tentacles. Jung awoke with a craving for knowledge. The creature seems to have been a numinous symbol for him, leading him on to further development. Having decided on science for matriculation, he later settled on medicine at university, although he felt this to be a compromise. It was when reading a book on psychiatry for his exams that Jung

> had to stand up and draw a deep breath. My excitement was intense, for it had become clear to me, in a flash of illumination, that for me the only possible goal was psychiatry. Here alone the two currents of my interest could flow together and in a united stream dig their own bed. Here was the empirical field common to biological and spiritual facts, which I had everywhere sought and nowhere found. Here at last was the place where the collision of nature and spirit became a reality. (Jung, 1963, p. 111)

Jung's sudden flash of illumination seems to have been the outcome of a long and painful process, of the sort one might expect to encounter in someone struggling with a sense of vocation. For, a little later in the passage I have just quoted, Jung, interestingly, says: 'I knew—and nothing and nobody could have deflected me from my purpose—that my decision stood, and that it was fate'.

Without being explicit, Jung, I think, may be alluding to the self. Jung writes:

> The self is not only the centre but also the whole circumference which embraces both conscious and unconscious; it is the centre of this totality, just as the ego is the centre of the conscious mind. (CW12 para 44)

Jung's use of this word to denote several different meanings has been elucidated by Redfearn. He points to the common denominator running through Jung's work: 'a sense of something super-ordinate to the conscious "I" with great potency and with organising characteristics' (Redfearn, 1985). The something may be a God-image, it may refer to the total personality, it may be a compensatory symbol leading to an expansion of the personality. Whatever it is, it requires the conscious, executive part of the personality, the ego, to engage with it, to form an ego–self relationship, a sort of open road between 'I' and the unconscious. Jung writes:

> the psyche is transformed or developed by the relationship of the ego to the contents of the unconscious. In individual cases, that transformation can be read from dreams and phantasies. In collective life it has left its deposit principally in the various religious systems and their changing symbols. Through the study of these collective transformation processes and through understanding of alchemical symbolism I arrived at the central concept of my psychology: the process of individuation. (*MD&R*, p. 200)

It is generally thought that this relationship between 'I' and the unconscious, which Jung intimates is both priceless and vital, has its roots in the relationship between the baby and its mother. The baby is at first totally dependent on its mother, who tries for the first few months to adapt to the infant as much as possible, only gradually introducing fragments of frustration at a speed that the infant can tolerate. During these early months, the mother also offers a mirror-role for the baby, acting as a medium of inter-communication between mother and baby and meeting an urgent need of the baby. Winnicott describes it thus:

> What does the baby see when he or she looks at the mother's face? I am suggesting that, ordinarily, what the baby sees is himself or herself, in other words the mother is looking at the baby and what she looks like is related to what she sees there. (Winnicott, 1967b, p. 232)

Winnicott is referring to the mother's role in valuing, validating and understanding her baby's experience, feelings and sensations. The therapeutic task becomes,

> by-and-large . . . a long-term giving the patient back what the patient brings. It is a complex derivative of the face that reflects what is there to be seen. (Winnicott, 1967b, p. 131)

All these functions are taken in by the baby and form the

basis of this inner ego–self relationship. If the maternal environment is sufficiently responsive, facilitating and adaptive to the infant, then feelings of love and hate intertwine around the same person, the mother, so that destructive impulses cohabit with concern and the wish to make reparation. For by this time, the baby is worried about the effects of the attacks it has made in fantasy or actuality on the mother. Within this state of affairs is born the feeling of gratitude. Both the wish to make reparation and the feeling of gratitude form part of the bedrock of the wish to help others, although it must be remembered that that wish can arise out of a different urge—a reversal, an attempt to meet in others unmet needs in oneself.

Something else that arises out of this ego–self relationship is what the late Kenneth Lambert called the 'agape-factor', an attitude that informs the professional approach of those in the helping professions. The word agape is taken from 1 Corinthians 13.4–8. Lambert gives the Authorised Version translation and then a more literal one:

'Charity suffereth long and is kind, charity envieth not; charity vaunteth not itself, is not puffed up. Doth not behave itself unseemly, seeketh not her own, is not easily provoked, thinketh no evil. Beareth all things, believeth all things, hopeth all things, endureth all things. Charity never faileth.'

'Agape defers anger, is long suffering, or long-tempered, and is kind in demeanour or plays the part of a kind person; does not envy; agape does not play the braggart; is not inflated with pride, is not vain; does not behave unmannerly or unseemly (a-schematically); does not seek its own advantage; does not fly into a rage quickly, does not keep an account of evils suffered; is not glad over injustice or wrong, but sympathises with the advancement of truth; roofs over or keeps out the weather; believes all things; hopes for all things and stands ground in all things. Agape does not fail or fall down.' (Lambert, 1981, p. 34)

St Paul was writing to people discharging a pastoral role under difficult conditions, and was making the point that most, if not all, of the activities of the pastor are rendered futile unless grounded in agape. The first translation of the passage can be read as extremely persecutory; the second is more down to earth, but still leaves agape high on a pedestal, idealised and unattainable. The feeling about this changes if we assume some integration of the shadow, so that, for example, a wish to punish and reject a client who 'refuses' to change or 'see the light' can be acknowledged and contained, and not enacted.

Lambert, who is addressing analysts and therapists, goes on to consider the agapaic attitude in terms of ethical injunctions, persona considerations and the maturity of the pastor. Ethically, the pastor is enjoined to avoid exploiting those who entrust themselves to his care (agape does not seek its own advantage) and to stick to the task (agape does not behave a-schematically). We will return to the first of these in Chapter 5 and to the second in Chapter 3.

Being long-suffering and not flying into a rage quickly do not refer to acquiescing passively to abusive parishioners, smiling sweetly at the incompetent organist, or spending yet another hour on the phone with a demanding, hysterical client. These qualities warn, Lambert suggests, 'against the hasty, unconsidered and untimely expression' of anger or rage. Jung gives an amusing illustration of this. He is reminiscing about an obsessional patient, who had taken to slapping her employers!

> She was a very stately imposing person six feet tall—and there was power behind her slaps I can tell you! She came then and we had a very good talk. Then came the moment when I had to say something unpleasant to her. Furious, she sprang to her feet and threatened to slap me. I, too, jumped up and said to her, 'Very well, you are the lady. You hit first—ladies first! But then I hit back!' And I meant it. She fell back into her chair and deflated before my eyes. 'No-one has ever said that to me before', she protested. From that moment on the therapy began to succeed. (*MD&R* p. 140)

This example raises all sorts of interesting questions. Is that sort of spontaneous gesture appropriate? Had Jung actually slapped the patient, might she have experienced his actions as vengeful? If she was compelled to slap people, as Jung suggests, was she really going to slap Jung or was she going to slap whoever or whatever Jung stood for? I think the lesson lies in Jung's determination to establish the limits within which he was prepared to work. Defining those limits in that instance included a spontaneous and angry response, which was, none the less, considered. He did not simply slap her, shout at her or throw her out. Perhaps experience was his keeper; perhaps he also knew the extent of his hate, an indispensable emotion for becoming and remaining separate.

This brings us back to the maturity of the pastor. I am not happy with the word maturity because it implies a sense of stasis, a fullness or completion, a goal as distant on the horizon as the misunderstood notion of individuation. It may be more realistic to expect that the destructive effects of envy, the defensive aspects of pride, the enactment of vengeful feelings towards those that disappoint, and delight in the misfortunes of others may be sufficiently conscious. The pastor would then be able to exercise more choice and control over the use of his self in his roles as symbol of 'being', model of 'doing', and mediator of understanding. Pastoral work involves recognising and accepting both the rational and the irrational in worker and client; it also evokes strong feelings in both parties and requires the pastor to use those feelings in a disciplined way.

A cursory sifting through the tabloid press will quickly reveal the condemnation and scapegoating of the pastor who gets carried away by bewildering feelings, and errs too far from the image projected on to him by the laity and the expectations of society-at-large. The institution of the Church, the projections from the laity and the internal moral beat of the pastor can interact collusively to instil into the pastor a real dread and terror of being 'found out' and cast out. Because the relationship between the private self and the public role is so close and intense, criticism, confrontation and firm management can be experienced as a most painful attack not on professional skills, but on the inner self of the pastor, who is sometimes left feeling psychically annihilated, especially when the persona is inadequate. In such a situation, Jung's words may seem of little comfort:

But when one follows the path of individuation, when one lives one's own life, one must take mistakes into the bargain; life would not be complete without them. There is no guarantee — not for a single moment — that we will not fall into error or stumble into deadly peril. We may think there is a sure road. But that would be the road of death. Then nothing happens any longer — at any rate, not the right things. Anyone who takes the sure road is as good as dead. (*MD&R*, p. 277)

Jung reminds us,

The psychotherapist learns little or nothing from his successes, for they chiefly confirm him in his mistakes. But failures are priceless experiences, because they not only open the way to a better truth, but force us to modify our views and methods. (CW16 para 73)

Hobson goes further: 'We need to say constantly "I fail". To say "I am a failure" is blasphemy, the collapse of an idealisation mistakenly adopted as an ideal' (Hobson, 1985, p. 278).

The pastor is faced almost daily with people who are not only very disturbed; they are also very disturbing. He is also required to negotiate successfully switches between various roles within a day or less — administrator, spiritual adviser, businessman, counsellor, parent, committee member, leader in worship, etc. The stress on the person in role cannot be underestimated and, as Eadie has pointed out, takes its toll. There is, therefore, a case to be made for offering the pastor opportunities for gaining self-knowledge and for exploring the balance between the professional and the vocational. Some psychodynamic awareness can aid these processes.

I envisage a range of opportunities, which might include:

(1) A management structure that can monitor and evaluate the pastor's use of time, the social and ecological conditions in which he operates, the management of his work.

(2) A relationship with a supervisor or group that is, on the whole, benign, challenging and supportive. This would gradually be internalised by the pastor and then act as a

source of nourishment and reference and be invoked during the working week.

(3) Access to courses in which the pastor can gain understanding relevant to the attitudes and behaviour of parishioners, and which explore the complex dynamics that operate within and between institutions.

(4) Personal therapy — individual, marital or group — where the primary aim is deepening personal awareness and unblocking development. This would enhance the pastor's capacity to respond agapaically to the various demands made upon him, and minimise the intrusion of his own psychopathology into the space between pastor and client.

All four settings offer opportunities for the sharing of strengths and the acknowledgement of weaknesses and failings. It is to failing that I wish to return. A passage of Winnicott comes to mind:

> Human beings fail and fail; and in the course of ordinary care a mother is all the time mending her failures. These relative failures with immediate remedy undoubtedly add up eventually to a communication, so that the baby comes to know about success. Successful adaptation thus gives a sense of security, a feeling of having been loved. . . . It is the innumerable failures followed by the sort of care that mends that build up into a communication of love, of the fact that there is a human being there who cares. (Winnicott, 1968b)

Once that feeling of care has been experienced, then the pastor is more ready and able to care for and contain the developing individual.

TWO

Developing as an Individual

Man born of desire
cometh out of the night,
A wandering spark of fire,
A lonely word of eternal thought
Echoing in chance and forgot.
Robert Bridges

It is probably true that throughout the course of history the number 'four', like the shape of the wheel or the cross, has had a symbolic significance that is almost universal. There are four cardinal points to the compass, four elements, four seasons, four temperaments. Mandalas are sacred/magical symmetrical structures divided and subdivided into four, which Jung came to understand as symbols of wholeness or completeness. The number 'four' also pervades his own psychology. There are the four functions, the four forms of the female psyche, the four phases of analysis.

It comes as no great surprise, then, that Jung should conceive of life as divided into four broad stages, subsumed under two larger halves, each with its own specific task: childhood and youth thrusting out into the world and developing the ego; mid-life and old age enshrining a search for meaning and purpose and a move away from the inter-personal to the intra- and supra-personal. Jung compares life with the journey of the sun through an arc of 180 degrees:

> The first quarter, lying to the east, is childhood, that state in which we are a problem for others but are not yet conscious of any problems of our own. Conscious problems fill out the second and third quarters; while in the last, in extreme old age, we descend again into that condition

34

where, regardless of our state of consciousness, we once more become something of a problem for others. (CW8 para 795)

Problems arise when the individual, at whatever stage of life, tries to cling to the aspirations, achievements, values or behaviour appropriate to the previous stage(s), as in the following example.

Adam:

Adam was a handsome man of forty-seven, greying temples lending an air of distinction to his immaculate presentation of himself. He was a witty and entertaining raconteur, generous in his hospitality and delighting in the sociability of running a restaurant, which afforded him considerable success and a high standard of living. He lived on his own in a luxury apartment and drove a sports car.

He was the youngest of four children, parented by a father, a busy pastor, and a mother who devoted her time to being a wife and mother. When Adam was seven, he was dispatched to boarding school, where his feelings of rejection surfaced in the form of a chronic but subtle war against authority. At fourteen, a time when Adam was looking for a greater sense of containment and direction, his father died, leaving the boy with the task of trying to separate from a mother who was desperately trying to cling on to him. He went to art school and then into advertising. He flitted from job to job, often charming his way in and then becoming quickly bored.

A large number of brief sexual relationships left him feeling empty until he met a beautiful Italian woman, some years his senior, at drama school. Their childless marriage broke up a few years later, and Adam found himself darting around from one affair to another, his behaviour almost encouraged by the loneliness of theatrical digs and endless travelling. He finally settled down to life as a restaurateur, but remained deeply lonely. His excessive generosity, perhaps hiding his own neediness, nearly bankrupted him in his first restaurant, where friends were lavishly entertained at his expense. Privately, he pursued women now much younger than him, struggling to retain his youthful athleticism in the gymnasium, and continued to dress as an elderly adolescent.

To his acute embarrassment, he was sitting in his restaurant one night with some friends when he suddenly started to retch, and this symptom, a Job-like affliction for a restaurateur, persisted and finally brought him to counselling. Among the many feelings and experiences he talked about in his first session was his fear of advancing age and death, of which he saw his symptom as a symbol. His dreams were peopled by mocking groups who rejected him, and whom he came to understand as parts of himself wanting to reject an aspect of himself—namely, his outmoded adolescence.

People who seek pastoral help often do so either because they are clinging to attitudes, patterns of relating, ways of being and doing that are no longer appropriate to the present; or because their development and growth are blocked by anxiety, fear of failure or fear of loss. Clearly, these categories overlap, the second often explaining the first. Using a schema of human development, the pastor can more easily detect points at which an individual has got stuck, or points to which an individual has jumped, missing out stages in between.

Jung's description of the life-cycle is too broad to be of much use in a work setting; but his ideas about the second half of life are often very meaningful to people, and we shall return to these in due course.

I intend to view the developing human being from two perspectives: instinctual life; and the negotiation of developmental tasks.

Instinctual life

In his essay 'Psychological Factors in Human Behaviour' (CW8), Jung posits the instincts as prime mainsprings of psychic life. In that paper, he cites five; elsewhere he adds a sixth. The five are: hunger, sexuality, activity, reflection, and creativity. The first three lend themselves to transformation; for instance, hunger may be transformed into terrific ambition; bisexuality may become heterosexuality or homosexuality; activity, which may start as restlessness, turns into play and a myriad of pursuits. Jung saw reflection as the cultural instinct whereby a stimulus becomes an experience. He saw creativity as having a lot in common with both activity and reflection, but he warned that an individual could get carried away by it to the point of self-destruction.

Instinctual life takes place within the context of three balances: conscious–unconscious, extraversion–introversion, spirit–matter. The actual behaviour of the individual, the way the instincts manifest themselves, will, said Jung, be largely determined by how conscious an individual is. The less an individual is conscious, the more prone he will be to compulsive instinctual processes. To put this another way: the less aware that I am of a destructive sub-personality within myself, the more likely I am constantly to break things, mismanage arrangements, etc.

Extraversion–introversion

determines the direction of psychic activity, that is, it decides whether the conscious contents refer to external objects or to the subject . . . it decides whether the value stressed lies outside or inside the individual . . . it builds up habitual attitudes, that is, types with recognizable outward traits. (CW8 para 250)

Spirit–matter or upwards–downwards is the modality through which the contents of consciousness are perceived. A dream of being on top of a hill, for example, might be perceived as referring to being in an exalted position close to God (spirit) or as being hungrily involved at the breast (matter). Either way, it is the use the dreamer makes of the image that will hinder or abet development.

Elsewhere, as I have said, Jung writes about the spiritual as an instinct. 'The spiritual appears in the psyche also as an instinct, indeed as a real passion . . . it is a principle sui generis, a specific and necessary form of instinctual power' (CW8 para 108).

The negotiation of developmental tasks

Jung's notion of opposites, the tensions between them and the way they are regulated throughout life, form the bridge to the work of the psychoanalyst Erik Erikson, who has developed an epigenetic chart, which embraces 'ego qualities which emerge from critical periods of development—criteria . . . by which the individual demonstrates that his ego, at a given stage, is strong enough to integrate the timetable of the organism with the structure of social institutions' (Erikson, 1950, p. 238). This chart is reproduced as Figure 2.1.

The vertical axis represents a kind of synthesis of Freud and Jung, the latter being more evident in stages F, G, H. Although the diagonal line signifies a developmental sequence, Erikson is at pains to point out that the sequence is not necessarily linear; it may indeed be spiral. Furthermore, it is more optimistic than classical Freudian theory, since it allows for second and more chances at every stage of development. Similarly, the empty boxes allow space both for the influence of experience and for the unfolding of potential. Erikson is insistent that his stages do not represent achievements; rather, the developing individual will arrive at 'favourable ratios' out of each pair of opposites. The outcome of a 'favourable ratio' is a particular strength, which is allied to a particular 'basic virtue'. These are institutionalised in so far as they evolved with man's development and form a groundbed of traditional and universal values, which sustain culture and society. A poor outcome represents pathology.

Table 2.1

1   Basic trust v mistrust: drive and hope
2   Autonomy v shame and doubt: self-control and will power
3   Initiative v guilt: direction and purpose
4   Industry v inferiority: method and competence
5   Identity v role confusion: devotion and fidelity
6   Intimacy v isolation: affiliation and love
7   Generativity and stagnation: production and care
8   Ego-integrity v despair: renunciation and wisdom

In this section, I will use Erikson's stages *only* as a framework within which to survey briefly the life-cycle.

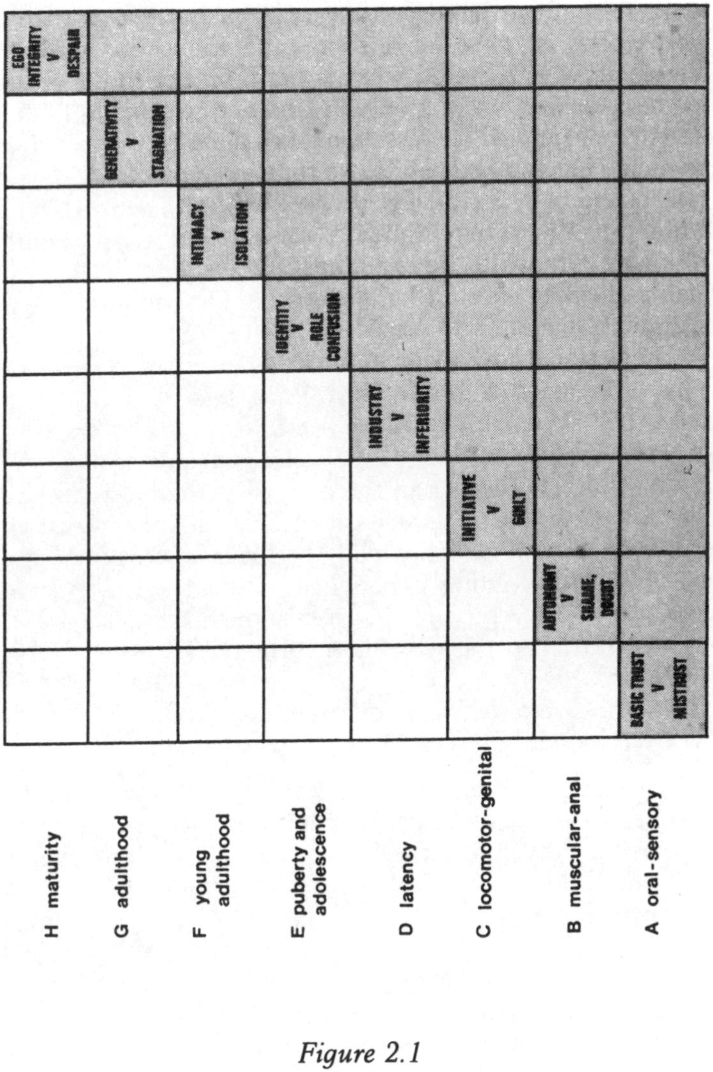
EGO INTEGRITY V DESPAIR
GENERATIVITY V STAGNATION
INTIMACY V ISOLATION
IDENTITY V ROLE CONFUSION
INDUSTRY V INFERIORITY
INITIATIVE V GUILT
AUTONOMY V SHAME, DOUBT
BASIC TRUST V MISTRUST
1
2
3
4
5
6
7
8
H maturity
G adulthood
F young adulthood
E puberty and adolescence
D latency
C locomotor-genital
B muscular-anal
A oral-sensory

Figure 2.1

1 Basic trust v mistrust

For the first few months of life, the infant, though biologically separate from the mother, appears to be merged with the environment, so that he has no capacity to differentiate between what is him and what is not him. For much of the time he is asleep, waking only to feed and to play, activities through which much conversation takes place between mother and child. The mother's ability to tune in empathically to the needs of the baby enable her to meet his needs and to adapt to him in a way that builds a sense of consistency and continuity. Gradually, he can take it for granted that she will reliably alleviate his states of distress, and he can also take it for granted that she will return after periods of absence. This is because she is now inside him. He has introjected, or taken in his experience of his mother. Trust has been won and established. Outside and inside are differentiated. Much of the work of differentiating takes place in and around the mouth, which is the part of the body that the baby uses to relate and to explore. This self–other division is sharpened by the arrival of teeth, which usually preludes weaning and the end of blissful feeding experiences, 'this stage seems to introduce into psychic life . . . a sense of inner division and universal nostalgia for a paradise forfeited' (Erikson, 1950, p. 241).

Jung brings this to life in different colours in his chapter 'The Dual Mother' in *Symbols of Transformation*:

> in the morning of life the son tears himself loose from the mother, from the domestic hearth, to rise through battle to his destined heights. Always he imagines his worst enemy in front of him, yet he carries the enemy within himself—a deadly longing for the abyss, a longing to drown in his own source, to be sucked down to the realm of the Mothers. His life is a constant struggle against extinction, a violent yet fleeting deliverance from ever-lurking night. This death is no external enemy, it is his own inner longing for the stillness and profound peace of all-knowing non-existence, for the all-seeing sleep in the ocean of coming-to-be and passing away. (CW5 para 553)

Jung's awareness of ambivalence towards life is mirrored by Winnicott's attempts to rescue mothers from idealisation through his coining the phrase 'good-enough mothering'. He once remarked that there was no such thing as a baby, by which he meant that a baby is essentially a part of a relationship. Without dependence on a 'facilitating environment', the inherited potential of the infant could not be realised. The infant moves from 'absolute dependence' through 'relative dependence' and then 'towards independence', a process that comes about through the mother gradually failing, in much the same way as a counsellor or pastor has gradually to fail the dependency needs of a client, if any growth is to take place.

However, it is sometimes true that:

> The mother who is not good enough is not able to implement the infant's omnipotence, and so she repeatedly fails to meet the infant gesture; instead she substitutes her own gesture which is to be given sense by the compliance of the infant. This compliance on the part of the infant is the earliest stage of the False Self and belongs to the mother's inability to sense her infant's needs.
>
> Through this False Self the infant builds up a false set of relationships, and by means of introjection even attains a show of being real, so that the child may grow to be just like mother, nurse, aunt, brother or whoever dominates the scene. The False Self has one positive and very important function: to hide the True Self, which it does by compliance with environmental demands. (Winnicott, 1960b, p. 145)

Such a person is always seeking, albeit unconsciously, another opportunity for his true self to unfold into life, but his sense of trust is minimal. We can contrast the following two people, one of whom is basically trusting and the other of whom seems only to know the chill of suspicion.

Ben:

Ben was someone in his late thirties, who, because of the political climate, found the bureaucratic restrictions and the increasing frustration of his clients in a social security office gradually alienating him from his work to the point at which he decided to resign. He belonged to an unorthodox church, where he had made a reputation for himself as someone who could use drama and humour as a way of addressing human and spiritual issues. The priest and members of the church were not at all surprised to hear of his resignation and encouraged him in his wish to train as a clown and juggler. Nor were they surprised to learn that at his first clown workshop he had been required to stand on the inside sill of a window sill and to lean back into the room until he fell off, like a felled tree, trusting to be caught by his teacher and fellow students.

Marion:

Marion was fifty-six when she was referred for counselling by her vicar after the death of her adoptive mother. She had been adopted at the age of six months by a single headmistress of a girls' boarding school. She was brought up in a closed and closeted context by a woman whose servants remember her with a shudder, so cold and puritanical was she to all and sundry. The mores of the time and the school's affiliation with the Church both underpinned a rigid personality, which seemed to have little space for a small girl with her emotional needs. Rather, this woman seems from all accounts to have needed her adopted daughter to complete her. Marion was kneaded into an image her adopted mother had of her. Later, strings were added, and Marion was able to perform brilliantly like a puppet socially and at work. But all the time, she was aware of what she called 'my jumble' within her, a jumble that she felt was really her. Her compliance was transferred straight into the counselling, so that it was a very long time indeed before the counsellor got a glimpse of the real person inside.

Marion's case points among other factors to the absence of a father. The father's importance in the development of the individual is at last enjoying the interest and attention of psychologists and of the public. It is beyond the scope of this book to go into this area in any depth. But I would like to draw attention to the work of Abelin, who maintains that at around the age of four months the child turns to the father, who in turn can give his child a sense of joy about himself/herself and who can contribute to the child's gender and social identity. Fathers act as mediators between mother and child and offer a way out from total entanglement with the mother (Abelin, 1975). The father's body is significantly different from that of the child and of its mother, and so the father comes to be the first significant other. He is also the first representation of masculinity, and in this role is the purveyor of triangulation, which leads to the establishment of gender identity and choice of partner. In talking about the symbolic inner figure of the father, Jung writes:

> Just as the mother archetype corresponds to the Chinese yin, so the father archetype corresponds to the yang. It determines our relation to man, to the law, and the state, to reason and the spirit, and the dynamism of nature. 'Fatherland' implies boundaries, a definite localisation in space, whereas the land itself is Mother Earth, quiescent and fruitful. The father . . . represents authority, hence also the law and the state. He is . . . the creative wind-breath — the spirit, pneuma, atman. (CW10 para 65)

I want to stress that Jung is writing of the symbolic inner figure of the father, not of the actual father. It is necessary to emphasise the distinction because of the confusion arising from people's experience of masculine mothers, mothers who seem to be more like fathers, or so-called phallic mothers, who seem powerful, erect and penetrative.

2 Autonomy v shame and doubt

Between six months and two years, the child develops from an infant into a toddler. There is decreased bodily dependence on mother and an active turning towards the outer world. Paddling around the floor, crawling and self-righting enable the child to explore the environment, but also lead to an increased awareness of being separate from the mother. Many of these maturing functions are expressed in close proximity to mother and are the natural sequelae of earlier states of relaxed unintegration, which Winnicott called:

the capacity to be alone . . . one of the most important signs of maturity in emotional development. . . . It is only when alone (that is to say, in the presence of someone) that the infant can discover his own personal life. . . . When alone in the sense that I am using the term, and only when alone, the infant is able to do the equivalent of what in an adult would be called relaxing . . . to become unintegrated, to flounder, to be in a state in which there is no orientation, to be able to exist for a time without being either a reactor to an external impingement or an active person with a direction of interest or movement. (Winnicott, 1958, p. 34)

From this early state, the child continues to grow in proximity to the mother, and although he explores further and for longer, he returns to her for what Mahler (1969) calls 'refuelling'. Increased separation anxiety goes hand in hand with joy at escaping from the engulfment of mother, who can now be recognised and enjoyed from afar.

As language develops rapidly, the words 'me' and 'mine' become important, and the child is no longer so willing to share what is his. Possessiveness and acquisitiveness loom large. At the same time, the child begins to experiment more actively with saying and meaning 'no', something that has its precursors in averting the eyes. Battles with authority sometimes take place in the field of toilet training, where the child works out conflicts between letting go and holding in, and where ways of seeking and losing mother's love and approval of the precious products are sorted out. The child's explorations into the world, his striving for autonomy and separateness proceed quite naturally, given a good-enough environment. Scorn, contempt, harshness in language or action, when repeated often enough, lead to intense shame and self-disgust, which can so easily become self-contempt. When this level and degree of repudiation of aspects of the personality have been reached and achieved, the person and those s/he comes into contact with are often left with the feeling that irreparable damage has been done.

Melanie:

She came for help because of a chronic despair, manifesting itself in strong self-destructive impulses, against which she guarded by avoiding tube trains and high buildings. She also sold her car, fearing that the impulse to drive along the wrong side of the road would overwhelm her. She was successful at work, and lived with her business partner in a relationship in which her emotional paralysis was felt by him to be enragingly withholding to such an extent that he would beat her, and his violent outbursts felt like the treatment she had received from her father, whom she could never please. Actually, it was worse than that. Her father punished her by slapping her on the legs, and then feeling remorseful. She could never get it right. If she was unhappy, she was accused of sulking; if she cried, she was told she would be given something to cry about; if she smiled acceptingly, she was criticised for not taking the matter seriously. Her mother seems to have colluded with this sadistic father, and was often absent from the house on missions of mercy to friends and neighbours. Melanie grew up feeling that almost all her impulses and feelings were unacceptable, because they met with violent condemnation. With help, she gradually found ways of reapproaching the repudiated child within herself.

The achievement of unit status, of separation from mother and father, had not been possible for Melanie. She could not live in the here-and-now, only in the there-and-then about which she had to ask endless questions. She was stuck in a prison of yesteryear, where awful things happened to her. She had proved to herself Winnicott's assertion that:

> The most aggressive and therefore dangerous words in the languages of the world are to be found in the assertion 'I am'. It has to be admitted, however, that only those who have reached a stage at which they can make this assertion are really qualified as adult members of society. (Winnicott, 1966)

In other words, he was suggesting that quite intense persecutory fears emerge quite normally when awareness of separateness from the mother is well developed. Painters, composers and artists of all kinds are usually very aware of these fears. If the more ordinary mortal cannot resolve these fears, the stage is not set for grappling with the next pair of opposites.

3 *Initiative v guilt*

At first, the baby relates mainly through its mouth. Later, interest in the anal region is added as issues of control are negotiated. In the third phase of childhood, the child becomes increasingly aware of sexual differences and curious about genital differences. Freud described this as the phallic stage. In inter-personal terms, the child has progressed from a state of permitted omnipotence and one-ness with the mother, to a two-person relationship, in which there is awareness of himself as distinct from the other. Now he is faced with the task of negotiating three-person relationships both in terms of relating to his two parents, and in vying with his sibling(s) for the attention of the parent(s). Violently conflicting feelings swirl around as the child is plunged into the Oedipus Complex.

For the boy, this means struggling with loving and possessive feelings towards the mother, coupled with hostility and rivalry against the father, who may also be feared. For the girl, this means a struggle with the same sorts of feelings. The difference is that, for the girl, there is a change of love object from the mother to the father. This has then to be relinquished so that the girl can reidentify with her mother in order to move on into womanhood and motherhood. For both boys and girls, the Oedipus Complex has a positive and a negative form. In its positive form, there is rivalry with the parent of the same sex and a longing for exclusive possession of the opposite-sex parent. In the negative form, the whole thing is reversed. Both coexist in different proportions because of our inherent bisexuality. Some children of clergymen feel confused for a long time, particularly during adolescence, by their father's dress both in and out of church. They then tend to seek out less ambiguous father-figures in a way analogous to the children of military personnel, who can long for softer fathers.

The Oedipus Complex also means learning to cope with feelings of exclusion. The parents are a couple, and they have their own room and they sleep together in it. It is the setting of the so-called primal scene, where vast energy is generated by the meeting of opposites. The actual enactment of sexual feelings towards the parent of the opposite sex is, hopefully, prevented by the incest taboo, which helps all the parties concerned, particularly the adults, to inhibit these impulses not so much out of fear, which would then relegate them to the shadow, but out of love, concern for and thought about the other participants in the triangle. The quality of the relationship between the adults in the triangle and their unconscious motivations will play a large part in how much the incest taboo is broken.

For the child, these conflicts are resolved in part by identifying with the parent of the same sex. These identifications go hand in hand with the taking in of parental prohibitions, cultural, social and religious standards, and together help fill out that area of the personality known to psychoanalysts as the superego. In common parlance, we might call this the conscience, which can generate feelings of guilt and dread; the capacity for self-observation, which can range from being over-active and hyper-critical (the perfectionist) to being dormant and indiscriminating (the psychopath); the ability to form ideals, which can generate feelings of love or of inferiority.

Jung gave full value to the sexual feelings experienced at this stage in life, but added a vitally important symbolic dimension. The adult who seeks to return to the parent of the opposite sex does so in the hope of being regenerated (cf. Mahler's 're-fuelling') and reborn into a different attitude. The father's contained enchantment with his daughter, and the mother's with her son, plays a vital part in the child's growing celebration of his/her sexuality.

Emily:

A beautiful young woman turned up for one of her sessions on her birthday. As luck would have it, just after she had settled down, the doorbell was rung repeatedly and insistently.

The analyst said that he felt too distracted by the noise and told his patient that he was going to investigate. When he returned to the room, he was more than a trifle taken aback to find Emily standing nude in the middle of the room. With extraordinary sensitivity for her need at the moment, he told her that he thought she was absolutely lovely, and then told her to get dressed and they would continue with the session. She was deeply moved by his response, and later in the session recalled coming downstairs as a little girl on her birthday in a new dress, to be greeted by indifference from her father. She rushed back upstairs and had to be cajoled out of her room by her mother. But the experience had left a mark indelible until her birthday many years later within the therapeutic relationship.

Her healthy exhibitionism had not met with a mixture of enchantment and self-containment by her father, and this had seriously affected her sexual development, so that she presented herself as a dowdy, prematurely middle-aged woman. Her sexuality had gone to sleep.

4 *Industry v inferiority*

Freud thought that there was a period in childhood when sexuality did actually go to sleep quite healthily and naturally. He called this the latency stage. It is important to understand that, while many psychologists talk of 'stages', they do not intend to create discrete compartments through which people progress in a unified fashion. Children develop in their own way and at their own speed. This is clearly seen as the child moves out of the family home into playgroup or nursery school or school proper. If all goes well, the child at this stage takes on a new 'shape'. The peer group begins to assume a new kind of importance, a bridge to independence, a chance to consolidate sameness, and a forum in which to exchange lavatorial jokes, compete and test out newly acquired skills. Neighbours, relatives and godparents, among others, might begin to comment on a very definite character shape, who has developed various ways of coping with his inner and outer world and who can or cannot amalgamate pressures from within and without in a productive way.

Harvey:

Harvey was fifty when he arrived home one day and told his wife and adopted daughter that he had been made redundant. He had been working for years without promotion in the public-relations section of a large company, where his begrudging attitude to work and his absence on the slightest pretext had not gone unnoticed. His wife had been deeply disillusioned by his lackadaisical attitude both to his work and to his responsibilities as a husband and father. He, on the other hand, had never forgiven her for what he assumed to be her infertility, which had left him unaffirmed as a man. That feeling was exaggerated by the scorn and disrespect of his daughter, who seemed to throw herself into life. His inferiority found compensation in the garage, which housed a huge model railway, and with which he whiled away hours of time in his imagination as station master, driver, etc.

Harvey came from a small family. He grew up with an elder sister from whom he always felt estranged. Although naturally intelligent, he found the confines of the school curriculum too constricting, but lacked the confidence to branch out on his own along lines that interested him. His father, a civil servant, saw in his son all that he disliked in himself and exacted the highest standards of conformity from him. His mother slaved away mechanically in a fashionable department store, and shared her husband's concern about the opinions of their neighbours. Harvey grew up feeling that he could never live up to his parents' standards, and spent his life underachieving, forever dissatisfied with his lot, and in awe of successful men.

Harvey is a not untypical example of a child born into contemporary society, where he is not only introduced to what we may think of as old-fashioned technology, but he is also required to grapple with an awareness of the agglomeration of vast amounts of energy (nuclear), ecological changes and hazards, an expansion of simulation (robots, computers, etc.), and an indefatigable push in the world of athletics and sport towards the bounds of possibility. Harvey could not cope. For him, joy, pride in achievement, and the capacity to fail in order to learn did not comingle at this age. On the negative side, difficulties in physical co-ordination and in learning, which so often leave the sufferer with a deeply depleted sense of self-esteem, contributed to anxieties about relating to the peer group, which takes on a numinosity, an awesomeness of its own in the next stage.

5 *Identity v role confusion*

> . . . They come then as birds in an irresponsible plumage
> Moulting their childhood for always,
> Half predatory, half
> Laughing . . .
> Ripeness that dares not open, that fears its own
> Promise, skin mercilessly
> Alive with star-points of sensation, angel-
> Senses aroused like petals outcurving
> After the first prolongation of the look in impossible
> mirrors
> With disquiet and admiration . . .
> (Iain Fletcher, *Faber Book of Modern Verse*, Faber 1960)

Few people claim to have enjoyed their adolescence. Some idealise it; others shudder at the recollection of it; still others look into the middle distance and mutter about their 'misspent youth' before hurriedly changing the subject.

Fletcher captures vividly a core concern of the adolescent — the fascination with and the alienation from the body. A primary task facing the adolescent is acceptance of the body. Anxieties about achieving this are often expressed in attacks on the body — excessive dieting, overeating, self-mutilation, etc. Adolescents quite suddenly find themselves in possession of heightened physical power, strength and, often, co-ordination (despite subjective feelings of awkwardness or gawkishness). Growth takes place unpredictably and is sometimes not synchronous with the onset of menstruation in girls or the first seminal emissions in boys. This adds to the feelings of confusion and to the agonies girls undergo in relation to the size of their breasts and boys to the length of their penises.

The adolescent is faced with the second task of integrating

major changes in his self-image and of coming to terms with powerful sexual feelings. There is a great increase in masturbation, which acts as a release of sexual tension. But more importantly, it provides a container in which experiment-ation can take place accompanied by rich fantasy, and not necessarily enacted aggressively or impulsively. Masturbation ideally acts as a bridge to mature sexual relationships, although it can become an end in itself, and contribute to social and sexual isolation.

Just as the self-image changes drastically, so the experience of the self is often felt to be fragmented so that various sub-personalities (a willing helper, a layabout, a hero, etc.) seemingly fail to relate. For instance, an adolescent may genuinely promise to do something and then fail to do it. These two sub-personalities are felt to have nothing to do with each other. This dilemma is often resolved by belonging to a gang or group, where each member can be seen by the adolescent to embody his various selves. The gang, therefore, acts as an externalised community of selves, until such time as the adolescent feels able to take these sub-personalities back into himself and integrate them. By so doing he works towards the third task of adolescence, finding his own sense of identity, his strengths and weaknesses; he achieves a new synthesis.

The gang is also the space between the childhood world of home and the adult world of work and sexual relationships. The adolescent's fourth task is to struggle for independence and emancipation from the family. The necessary rebellious-ness of adolescence has its precursor in the toddler saying 'no' as a way of separating. The parents have to be overthrown; but the parents also have to survive, otherwise the adolescent is left feeling guilty, out of control and uncontained. Winnicott wrote about meeting the 'adolescent challenge':

> understanding has become replaced by confrontation. . . .
> Confrontation belongs to containment that is non-retaliatory, without vindictiveness, but having its own strength . . . a grown up person stands up and claims the right to have a personal point of view, one that may have the backing of other grown-up people. (Winnicott, 1968a, p. 173)

With such strenuous demands being made on adolescents (and their carers!), it is not surprising that quite intense dependency needs arise, often causing consternation in parents. At the other end of the spectrum lies a sub-spectrum of minimal to extreme pathology, most of it short-lived, but none the less worrying for the adolescent and his family. I am referring to frequent somatic complaints at one end and to complete withdrawal, or major delinquency or psychosis at the other.

Brian:

Brian was born illegitimate. His mother was a teenager, unable to look after him, and so she placed him in a children's home, some time between his fourth and fifth month. When he was four, he was adopted by a clergyman and his wife, who had been advised not to have children because of congenital disease in the man's family. The adoption took place after the prospective parents had made several visits to the children's home to try and forge a relationship with Brian. He shunned their advances. When he finally went to live with them, he remained silent and withdrawn for some time.

The adoptive parents persevered and seemed to win through until Brian reached puberty. He developed crippling anxiety attacks, with symptoms of diarrhoea, incontinence, palpitations and sickness. He was prescribed medication, to which he became addicted over the next twenty years. His compulsive rituals served to ward off unacceptable hostile and sexual impulses, particularly terrifying images and guilt about masturbation. He became preoccupied with writing lists and with endlessly tidying his room.

An interest in the military surfaced, and he read avidly about new weaponry as well as keeping a large map on his wall on which he plotted troop movements over Europe. He was involved in the life of the church, and was considered by some of the parishioners to be too spiritual. His parents felt out of their depth, knowing that all was not well. They felt guilty about not having done enough for him, and bemused by his curious interests. Underneath, they also felt quite helpless.

Brian went to university, where his defences collapsed and

he broke down, unable to cope with work and continuing his social withdrawal, which had coincided with the eruption of his symptoms. He later returned, finished his studies, and spent his spare time with a reserve wing of one of the armed forces, which gave him the opportunity to enact playfully attacks on his projected enemy. He had passed through adolescence, but his conflicts had disappeared through complex defence patterns, and all reappeared some years later in his marriage, in his work, and in relation to everything mechanical. Wife, colleagues and machinery all came to symbolise longings for dependency cancelled out by terrors of abandonment (a repeat of his early trauma).

Brian's adolescent breakdown was determined in part by early environmental failure, but the eruption of symptoms in adolescence illustrates the all-too-typical stress to which the adolescent is subjected by the upsurge of instinctual energy and its concomitant fantasy.

6 *Intimacy v isolation*

Brian was one of those people for whom intimacy can suddenly flip over into the subjective experience of utter isolation and desolation. The sound of mother's voice suddenly becomes the scream of the institution's electric bell, calling the children to lunch.

There are others, known to pastors and therapists of every persuasion, who, like porpoises, dive in and out of relationships of sexual intimacy, but who feel profoundly isolated. Love and sensuality have not fused. Others feel driven into isolation by irrational fears of being swallowed up or of being engulfed by or engulfing the other, of losing a precarious identity that they have struggled to forge.

As adults who have emerged from the doldrums of adolescence, all these people, along with everyone else, at some level within themselves are searching for someone else with whom to have a mutually loving and genital relationship and have been trying to listen to or escape from their vocation, that is, to avoid listening to the voice within. We will look first at relationships.

Morley (1984, p. 30) has amplified Erikson's ideas and describes four pairs of opposites, or four continua along which each individual will try to find the most comfortable position. He suggests that attempts, even if unconscious, to locate this position form the 'emotional task' within the relationship. The four pairs are:

Attachment v detachment
Commitment v disengagement
Intimacy v alienation
Similarity v difference

To my mind, they provide a useful perspective in which to think about encounters (meaningful and time-limited) and relationships (attachments lasting through time), including those where the choice of partner is homosexual. The perspective is useful as long as one bears in mind the compensatory nature of the unconscious whereby, Jung asserted, any tendency towards one-sidedness at a conscious level will be counterbalanced in the unconscious:

... the last and most formidable opposition, which the alchemists expressed very aptly as the relationship between male and female. We are inclined to think of this primarily as the power of love, of passion, which drives the two opposite poles together, forgetting that such a vehement attraction is needed only when an equally strong resistance keeps them apart. (CW14 para 104)

Furthermore, the search for a comfortable position on Morley's continua is almost bound to be full of conflict.

In a situation of conflict a person can be paralysed or commute at speed between the opposing states, or be pulled on to one side of the conflict. Someone who has problems with commitment v disengagement might, for example, fear commitment as entanglement in dependence and be terrified of disengagement as imprisonment in isolation. Such a conflict is characterised by the affect of futility. If the person can sustain the conflict, a function comes into play which mediates the opposites by forming a compensatory relationship with each. This function was called by Jung the transcendent function, a term he borrowed from mathematics, although he originally used it to denote a function that transcended time, space and destructive tendencies. It was also called transcendent because it makes possible the transition from one attitude to another and links conscious with unconscious, thus producing a new synthesis. To return to Jung:

> The conflict between the opposites can strain our psyche to the breaking point, if we take them seriously, or if they take us seriously. The tertium non datur of logic proves its worth: no solution can be seen. If all goes well, the solution, seemingly of its own accord, appears out of nature. Then and only then is it convincing. It is felt as 'grace'. Since the solution proceeds out of the confrontation and clash of opposites, it is usually an unfathomable mixture of conscious and unconscious factors, and therefore a symbol, a coin split into two halves which fit together precisely. (*MD&R*, p. 309)

The symbol provides a new point of view, hinting at new possibilities, beckoning in faintly discernible directions, but none the less enabling the person to become unstuck, reoriented and to move on through life, armed with new meaning and a different attitude in an area that may be unknown. Such an approach is based on a capacity for psychic relatedness, which Jung called Eros, and which underpins much of Jung's thinking. Eros came to mean, for Jung, relatedness, love and intimacy, and is characteristic of the female principle. Its opposite is Logos, denoting discrimination, insight and judgement and hallmarking the male principle. Eros and Logos are often co-habitees in the same person. Within the person, the erotic relation is between conscious and unconscious, 'I–myself' and what is felt to be greater than me, and is to be found in the conjunction of opposites. But this inner relatedness, which enhances the process of individuation, cannot take place in a vacuum:

> The unrelated human being lacks wholeness, for he can achieve wholeness only through the soul, and the soul cannot exist without its other side, which is always found in a 'You'. (CW16 para 454)

Thus it was that he considered marriage (and I include relationship) as a psychological relationship, in which the way the pair relate to each other depends on their particular blend of consciousness/unconsciousness, or, as Morley puts it, the comfortable position between similarity and difference. A surfeit of similarity, or illusions of oneness, are probably as poisonous to a marriage as a relationship in which differences are so stark and jagged as to preclude any relatedness.

Jung proposed a model of marriage as a relationship between 'container and contained' (CW17, para 331c). The container (of either sex) refers to a personality more complex than that of the contained (also of either sex). For ease of explanation, I shall take the container to be the male partner, and the contained to be the female. The container feels that the various parts of his personality do not fit together in a harmonious way, and he therefore seeks containment in the more simple personality of the contained. She possesses an inner sense of at-oneness with herself, but feels dependent on the container to a degree that makes her feel insecure. In addition, she seeks simple answers from the container, whose complexity cannot accommodate simplicity. The container may try to find a way out of his dilemma by looking outside the marriage for someone to match his complexity and help him to achieve inner wholeness. What he desperately needs at that time is for himself to be contained within the relationship, but this is not possible since he is the one who provides the containment. Some form of breakdown might then occur, the purpose of which is to enable him,

> to become conscious of the possibility of an inner integration, which before he had always sought outside himself. (CW17 para 334)

Similarly, acknowledgement of failure by the contained forces her

> to recognise that the security she was so desperately seeking in the other is to be found in herself. In this way she finds herself and discovers in her own simpler nature all those complexities which the container had sought for in vain. (CW17 para 333)

Nick and Julie:

Nick and Julie were a middle-aged couple who were fairly entrenched in a pattern in which Julie acted as container and Nick as contained. Julie came from a rather upper-class background which encouraged her pursuit of individuality. After graduating in social sciences, she rose quickly up the hierarchy of personnel management, and from her exalted position scanned the social scene for a suitable man. Her left-wing ideology took her to a conference where she heard an amiable-looking priest speaking under the banner of the 'Greens' about acid rain and pollutants spewing out of the industrial complex that lay across the river from his parish in Wales. They fell in love, he with her dynamism and she with his beneficence, married, and settled under the cloud of yellow smoke that hovered permanently over the valley.

Children arrived quickly, and while Julie devoted herself to bringing them up and settling into a backseat role of being a vicar's wife, Nick became more energised and innovative in his work and was noticed by the powers-that-be. He was nudged through the diocese into more interesting jobs in places less polluted and finally settled down comfortably and effectively as archdeacon. The last of the children left home, and the power behind the throne suddenly surged up. Julie threw herself fully now into her personnel work, which had until then been part-time. She recapitulated her earlier rise up the promotional ladder, and a combination of occupational flair, humour, diplomatic assertiveness and elegance opened up all sorts of possibilities for her. She felt herself expanding socially and sexually, and became pushy and dominant at home, from which her work took her away for the odd week.

She became troubled by a growing materialism, the odd sexual fling which she could rationalise in terms of the sycophantic women that consumed hours of time with her husband in his study, and a general feeling of unease arising from the clash between her mode of life and her professed Christian values. Temptation came in the form of a recently divorced psychiatrist, an intense man, unconventional, unpredictable and unfathomable. A close friend counselled Julie to give the man a wide berth, saying that there are none madder than psychiatrists. Julie took no notice, but she carelessly left directions for a rendezvous with her lover by the phone. After some terrible rows and mutual recriminations the couple did sufficient work within and between themselves to enable them to forge a new and different equilibrium.

Both partners of that marriage were ambitious, although Nick's drive was less apparent. But there was also an unbridled quality in Julie, which swung into its opposite when she married, and only resurfaced in middle age when the children had left home. It enhanced an elusive, seductive side of her personality, and it was this that lured the psychiatrist to her and challenged him to capture and school her.

Jung's model omits two factors. One is the possibility of the marriage acting as container for both partners, who can then increasingly differentiate themselves from the image of the other. The second is that in a marriage container and contained can interchange. One partner can contain some aspects for the other which feel uncontainable and vice versa.

As in most cases, Nick and Julie had fallen in love with the image of the other. But the images are psychic images. The psyche is peopled by many 'Others', any of whom and parts of whom can be projected on to a person and then a partner. Three such 'Others' are the shadow, the anima and the animus.

> The shadow can be realised only through a relation to a partner, and anima and animus only through a relation to a partner of the opposite sex, because only in such a relation do their projections become operative. (CW9(ii) para 42)

Jung is describing a process in which masculine figures in the woman's, and feminine figures in the man's, psyche are projected on to an actual person whose personal qualities will attract the projection. These images come from the basic inherited structure of the psyche and are often encountered in dreams and fantasies. In their positive form they act as psychopomps or soul-guides and invite exploration of what is different from or other than the conscious attitude — in other words, the unconscious. In their negative aspect, they take possession of the man through moodiness, and of the woman through opinionated views. In relation to couples,

> When animus and anima meet, the animus draws his sword of power and the anima ejects her poison of illusion and seduction. The outcome need not always be negative, since the two are equally likely to fall in love (a special instance of love at first sight). (CW9(ii) para 30)

The psychological task is to retrieve the projection, to repossess or own those qualities that are perceived to be in the other and experienced as animating. The person is then enriched. Such enrichment can be fostered by the two people actually getting to know each other, a process that may or may not result in a lasting friendship or partnership.

We have spent some time looking at relationships; I now turn to vocation, to ponder some of the difficulties people have in valuing the voice within. Many people come to a pastor or pastoral counsellor because they feel impoverished of meaning and purpose. They have discovered that there is a profound dissociation in them between what they do for a living and what they secretly want to be.

Harry:

Harry was one of five children of a conservative, conventional family. His father had been head boy at school, captain of rugby at university, the youngest captain in the Navy during the war, and had ended his working career as a director on several boards. He seemed a giant of a man. Mother paled into insignificance by comparison. Both parents were rather cold and aloof, and the care of the children was delegated to nannies and boarding schools. As a child, Harry addressed his father as 'Sir'. This formality continued into adult life, and was supplemented by memos from father to son about Harry's finances and by a fearfulness that did not allow Harry to smoke in front of his father.

From his days at prep school, Harry had been aware of himself as two people: a 'Yes, Sir' person and an 'Up yours' person. The former obeyed most rules, stood by convention, and was adept in the niceties of social intercourse; the latter spent many an hour plotting the downfall of his oppressors. In later life, at his father's 'suggestion', he went to theological college with a view to taking Holy Orders. He was thought of as a diligent student, and someone who would be well-suited to a small parish in somewhere like Norfolk. But this outer picture did not at all correspond with Harry's inner state. Secretly he smoked pot, became an accomplished jazz bass player, and toyed guiltily with the idea of becoming a freelance translator. Modern languages were his passion in life. The struggle within him intensified until one day he returned to the college blind drunk.

By now, his studies had deteriorated and he was feeling more and more ill at ease within himself and with his fellow students. The principal referred him to a counsellor at the university health centre, who asked him what he really wanted to do in life. After a lot of work in his counselling, he was able to give more expression to the suppressed rage against his father. This freed him to break out of his internalised prison and to indulge his secret ambition and unleash his considerable creativity.

> What is it, then, that inexorably tips the scales in favour of the extraordinary? It is what is commonly called vocation: an irrational factor that destines a man to emancipate himself from the herd and its well-worn paths. True personality is always a vocation and puts its trust in it as in God, despite its being, as the ordinary man would say, only a personal feeling. But vocation acts like a law of God from which there is no escape. . . . He MUST obey his own law, as if it were a daimon whispering to him of new and wonderful paths. Anyone with a vocation hears the voice of the inner man: he is called. (CW17 paras 299–300)

7 *Generativity v stagnation*

It is always a living relationship between persons that gives the elbow room which is necessary for true growth. True growth gradually, and in the course of time, carries the child or adolescent on to an adult sense of responsibility, especially responsibility for the provision of secure conditions for the small children of a new generation. (Winnicott, 1960b)

The flight of time through the years from the mid-twenties to the late thirties brings in its trail the transition from physical union in order to have children to psychic union, or coniunctio, particularly with the contrasexual image of anima/animus in order to continue individuating.

For many, a lasting relationship comes to fruition in the form of children, who will continue the family line and will contribute to ensuring the survival of the species. The adult becomes a parent and, in most cases, experiences himself simultaneously as a father to his child, and a son to his parents. In addition he has an adult-to-adult relationship with his wife, from whom he sometimes seeks mothering in much the same fashion as she seeks fathering from him. The couple feel incomplete as a couple and the individuals in it often feel unfulfilled until the arrival of a child. The first pregnancy may confirm both partners in their sexual identity. For the mother, her first pregnancy may be a landmark akin to her first period, the losing of her virginity, her menopause. The external changes, often felt as disturbing to self-image, brought about by pregnancy are paralleled by psychic changes. Oedipal longings can be forsaken as the hope of a real child from her husband (as against a fantasised child from her father) fulfil childhood longings. Loss of freedom in the outside world, coupled with resentment of the husband's continuing freedom, can be echoed inwardly in anxieties about the child becoming separate and free.

Archetypal images of the feminine often crowd in on the mother, so that one day she feels herself to be the good, bearing and releasing mother, and the next day she is afraid of ensnaring and devouring aspects of herself in relation to her child. Motherhood becomes a three-generation experience. Her inner mother will exert pressures that clash with her baby's needs. Sometimes she will identify with her mother; sometimes with the baby. The father's involvement and support are not only beneficial to the baby, but they also help the mother to look after the needs of the child. At the same time, he can emphasise the adult relationship between himself and his wife and rescue her from her 'primary maternal preoccupation'. For both parents, the arrival of the child outside reactivates a relation with the child within. The more the latter is despised or hated, the harder it will be for the parent to meet the needs of the former.

Parenthood brings with it a reappraisal of one's own parents who, as grandparents, can enjoy their grandchildren free of the responsibility of being primary carers, and who can make reparation for any damage they fear they inflicted on their own children. The older generation serve to remind the new generation of parents of the gradual decline in physical and mental powers, a decline that contributes to the increasing intensity of the inner gaze on a field of vision that seems to need more and more attention. Jung talked about a mental transformation, which not infrequently occurs in the second half of life. It is sometimes precipitated by the loss of one or both parents, but this is by no means a necessary condition.

In 1913, at the age of thirty-eight, Jung broke with Freud. The event plunged him into what he called his 'confrontation with the unconscious', a courageous undertaking that acted as the well-spring for the rest of his creative activity over the next fifty years. Feeling that he was subject to a state of disorientation, menaced by madness and in danger of being swamped by his fantasies, he devised various techniques including stonebuilding, the recording and painting of his fantasies, internal dialogues between the personified figures that emerged from his unconscious, and the painting of mandalas. All these enabled him to 'take an objective view of the things that filled my being' (*MD&R*, p. 190).

In Jung's case, the mental transformation was dramatic. Elliot Jaques (1965) has made the interesting observation that highly creative people, using whatever medium, tend, by the time they have reached their mid-thirties, either to die (e.g. Mozart, Raphael) or to produce work that is radically different from their early work (Beethoven, Shakespeare). There is a shift in the survivors from the exuberant, youthful quick-fry creativity of their early years to a way of working that depends for its effect on simplicity, economy and slow-cooking. Jaques sees the possibility of moving into what he calls 'sculpted' activity as based on the successful reworking through of the 'depressive position'. This is a psychological mode of relating attained by the infant when he can recognise that the mother who meets his needs (the good mother) is also the mother who frustrates him. The infant is then faced with guilt over damaging her, fear of losing her, and a growing sense of concern for her and responsibility for himself.

Middle age remains the time when one's own parents tend to die. The loss of parents and the work of mourning perhaps lead on into a reflective attitude to the past and a corresponding drop in appetite for the pleasures of youth.

What about gay relationships? Is it a heterosexual prejudice that gay couples generate little or nothing, or that they degenerate into stagnation? Little is known about long-term homosexual relationships, other than that some produce out of their own coniunctio some sort of child, however symbolic.

It seems clear, though, that intense and profound feelings in someone for a person of the opposite or of the same sex are not indicative of a sexual orientation. Our bisexuality allows for these intense feelings, with which we all have to work so that they can be accepted and enjoyed without shame or guilt. There are homosexuals who have been so severely damaged that they are on an everlasting quest for someone who will mend this early damage. Such a partner will ideally reflect back to the searcher an unblemished mirror image of himself. This is largely impossible since the person behind the image is seldom satisfactory; the searcher then receives back a distorted image of himself, which sends him once again on his quest. Other homosexuals are unconsciously fettered to their mothers, or else have identified with their mothers in order to obtain their father's love. Those who cruise around in public places or have sexual encounters in public toilets are often engaged in a compulsive search for the father.

Whatever the motivation towards a particular sexual orientation (a process I do not wish to oversimplify), it seems reasonably clear that stagnation in a relationship or separation can be avoided where there is an optimal degree of psychological difference (which can, of course, be enhanced by anatomical difference) in terms of emotional make-up, functions, attitudes, values, etc.

8 Ego-integrity v despair

There is a Japanese haiku that reads:

Sitting quietly, doing nothing,
spring comes, and the grass grows by itself.

This implies a natural rhythm in life, a kind of universal path that the flight of time takes and that, through the process of evolution, has become ingrained in us. Very many people begin to dream of death in their fifties because unconsciously they still believe that death will overtake them in the seventh decade. Others are held by an image, like, for example, a patient of mine who had a vision of a wood in autumn, in which the trees, blazing in their autumn splendour, were surrounded by daffodils. Yet others become preoccupied with opposites like 'impermanent-eternal'.

Retirement presents a challenge in the form of an acute loss of the identity that a social role offered. In Jungian terms, we might talk of an over-identification with the persona, which, when stripped away, leaves the person defenceless and severely depleted of a source of self-esteem. Many organisations are beginning to come to terms with the deep sense of loss that employees feel when they retire, and are working at ways of weaning the employee from his source of purpose and well-being—in much the same way as a mother gradually weans her baby from the breast.

Gutmann considers that, 'over time and across gender lines, a massive transcultural gender shift seems to take place. The husband, who used to support his wife both physically and emotionally, now becomes more dependent on her as a kind of maternal authority' (Gutmann, 1977). Both partners seem to swap roles to some extent, the woman becoming less affiliative and more managerial, and the man more drawn to supportive and non-conflictual relationships. In the sexual sphere, each individual has to accommodate to waning genitality and to a loss of the reproductive function.

This may have alarming consequences for partners and sometimes children and neighbours. Men in particular manifest tendencies towards exhibitionism, masturbation, interest in pornography, as well as sexual behaviour that partners experience as intrusive, unloving and embarrassing.

Geoffrey and Brigid:

Geoffrey was a retired pastor, the father of three boys and a girl. His wife was a retired teacher. The marriage had not been very happy since the birth of the third boy, who had needed repeated heart surgery. Geoffrey was convinced that this boy was conceived out of wedlock, and considered the child's illness as proof of his suspicion. When the children had all left home, Brigid started drinking and became very depressed.

She was admitted to a psychiatric hospital, where she was dried out and given ECT. Her depression lifted, although she now complained of being forgetful. She managed to return to work, from which she retired shortly after her husband. They bought a flat that overlooked a harbour, and enabled Geoffrey to live out vicariously a lifelong ambition to sail around the world.

They were in their late sixties when, one day after lunch, Brigid awoke from her regular snooze to find her husband standing naked before her in the sitting room. She was none too pleased at the resurgence of his libido after such lengthy abstinence, and rejected his advances.

This seemed to make things much worse. He would suddenly undress at breakfast or fondle her too intimately on the bus. She went to the GP, who, recalling her psychiatric history, took her not very seriously, and sent her away with reassurance and an appointment in a week's time. Things came to a head one day when Brigid announced that she was going shopping on her own. Geoffrey pleaded to accompany her, but she was adamant in her refusal. We can imagine her alarm and dismay when she saw Geoffrey in the distance loping towards her—once again completely naked. He was admitted to psychiatric hospital, where he became hopeless and apathetic.

Brigid, relieved of his pestering, none the less felt utterly abandoned and returned to the bottle for solace. An accidental fire in the flat alerted a community psychiatric nurse to her distress and she was readmitted to the same hospital as her husband, who refused to have anything to do with her for some weeks. The couple were referred to the hospital chaplain. He, however, felt too near to retirement himself and was frightened by the downfall of a former colleague.

The couple's reconciliation and ultimate rehabilitation into sheltered housing came about after a series of group discussions for volunteers at the hospital run by a social worker. The two volunteers involved with Geoffrey and Brigid were enacting in the group the marital relationship — but not quite to the degree it had reached at home!

The final years of life are often beset by illness and circumscribed by failing strength. Partners, family and friends die, increasing the danger in the bereaved of isolation in grief and making them feel vulnerable to the fantasised envy of the departed for the living. On the other hand, many elderly people attain a wisdom and compassion that are selfless and foster tolerance towards self and others, and therefore promote dialogue. They enjoy respect from younger people, for whom they carry projections of the archetypal images of Wise Old Man or Woman, personifications of the spiritual principle in positive or negative form.

The death of others, particularly loved ones, tends to bring home the reality of one's own mortality. But preparation for death remains an internal affair, taking place in a social context, which is often antipathetic to such activity. Jung wrote,

> As a doctor I am convinced that it is hygienic — if I may use the word — to discover in death a goal towards which one can strive, and that shrinking away from it is something unhealthy and abnormal which robs the second half of life of its purpose (CW8 para 792).

It is interesting, then, that in 1966 Mary Williams published a paper called 'Changing Attitudes to Death'. From a review of psychological abstracts between 1931 and 1961 she concluded that death remained a taboo subject in Western culture and had, consequently, accumulated the charge of a repressed content seeking expression.

Death has reappeared over the last twenty years from its psychic exile. Williams attributes this to the threat of total annihilation raised by nuclear power and nuclear tests on all sides. The possibility of genocide has brought death home to us. Paradoxically, while those most likely to encounter death are dispatched to homes and hospitals to die out of sight, the media abound with coverage of war, murder and suicide, again giving the world constant reminders of death. It is ironic that the management of the preparation for death, of dying and of mourning have increasingly passed over into the hands of specialists/professionals, who, perhaps, have taken over this role from the churches.

Jung saw death both as 'a fearful piece of brutality', and 'a joyful event . . . a mysterium coniunctionis. The soul attains, as it were, its missing half, it achieves wholeness' (*MD&R*, p. 291). The opposites are finally transcended and the cycle of change has come to an end.

THREE

Containing and Resisting Change

———

The powerful light that has been banished returns. There is movement, but it is not brought about by force ... but is characterised by devotion; thus the movement is natural, arising spontaneously. For this reason the transformation of the old becomes easy. The old is discarded and the new is introduced. Both measures accord with the time; therefore no harm results. ('The Turning Point', *I Ching*)

A pastor introduces a parishioner to his supervision group:

Alfred:

'It was a cold November evening, an evening made colder by a power failure and a wind that moaned its way through the house. At the appointed minute, the door bell rang, and I found myself peering out into the dark, my torch finally alighting on a diminutive figure, almost totally enveloped by a trench coat, tailored for a much larger person. I was immediately enamoured of the warm heart Alfred wore on his sleeve, and by his humorous approach to the situation. "Lots of archetypes at work tonight", Alfred exclaimed as we shook hands and I showed him into a rather large, candlelit room, the flames flickering in the draught. Alfred unwrapped himself and sunk, or rather disappeared, into an armchair, allowing the briefest glimpse of his balding head.

'As we both grew accustomed to the light and eyed each other up and down, I could make out a distinctly boyish and beardless countenance from which boomed a hearty sonorous man's voice. I noticed in myself, almost as soon as we had sat down, a fantasy about my grandfather, who had been a rector

68

in the depths of Dorset; I imagined him sitting in the huge, supposedly haunted rectory, listening in candlelight to a parishioner.

'Within a few minutes of Alfred and I meeting each other, something both personal and yet distinctly impersonal had been constellated between us—something that I formulated to myself at that early point in the interview in vague terms of feeling powerful, idolised, impotent and humiliated. I even found that I had sunk down in my chair, embarrassed by my relative height, and perhaps sensing the possibility of an envious attack. There was also something religious in the air, religious in the sense of a "careful consideration of unknown dangers and agencies" (CW7 para 164).

'This man-boy in his clownish outfit related to the rich effusions of his unconscious as a participant in an unfolding drama, from which he could draw a wealth of meaning. But as we talked, we could begin to map out some of the unknown dangers and agencies.

'Alfred was sandwiched between an elder brother and a younger sister. When I met him, he was forty years old, single and a bachelor. At the chronological time of his climacteric, he had come to me for help in adapting to, withstanding and developing through a medically induced adolescence. This enormous task overlay almost thirty years of suffering taunts, jeers and insults evoked by his size and, I think, by the anxiety induced in strangers who, like me, were immediately faced with their own sense of freakishness, deeply unconscious though that might be.

'It transpired that Alfred had never attained to puberty, a failure that his father, a minister, had interpreted as a punishment meted out by God to the family. Both family and local congregation went to great lengths to put an end to divine retribution, and finally a date for a miracle was revealed to Alfred's father. Family and faithful congregated; the day came and went and Alfred was left with his shrivelled poogloo (mother's euphemism for his penis). As if this was not humiliation enough, Alfred consented to go through the whole ordeal again, because once again his father had been "spoken to". By now he was studying modern languages at university and was struggling to reconcile an intellectual, rationalistic ambience with the superstitious religiose atmosphere of his patriarchal family.

'In despair after a second dethronement, he approached a counsellor, who skilfully helped him to separate a bit psychologically and then to seek medical help. He was given hormone injections for two years, developed secondary sex characteristics and was plunged into the *sturm und drang* of adolescence.

'In a nutshell, I might say that his development had been skewed or one-sided. Physical stuntedness had been compensated excessively perhaps by a keen intellect and an absorption in matters spiritual as well as an enviable capacity to laugh at himself. A charitable outlook intertwined with a youthful naivete made him gullible and prone to exploitation and the denial of his own needs. At our first meeting, his booming voice seemed to symbolise an unfamiliarity with the bodily, the instinctual; and it also signified to me that, just as his voice was seeking a body to contain it, so also was he seeking someone who would "contain the adolescent growth processes . . . and survive intact, without changing colour" (Winnicott, 1968a, p. 169). He came to me just after he had been rejected by a girl.'

This is a fairly typical example of a parishioner approaching his pastor for help at a time of personal crisis, which is so often an opportunity for inner change. But change is painful; it is a temporary state of feeling a bit dismembered; it always involves loss; and it is archetypal and, therefore, potentially good and bad. Jung once said,

> God is the name by which I designate all things which cross my wilful path violently and recklessly, all things which upset my subjective views, plans and intentions and change the course of my life for better or worse. (Jung, 1961)

The pastor is often faced with people who want or seem compelled to change, and this change can take many forms which range from wanting to be a 'better' person in little ways, to making quite a massive change, such as being converted. All these changes can be seen within the context of the process of individuation, which means

> becoming a single, homogeneous being, and, in so far as 'individuality' embraces our innermost, last, and incomparable uniqueness, it also implies becoming one's own self. We could therefore translate individuation as 'coming to selfhood' or self-realisation. (CW7 para 266)

This chapter will unpack the notion of change, the means whereby change can be contained, and some of the ways it can be resisted.

Images of change:
Through the cold winter earth, a crocus finds the strength to push its way towards the light.

A depressed artist has an idea to paint a series of watercolours of an apple as it putrifies. Towards the end, she notices a maggot emerge—a symbol of new life.

The butterfly, delicate and elusive, undergoes a complete metamorphosis, consisting of a four-stage life-cycle.

A hospital chaplain witnesses the slow and devastating deterioration of a young person dying of AIDS.

A forester looks sadly at trees watered and damaged by acid rain.

A brilliant musician lives imprisoned in the present moment, some of his brain affected by a virus. He has lost all sense both of personal continuity and of its paradoxical companion, change. None the less, he ages.

From these images, we can discern changes that are healing, in the sense of giving a person a feeling of being more whole, and changes that maintain divisions within the person or between people, and sometimes lead to disintegration. In the first group, I am thinking of a shift in attitude; the modifying of a defence; the discovery of a new capacity; the reclaiming of qualities projected on to others; perceiving and freeing oneself from a previously unconscious pattern of relating or of behaviour; arriving at an insight; having a religious experience, etc. Many of these changes involve painstaking and laborious work. They are often sparked off by encountering someone else, whose wisdom, personality, knowledge or way of seeing things is somehow liberating or inspiring. But the flow is never one-way,

> For two personalities to meet is like mixing two chemical substances: if there is any combination at all, both are transformed. (CW16 para 163)

It was in alchemy that Jung found a rigorous working-out in projection of something that he considered to be a basic psychic process—transformation.

> The alchemical idea of transformation is rooted in a spiritual concept of value which takes the 'transformed' as being more valuable, better, higher, more spiritual etc. (CW14 para 613)

Jung envisaged transformation as the fourth stage of therapy (an idea not currently held) and as part of the process of moving towards completeness or wholeness, not perfection. In his book *Symbols of Transformation*, he illustrates the process with accounts of night sea journeys, descents into the underworld, and rituals of death and rebirth.

Sometimes, changes are negative. There is adaptation at the expense of loss of soul; personal loss does not lead to grief but to depression; defences collapse and result in personal breakdown; attitudes harden; the new is shunned with fear; a very one-sided approach suddenly swings into its opposite with little integration taking place (like a sudden conversion or a swing from depression into mania); a person gets caught up in meaningless changes to outer life, while really seeking meaningful transformation of inner life. Bitterness sets in.

> Indeed, bitterness and wisdom form a pair of alternatives: where there is bitterness wisdom is lacking, and where wisdom is there can be no bitterness. (CW14 para 332)

This bitterness replaces suffering, which is our constant companion in life, and which seems from all the great traditions necessary if we are to move towards wholeness, holiness or creativity. Edinger sees this suffering as the core of the Job archetype (Edinger, 1986, p. 1). He suggests that once the individual, like Job, descends into the dark night of the soul, he has three options. The first is to despair and commit literal or psychological suicide, and become bitter. Or the person may seek refuge in a creed or community that will repress or suppress the doubts into which he has been plunged. Or a numinous encounter between ego and self may occur. This is the Job archetype. It consists of:

(1) An encounter between the ego and a superior being.
(2) The ego being wounded or suffering as a result of the encounter.
(3) The ego enduring the ordeal and searching for its meaning.
(4) A divine revelation, by which the ego is rewarded with some insight and an enlargement of the personality.

This enlargement of the personality is very visible in Jung, who had long and deep experience of experimenting with his own nature during his intensive self-analysis following the break with Freud in 1913:

> the widening of consciousness is at first upheaval and darkness, then a broadening out of man to the whole man. (CW14 para 209)

His experiment was his confrontation with the unconscious, an experiment that did not take place in a vacuum. He very much needed evidence to substantiate his ideas and searched around in vain until a dream in 1926 pointed him towards alchemy, a discipline that lent itself as the historical foundation, which had previously eluded him. The transformation of matter into spirit constituted the basic aim of alchemy, along with attempts to transmute base materials into gold or the philosopher's stone. The alchemist, known as the adept, worked with a mystical sister, who might be real or imaginary, to produce a coniunctio of disparate elements in the vas. Symbolically, the elements were seen in terms of opposites which, in the process of combining, transformed each other and produced a new third element. For this process of transformation, which constituted the opus or work, to take place, the vas or vessel had to be tightly, hermetically sealed.

The usefulness of the alchemical metaphor lies not only in the reverence with which the adept proceeds, but also in discussing the relationship between pastor and client. Within the metaphor lies the fundamental idea that the pastor is both a complete person in himself and someone who contains within himself projections of unconscious inner contents of his parishioner. This is a notion that we will explore further on in greater detail.

Jung writes:

> The *vas bene clausum* is a precautionary measure very frequently mentioned in alchemy, and is the equivalent of the magic circle. In both cases the idea is to protect what is within from the intrusion and admixture of what is without, as well as to prevent it from escaping. (CW12 para 219)

Again, a little later, Jung states:

> Another, no less important idea is that of the Hermetic vessel . . . typified by the retorts or melting furnaces that contained the substances to be transformed. . . . For the alchemists, the vessel is something truly marvellous: a vas mirabile. Maria Prophetissa says that the whole secret lies in knowing about the Hermetic vessel. 'Unum est vas' (the vessel is one) is emphasised again and again. . . . It is a kind of matrix or uterus from which the filius philosophorum, the miraculous stone is to be born. (CW12 para 338)

In pastoral counselling the *vas bene clausum* refers to all those aspects of the professional relationship that offer containment to the client. It is therefore primarily the pastor's responsibility, since he knows from his training and his experience that a feeling of trust cannot develop within a framework that is flimsy or unpredictable. The relationship might be compared with that of Japanese Sumo wrestlers. Vast men weighing over thirty stone can only crash into their opponents with all their might because they have absolute confidence that the ring in which they fight will not give way beneath them.

Anthropology contributes the notion of *rites de passage* to the management of change. Leach tells us that most transition rites have three phases (Leach, 1976). The person changing status (wife to widow, adolescent to man) is first separated from their former role by moving from one place to another, changing clothes, or ritual washing. Then, there is a period of social timelessness during which the person is kept apart from the main society (mourning, or a honeymoon). Finally, the person is connected with his new role in life, often by a reversal of the rituals in the first phase. Death and rebirth symbolism is often evident in many of these ceremonies, which help us to cross thresholds.

From religion, we have the notion of form or ritual, within which the encounter with the numinous can take place. Obedience or conformity to the form helps to clear a space within which the numinous can appear. Ritual and liturgy will be very familiar to readers. Suffice it to note here that Jung considered that the rites of religion constitute 'a sufficiently effective defence against inflation of the ego' (CW8 para 426). (See Glossary.)

Aspects of containment in pastoral care and counselling consist of a reliable and consistent relationship, sustained by an agapaic attitude. People seek help in crisis or at the end of a gestation period, often quite long, during which a vague sense of unease with themselves and their lives has crystallised out into something more definite, although subjectively it may feel formless, and therefore frightening.

Whichever the avenue by which the client approaches, each client will be in a state of loss, occasioned by giving up the image of himself as a coping, capable fellow, who had a good understanding of what made him tick. The move from independence, with the loss of pride and often quite deep feelings of shame, to dependence on someone comparatively unknown, often idealised, is quite momentous. It is a bereavement and contains within it feelings of disorientation. There is however an element usually lacking at a conscious level in the early stages of bereavement. It is hope, and the hope is to be accepted and understood by another, a potentially transformative experience, which takes place within a relationship. This relationship is bounded by confidentiality, time and space, and takes place, where necessary, within a network of inter-agency collaboration.

Confidentiality

Perhaps historically there can be no professional or vocational group so drenched in the fog of confidentiality as pastoral care, a fog that blurs what is seen and carries what is heard into the recesses of the soul. To speak to a pastoral worker in confidence means to speak to him with the conviction that what is revealed will be held in trust for him until such time as both parties can use it for the benefit of the client. The seal of the confessional has traditionally been hermetic; but outside the confessional, the ramifications of confidentiality are highly complex, and the boundaries of secrecy are seldom conveniently clear.

Jung was aware of the potential in secrets to enclose and to exclude, and was, therefore, aware of their power. When he was ten, he carved a little manikin out of wood, coloured and clothed it and embedded it in a pencil case with a special stone, the manikin's stone, that he had found in the Rhine. He placed the pencil case in the attic, forbidden territory, where he hid it on a beam under the roof,

> for no one must ever see it! I knew that not a soul would ever find it there. No one could discover my secret and destroy it. I felt safe, and the tormenting sense of being at odds with myself was gone. (*MD&R* p. 34)

At the time, he had no idea why he was doing what he was doing. It was only twenty-five years later that he came to see the manikin as a symbol of the creative impulse. After a further ten years of experience, he was envisaging the confessional as the prototype of analytical treatment and had linked together the ideas of sin, psychic concealment and repression:

> Anything concealed is a secret. The possession of secrets acts like a psychic poison that alienates their possessor from the community. . . . A secret shared with several persons is as beneficial as a merely private secret is destructive. The latter works like a burden of guilt, cutting off the unfortunate possessor from communion with his fellows. (CW16 paras 124 and 125)

It is not that difficult to relate to these ideas on a personal level; and it is even less difficult to relate them to a client or parishioner. But suppose we turn the whole thing up on its head, as in the following example.

Archie:

At the end of a year, Archie had settled uncomfortably into his role of curate to a vicar who was sound, experienced, conservative and nearing retirement. Archie was theologically and politically rather on the left, and, while he had alienated some of the older parishioners with his jeans and trainers, he had attracted into the church a small but powerful group of liberal, middle-class intellectuals, to whom he devoted much time and energy.

Soon after his arrival in the parish, he had been adopted by elderly twin sisters, who delighted in baking him cakes and knitting him socks and jumpers. They were also mischievously admiring of his 'unwelcome' views and prided themselves in desporting their own considerable intellectual prowess before him. As retired teachers of some repute, they were able to weather his extreme views with tolerance and veiled approval.

The happy relationship of this incongruous trio was rocked one winter's day when Ethel phoned to say that Amie was in hospital, with several bones broken as a result of a fall in the snow. Archie visited both sisters independently and took part conscientiously in Amie's plans for discharge, convalescence and re-entry into life with her sister. Eventually, Amie returned home. But Archie noticed that the playful, sparring atmosphere between them had been overtaken by an appalling gloom, broken only by sparks of irritability. He noticed that slips of memory and confusion over dates that had been occasional were now frequent. Ethel was stretched to keep up even a show of charity, let alone sisterly love, and Archie understood that she was plunged into a most terrible conflict over her sister's future. Most tragic of all was Amie's awareness of her degenerating mental capacities and her open longing for death.

One day, as if reading Archie's reluctance to continue his visits, Ethel phoned up and asked him to tea a week later.

Quite casually, at the end of the conversation, she asked for his views on the relative merits of the old and new orders of service for the dead. He enthused about the new and hung up, only to be filled instantly with a sense of dread. As an intellectual, he swept this aside, and rushed off to a school governors' meeting, for which he was customarily late.

His heart sank a few days later when an autopsy revealed that Amie's death was due to suffocation and an overdose of drugs and alcohol. The twins' allegiance to the principle of euthanasia had resonated in Archie's head, but its enactment within the warmth of human relationship troubled him deeply.

What would you have felt, said, done in Archie's situation? This is the sort of pastoral dilemma that throws up so many questions that, in order not to feel overcome by perplexity, we feel inclined to make pontifical pronouncements and assuage everyone's anxiety. It is more productive to keep alive one's doubts. It is possible in this case to make a few preliminary comments. The hermetic seal of the confessional was absent and the social nature of the trio's meetings blurred any need for an understanding about confidentiality. Euthanasia had been part of the humorous exchange between the three of them; the humour may have been a way of coping with an unspoken anxiety among them, which, in retrospect, could have been addressed.

Archie and Ethel had secretly hoped for Amie's death, but the despair over the situation had not been shared. Archie was torn between his head and his heart, abdicated his role of priest, and handed it over to Amie; deep down, he had known what was going to happen. With whom could or should this knowledge, even if it was of a mainly intuitive nature, have been shared? The police? A member of the Church hierarchy? A close friend? This particular dilemma touches on ethical, philosophical, moral and religious issues, which the reader may like to contemplate.

Jeremy:

The Church Army worker, recently trained in counselling, was baffled by Jeremy. He described him as someone who, having pressed the red button on the escalator, had no idea why everything came to a standstill. Jeremy had developed severe panic attacks after being arrested by the police for receiving a large quantity of stolen goods. Jeremy denied knowing that they were stolen, although he could not produce any paperwork that gave evidence of an above-board transaction.

The Church Army worker, Paul, was telephoned by Jeremy's solicitor, who requested a letter for the court saying that Jeremy's state of mind was such that he could not have known the goods were stolen. Paul said he would discuss the matter with Jeremy when they next met. Jeremy failed to arrive at his next session. Paul decided to write none the less, and then shared his letter with the GP, who was also writing to the court. The two congratulated each other on their letters and dispatched them.

At Jeremy's next session, Paul explained what had transpired. Jeremy was coldly angry. He had not given any permission for any communication behind his back. Nor had he given the solicitor Paul's name and number. Furthermore, a letter was superfluous because he was going to plead not guilty, and would consequently not receive a custodial sentence. Finally, how could Paul have written when he had no idea of what Jeremy's state of mind was at the time of the alleged offence?

Paul then pointed out that he had written to the court out of his conviction that a custodial sentence would only be harmful; using another aspect of containment, he also confronted Jeremy with his fantasy of magically controlling the court by pleading not guilty, an approach quite likely to infuriate the judiciary and result in a prison sentence. The process of confrontation offers containment in so far as it envelops a person within a sort of circular mirror, not allowing him to escape the experience of seeing what he is actually doing. He is faced by another person facing him with his words and actions. There is no running away; he feels contained, although he might hate that feeling.

By working on his own feelings, Paul was able to understand that Jeremy was unable to contain his anxiety and was infecting the people most important to him with it.

Hence, his wife was acting impetuously, his counsellor and GP had been panicked into precipitous action, and the solicitor was searching frantically for an escape from helplessness. The outcome of the infection was a break in the pastoral containment, leaving the client feeling very uncontained and unsure of whom he could trust.

In this case, the issues are much more straightforward. The principle that emerges is that the pastoral container cannot be broken without the client's considered permission.

At the end of a day, the pastoral counsellor is often left feeling weighed down not so much by information, as by the intensity of the day's emotional experiences, imagery, client material that might resonate uncomfortably within himself and, sometimes, a sense of responsibility. These and other factors can pressurise the counsellor into wanting to offload some of what he is trying to contain to his spouse, a friend in the pub or a supper party, where the humorous side of pastoral anecdotes can be a great release and relief.

Of vital importance is the principle that not only the client but also the client's material is treated with care and respect. Confidentiality can then be experienced as being in the service of both parties in the relationship. It can sustain, hold and support, like the mother's arms, but it can also set very firm limits, like the arms of a policeman controlling the traffic.

Time

In conscious waking life, we are bound by clock time. The unconscious, however, is timeless. The pastor's familiarity with the concept of eternity makes him particularly prone to being caught at the interface of time and timelessness. The experience of being asked for five minutes of one's time is not reserved for pastors or pastoral counsellors, although some of them are known to be very gullible to such requests. What is universal in these requests is a dissonance between what is said and what is meant.

The pastor is in danger of acquiescing resentfully to what he knows is often going to turn out to be a lengthy encounter. I say 'resentfully' because the giver in the situation is often flattered by the request, while at the same time feeling invaded and often caught between loyalties: the wish to be helpful to the client and the knowledge that his involvement is going to keep him away from an already existing commitment.

In order to function effectively, he needs to develop skills in containing both himself, his client and his family within certain time boundaries. These include working hours, a day off, adequate holiday periods and time-bounded interviews. A series of time-bounded interviews is often more helpful than a marathon sitting, during which attention wanes, and there is no chance to work through what has been discussed.

David:

A nineteen-year-old student of psychology was referred to a college counsellor by his head of department, who had noticed his bizarre appearance and depressed manner. David told the counsellor that he had become depressed when he fell in love with his girlfriend. He felt so awful in situations in which she left him, like the end of a weekend, that he was reluctant to become further involved with her. And yet he was crazy about her. The depression he felt was undermining his studies to the extent that he had failed his first-year exams and was now in a serious quandary. The counsellor searched around for a link between closeness and abandonment and quite soon found one. David's mother had died of cancer when he was five.

The father had been having affairs during his wife's terminal illness, perhaps as a manic defence against the impending loss. Within months of the mother's death another woman moved in to the house and later became David's stepmother. Other children supplanted him and when the reconstituted family moved to another house, David ended up in the smallest room.

The counsellor decided that she had to grab the bull by the horns and began to probe in the area of the defences surrounding the loss of the mother. Having made deep contact with David, she then suggested that his fears of involvement with his girlfriend were a result of the fact that he could not bear to get close to another woman and then face the possibility of losing her. David was at first aghast at this idea and then quite distraught. The counsellor, a woman, offered him twelve sessions with a fixed termination date. The two of them would focus on the conflict they had unearthed. Sessions missed by him would not be made up and immediate notice was given of holiday breaks.

The outcome was predictably good, since it was almost inevitable that the problem that the counsellor had encapsulated for the client would surface quickly in the counselling relationship and would assume exaggerated proportions as termination approached. The work was satisfactorily concluded and through it the client acknowledged further areas that needed exploration, possibly in a group setting. These included sibling rivalry, ushered in by the client's fantasies about who was going to take his place in the consulting room, and some difficulties with authority figures.

Failure to keep time boundaries often results in insufficient nourishment for the pastor, as Wendy's case illustrates.

Wendy:

The conductor walked into the pastoral support group dead on time. The assembled members subsided into a hush. The conductor noticed several surreptitious glances at the one empty chair and eventually said that it seemed difficult to get down to work because everyone was wondering where Wendy was, and was engrossed in feelings about her absence which for some reason they were keeping to themselves. This eased the atmosphere. Some members shared their feelings and their speculations about her absence, and the group was freed to get to work on the presentation of a case.

At 2.00 p.m., when the group had been meeting for an hour, the door flew open and in breezed the rather stunning Wendy, dressed in bright red and tossing back her long blonde hair as she deluged the group with apologies and plunged into an account of a difficult encounter with a client.

This man had been due for his appointment at 11.00 a.m. He had rushed into the office an hour late, saying that he had been kept waiting at the DHSS only to be given no money at the end of this time. He was in a terrible state. It was Friday, he had no money for the weekend; he didn't mind about himself, but he could not bear to see the children go hungry; he did want to talk about other things, but could Wendy please sort something out with the DHSS first. Wendy realised that her lunch hour had gone out of the window; it also occurred to her that she might even have to miss the group. But that did not matter. Like Harry, her client, she could not bear the thought of the children going hungry. She remembered having a drink with that man from the DHSS who was rather taken with her; she would give him a ring and possibly even go round to see him with Harry . . .

A senior clergyman in the group suddenly clapped his hands down on his knees and threw them up to his hair and made as if to tear it out. He berated Wendy for storming into the group late, disregarding and disrupting the lively discussion they had been having, and accused her of using her sexual airs and graces to protect herself from the wrath of the group. There was a deathly silence. Leonard had never before spoken like that. Wendy looked crestfallen and profoundly confused and tearful.

Gradually, other members, liberated by Leonard's outburst, were able to help Wendy to focus on what had happened. A greedy, disorganised client had left it to the last minute to seek money from the DHSS; his guilt at failing to procure it had been injected into Wendy, who had deprived herself of her lunch and of her own source of replenishment, the group, in order to become the all-providing, bountiful mother, depriving her client of frustration and totally unaware of the seductiveness contained in her suggestion of driving Harry round to the DHSS, where she would act as an all-powerful advocate and enhance his sense of helplessness and inappropriate dependence. The whole process had been mirrored in the group, where her attempts to elasticate the time boundaries had resulted in insufficient nourishment for her or any of the other members.

The normally extraverted Wendy fell into a depressed silence for two or three weeks, and then emerged like a butterfly from a chrysalis to carefully and painstakingly explore the many issues the group had raised. She was helped to experience the holding effect of time boundaries and so to be able to construct and maintain similar boundaries for her clients. Her work became less disorganised, and she addressed in a movingly humble way the flaunting of her sexuality as an escape from the hopeless and helpless feelings induced by so many of her clients.

Space

The containment of time intersects with that of space, the two forming a matrix of certainty and predictability that are mirrored in the reliability and consistency of the pastor.

The physical space in which pastor and client meet takes on a significance akin to the familiarity and safety of the pram, the child's room, the home, and later to all those derivatives of the womb, in which growth and development can take place. The sameness of the room, the placing of the objects within it and the ambience that all these go to create offer a containing space within which transformation can and does take place. Changes in setting, impingements upon it or accidents within it can all have severe and unexpected results.

Angela:

Angela's father had converted from Christianity to Judaism. During her childhood he had taught in the local school in Russia; her mother had been out working in a factory all day. And so Angela and her father were thrown together for the few hours between the end of school and the time when her mother got home from work.

After some weeks of work, in which I had noticed an almost unbearable stiffening of my muscles during sessions with her to the extent that I thought that I was going to fragment into little pieces, she told me one day of the terrifying times with her father in the attic, where he sexually abused her. I could at last make sense of my physical state: it mirrored her terror at being left alone with her father. We talked about her fear of being alone with me and how this was so like being with her father.

At the end of the session, she got up, went to the door to open it, and the handle disengaged from the lock, effectively imprisoning us in the room. Her panic was all too obvious. I made reassuring noises, leapt out of the window into the snow, and made my way through the garden and round to the front of the house. I returned to the consulting room to find Angela in a state of near collapse. It was as if in my absence from the room she had been left with my presence, symbolically the terrifying and longed-for presence of her father. I did my best to salvage the relationship and so did she, but the containment of the consulting room had in one moment been turned paradoxically into a prison with an open window. It no longer offered her the sanctuary and safety she sought, and she did not return.

Ideally, the pastor's working room will contain comfortable chairs of approximately the same height, be adequately heated (or cooled) and quietly lit. Personal effects should be minimal, since they impinge on the client's space. On the other hand, the room needs to express enough of the pastor for him to feel at home in it for long stretches of time. If possible, in-coming telephone calls should be excluded either by having the phone elsewhere or by installing an answering machine, so that interviews are not interrupted.

Similarly, intrusions from the family have to be ruled out. This is often difficult for partners and children to accept, but it reinforces the necessity for the pastor to be clear about time boundaries. My own long-suffering children got so resentful at one stage about my working in the house and being unavailable that they took to turning the volume of the television up and down in quick succession in the next-door room, so that eventually I was forced to come out of my room and read them the riot act—only to return and be accused by my client of being a callous and tyrannical father!

Containment is also offered in the way a client is referred on to another agency. A question is often posed by pastors embarking on their work: 'How can I refer a client who has already formed an attachment to me?' This is an important question and one that deserves careful attention.

The first duty of a pastor is not to harm. Harm can include storming through defences and unleashing overwhelming affects, aggressive outbursts or psychotic irruptions, to name but a few. It can also include raising false hopes, encouraging premature attachments, acting from possessiveness or omnipotence and creating expectations that are doomed to profound disappointment. On the other hand, the pastoral counsellor cannot hope to work with every client referred; nor will every client's particular distress come within the pastor's competence, for reasons of personality, experience or training.

Between the extreme of taking the risk of harming clients and the other extreme of accepting nobody for fear of harming them, there is a middle path—that of befriending. This is a process whereby the pastor offers support, an opportunity for a parishioner to share their feelings and problems in order to 'facilitate a self-awareness and an increased inner strength that will allow and encourage us to take care of ourselves, not just others, and to become reasonably good parents to ourselves whatever may have been our actual experience of childhood and growing-up' (Coate, 1989, p. 204).

If befriending is not viable and there is a possibility of *not* working with someone, then this should be stated as soon as this is known: 'I'm not able to work with you myself, so we will use the time to explore what is troubling you and to discuss what might help best.' That sort of approach signals a clear boundary for the client, who might then look relieved or disappointed, feelings that can be taken up immediately.

Suzie:

A parish worker had supported a single woman through the harrowing and extremely painful experience of nursing her mother to her death, the result of cancer of the brain. The disease had brought in its wake changes in personality and some confusion. Not long after her mother's death, Suzie had taken herself off for a year around the world and then returned to England, but to another parish. On her return, she phoned the original parish worker and asked to see her once about a very specific issue. The worker accommodated her and the two of them met.

Suzie came straight to the point. She had met a homosexual English man in America. He had declared his love for her and she had just received a letter from him, announcing that he was leaving his job in the States, selling up, and hoping to arrive in England in the spring, at which time they could get married and have a child—something both of them had actually discussed at length. Suzie was in a panic.

The parish worker listened intently. She had known about Suzie's confusion over her sexuality and had thought to herself that her homosexual leanings were leanings rather than fixtures, and possibly represented a defence against growing up. She also knew that Suzie's Canadian father had deserted when Suzie was eight, and that she, her one-legged grandfather and her Irish mother had returned to England from abroad and settled with a benign couple in the heart of the country. Later, Suzie had made contact with her Spanish grandmother, and had recontacted her father who had married a manic-depressive. The father's new wife had died in a psychiatric hospital, and the father now lived with a formidable Ukrainian, neither of them wanted anything to do with Suzie. The girl seemed rootless in a family sense, but also in an internal sense.

During this one interview, Suzie casually dropped a dream into the conversation, which strengthened the worker's hunch that Suzie wanted to explore her sexuality in depth. After some consideration, the worker came up with the idea of an analytic group, and gave her reasons for the suggestion. Suzie collapsed in tears. Acting on her intuition and her empathy, the worker quickly said that she could imagine that Suzie felt that yet again she was being pushed from pillar to post; how angry and disappointed that made her feel; and (very importantly) how those feelings might stop her thinking about the suggestion, let alone taking it up. This comment freed Suzie's anger, which in turn allowed her to think. By the end of the interview, she had gratefully asked to be referred for group therapy.

The point of giving this case study is to emphasise how important it is to search around for evidence of disappointment and anger so that those feelings can be expressed directly there and then. If they are not, it is more than likely that the client will not engage with the person to whom he has been referred. The new worker will be made to feel what it is like to be rejected, and the client may well disappear into a void.

Peter:

A GP left a message on the answering machine of his friend, the vicar (who himself had had a vasectomy), saying that he had advised one of his patients to contact the vicar for advice over whether or not to proceed with a vasectomy. No sooner had the vicar listened to the message than the door bell rang, and there stood Peter on the doorstep. The vicar took him in, made him a cup of tea, and invited him to talk.

Already, the vicar was feeling distinctly uneasy. There was something very strange about this man, who was balanced precariously on the edge of his chair, anxiously scanning the room while slurping his tea. After a lot of spluttering, Peter ashamedly confessed that he had been convinced that passengers on the bus were laughing at him. He had never felt like this before; and he still felt anxious with the vicar, whom he had known for some time. What on earth was going on? There was a menacing abrasive tone to his voice, quite unlike his usual personable manner. By now, the vicar was wishing he had never opened the door.

'I thought you had come about having a vasectomy', he said.

Peter exploded, saying he had never felt so humiliated in his life. He had gone to the GP, having taken Dutch courage, come clean with his dilemma, only to see the GP ring his bell for the next patient, and write the vicar's phone number on a leaf from a prescription pad.

'What the hell do you know about vasectomies anyhow, you sexless creep?'

Peter leapt to his feet and left the house, slamming the door behind him. He did not reappear at church, nor did any collaborative work between the vicar and the GP produce positive results. It was left to a pastoral support group to help the bewildered vicar with his feelings, and to help him reach an understanding of how Peter's persecutory feelings were a projection of his fury with the GP for approaching the issue in an apparently casual manner, and for referring the client with little obvious thought.

A referrer acts primarily as a bridge, spanning a gulf between the client and the new worker/agency. The ideal referral is made under conditions in which the client trusts the referrer and the referrer trusts the new worker/agency. The latter is not as frequent as one might hope, because of feelings of rivalry and envy that exist between some agencies and that can make referral break down. Where sufficient trust exists within the helping network, the client can feel very contained and held, even in cases like families with severe problems who might be involved in several agencies simultaneously.

We have explored what might facilitate change. A little self-exploration will reveal that we have an almost natural resistance to change. Resistance has its positive and its negative aspects. Unlike most of the defences that are intra-personal, resistance is an inter-personal phenomenon. The person trying to facilitate change will have the subjective feeling of 'being up against a brick wall', a feeling that Jung warns us to respect:

> When, therefore, there are strong resistances, the conscious rapport with the patient must be watched, and — in certain cases — his conscious attitude must be supported to such a degree that, in view of later developments, one would be bound to charge oneself with the grossest inconsistency. (CW16 para 381)

The notion of resistance took shape in Freud's mind when he was puzzling over a paradox handed to him by his patients. On the one hand, people came to him for help, actively wanting to co-operate with him in whatever way they could. All he asked them to do was to say whatever came into their heads. Most people complied readily enough with such a reasonable request, but invariably at some point fell silent. While consciously wanting to co-operate, unconsciously they were going on strike, and their unconscious was winning. It was this unconscious strike that he called resistance. Resistance is an interpersonal activity whereby one person (family, group etc.) puts up and keeps up a barrier against the potential influence of another person (family, group), who is experienced as a threat to equilibrium.

The resisting person may be afraid of unpleasant feelings (like shame); of being disoriented by change (artists going into therapy sometimes fear that they will not be able to create); of the loss of the familiar (the devil you know is better than the one you don't); of the loss of attention consequent upon recovery (clinging to illness); the vacuum made by the absence of self-punishment, which would have taken the form of symptoms or moral masochism.

Resistance is inter-personal, paradoxical and, as Roy Schafer has pointed out, bi-polar:

> While mounting this opposition has its negative aspects, such as denial, avoidance, dread, disclaimed action, it also has its affirmative, even constructive aspects, such as maintaining relationships, being faithful to ideals, maintaining pride, autonomy and achieving mastery. (Schafer, 1973, p. 283)

Jung says something similar:

> In particular, the view that the patient's resistances are in no circumstances justified is completely fallacious. The resistances might very well prove that the treatment rests on false premises. (CW16 para 237)

What are these false premises? In 1977, Hobson and Meares wrote a helpful paper called 'The Persecutory Therapist' (Hobson and Meares, 1977). Although addressed to psychotherapists, the content of the paper can be generalised out to anyone working in a pastoral setting. The authors describe a persecutory, downward spiral which sets up resistance in the client and acts as a kind of self-protection to the client. In being persecutory, the pastor would:

Be intrusive, by asking endless questions;
Be derogatory: 'I think that behaviour is rather childish, don't you?'
Be invalidating: 'You don't really mean that you hate your mother'.
Be opaque: 'You don't need to know about me; asking me questions is a way of avoiding talking about yourself'.
Be destructive to the structure by: Changing the setting (attacking the container); making unreasonable demands (like asking a mother to come at 3.30 p.m.); giving double

messages ('Feel free to get angry, but please don't get angry with me'); making conflicting demands ('We need to talk about your sexuality, but please do not mention your feelings for my wife').

But the client can be equally persecutory to the pastor, and one of the most common manifestations of this is the Negative Therapeutic Reaction (NTR). When such a reaction occurs, the pastor is likely to feel that all his patience, dedication and care have been ruthlessly discarded, and that all the work done has been thrown to the wind. This in turn is likely to provoke a retaliatory response, which can be checked if the pastor seeks to understand the purpose of such destruction.

In penal establishments, for example, 'inmates' are known to misbehave just before their release. This is often felt by the staff to be a defiant, obscene gesture, which makes them all feel they have failed. Closer inspection of the dynamics will reveal an acute anxiety in the inmate about losing the structure of prison life, about having to find a way in life, about reconciling with wife and family, about reconstituting a normal sex life, about a fear of reoffending. As a rough guide, the NTR occurs when the subject feels threatened by the loss of a relationship, or by psychic pain which feels unbearable, or by unconscious guilt about feeling all right. It is a phenomenon the understanding of which need not always be verbalised; like much psychodynamic knowledge it can inform the practice and management of a case.

To return to less malignant forms of resistance, I will give two examples—one arising out of individual counselling, the other occurring between two groups.

Aletheia:

Aletheia was a twenty-five-year-old single girl who was referred for counselling because of failure to achieve her potential. Working as a filing clerk, she had an ambition to do a course in pastoral theology, something easily within her potential from an academic point of view because she had got a good degree at university. With much patience and empathy, the counsellor lived through weeks of withholding silences and made what sense he could of fragmented communications from her. Then, a series of five sessions showed up a very clear pattern. (Often, the pastor has to wait a long time to see the shape of an emerging pattern.) By now, she was underway with her pastoral theology course, and, like everything else, it seemed doomed to failure. Over five sessions, the following themes emerged:

(1) She had phoned her parents to say that she was acting in a play, but they were not going to come.

(2) She had bought some paint to decorate the house but had done nothing with it.

(3) She had had an embarrassing rehearsal the day before.

(4) The local authority was giving her a difficult time over her grant.

(5) She could not start her other essays because she did not know what mark she had got for her first one.

(6) She had taken a Bible meeting at church very badly. A woman had come along and wrecked it (a shadow projection).

(7) Despite many gains at the play, such as meeting new people and being invited to do further acting, she complained that she had sat in a draught and ended up with a stiff neck.

(8) She wanted to do an essay on transubstantiation, but her tutor had given her the wrong books, including one that was unintelligible.

(9) She had given no thought to her research, an outline of which was due to be handed in quite soon.

(10) She had not written the required number of essays.

(11) She said she felt she was a pile of shit; that pissed her off; she felt even more pissed off when she prayed to God and asked him to forgive her for being a pile of shit.

The themes have a coherence to them. In each masochistic situation, there is someone (internal or external) inflicting suffering on Aletheia. There is also, as Masud Khan has told us, a third party, the witness, a role once assigned to God, and now given to the counsellor (Khan, 1979). The counsellor was in a dilemma. His gut feeling was to move from the role of witness to that of rescuer. He followed this feeling and was surprised to find an intensification of her suffering. Her resistance to change was finally traced back to a psychic cover-up of the loss of her father, who seems to have fallen in love with her younger brother when he was born. Her clinging to failure could then be seen, in Gordon's terms (Gordon, 1987), as the 'shadow-side of the need to worship and venerate' her father/tutor/counsellor/God. What the counsellor had to work with and work through in a painstaking but confrontative way was Aletheia's resistance to giving up her need to fail—something both self-destructive and designed, unconsciously, to punish her parents, particularly her father.

Working through is another technical term meaning to go over and over again the same thing until there is adaptation to change. Working through is the work of mourning, the work of giving up what is useless or lost. It is like the relentless, repetitive movements of the tides that constantly change the shape of the shore in an endless cycle of loss and gain, so that what was previously invisible, intangible, incommunicable is transformed and integrated into the self.

In a one-to-one setting working through is often possible. In an inter-group situation it is not so easy, and resistance to change is harder to manage. The resistance tends to precipitate out into various individuals who are perceived as obstructive, bound by tradition and inimical to innovation. Such people carry the anxiety about change for the group. To exclude them is no answer because the exclusion usually weakens the holding capacity of the container for change:

> the conflict . . . requires a real solution and necessitates a third thing in which the opposites can unite. Here the logic of the intellect usually fails, for in a logical antithesis there is no third. The 'solvent' can only be of an irrational nature. In nature the resolution of the opposites is always an energic process: she acts symbolically in the truest sense of the word, doing something that expresses both sides, just as a waterfall mediates between above and below. (CW14 para 705)

Austin and Zebedee:

Two churches stood within fifty metres of each other on the opposite side of a fashionable street. Both were large buildings expensive to maintain against the eroding effect of diminishing congregations. The minimal differences in doctrine were mirrored by a close similarity in membership of both churches. Furthermore, the pastors of both met regularly at various interdenominational working groups in the area, in one of which the idea of merging the two churches had been floated. Economically it made sound sense to sell off the older, though more beautiful, building to an American sect keen to purchase it and well able to afford it.

The pastors began discussions. Austin was extravert, confident and well known; Zebedee was introvert, diffident and recoiled from being in the limelight. The two personalities irritated each other from the start. But they persevered, and put the issue to church meetings. In public, the pastors not only appeared united, but seemed perplexed by the suspicion between the two groups, indignant about the infantile squabbles that erupted, and impatient over the slowness of the process.

The day came when both congregations attended their first service—in Austin's church (!). The two pastors co-conducted the service. The original congregations sat roughly on opposite sides of the aisle. The organist, assisted by his deputy (both of them a little eccentric), from Zebedee's church put the cat among the pigeons by playing music written by a Catholic mystical composer and by taking the hymns at funereal pace, a pace that reflected his sadness about the merger. Zebedee delivered a very boring sermon which did not fit into Austin's well-designed service.

The disastrous service was followed by a large lunch in which the two groups achieved a degree of pseudo-mutuality, a calm before the storm. The organist and his deputy were sacked soon afterwards for improper dress. The congregation from Zebedee's church insisted on having their own chapel in Austin's church. The scapegoating of the organist was followed by further scapegoating of Zebedee, who left and retired early.

Resistances and defences had combined to create an almost untenable situation. Zebedee's church had felt taken over by Austin's, and experienced a great sense of loss—of buildings, of ritual, of music, of identity, of independence. The change had disrupted an essential element of continuity in the lives of some of the congregants of both churches, and the positive aspects of change had been given much public airing with the negative feelings of loss split off and left to fester within individuals or within splinter groups. Each church had projected on to the other much of the bad ('They are no good at managing money'). The two pastors had been split—Austin being seen as decisive and effective, and Zebedee being seen as rather weak but more spiritual. Members of both churches were overly helpful to each other, falling back on reaction formation (the opposite to what one feels or fears) and contributing to a false elision of differences and the unproductiveness of pseudo-mutuality. Displacement had a heyday. Anything from the heating system to the tea urn acted as something on which to take out all the bad feelings that otherwise had nowhere to go.

In this highly complex process, which generated such powerful feelings, and, like most mergers, left in its wake some casualties, both pastors noticed an intensification of anxiety. In order to continue to function effectively in their roles they needed their defences. They also felt that they were being related to in a distorted way—in other words, that they were recipients of transference. Defences and transference form the content of the next two chapters.

FOUR

Defending Inner Space

From outside one will always triumphantly impress theories upon the world, then fall into the ditch one has dug; but only from inside will one keep oneself and the world quiet and true. (Franz Kafka)

At death, not only are the opposites transcended, but also one of the individual's travelling companions along the way, namely anxiety, finally dissolves. In this chapter, we will be exploring the different sources and the nature of anxiety and the various means by which we cope with it. These means are technically known as defence mechanisms and their purpose is the survival of the developing individual. They are, therefore, absolutely vital to the physical and emotional well-being of each one of us. They contribute to pathology when they are either inadequate or when they are excessively rigid.

My definition of defence mechanisms is as follows:

The defence mechanisms are ways and means by which the unintegrated infant, and later the developing individual, wards off anything which threatens biological and psychological equilibrium. Such threats include dangers to survival; pain; frustration; conflict; the onslaught of overwhelming imagery, feeling or impulsive behaviour; the severe attacks and punitive forebodings of conscience.

The defences operate for the most part unconsciously, and nearly all of them belong to what I have described as the executive part of the personality—the ego. While we tend to think of them as intra-personal phenomena, it is important to understand that they can and do operate inter-personally, in groups, institutions (see Chapter 6) and countries. A country having problems with the consequences of colonisation might project on to another country that was behaving invasively to a neighbour, all its greedy, grasping, crushing and power-driven impulses. Such a projection, if sufficiently enforced by the collective, would leave the first country feeling rather smug and self-virtuous and the second country feeling misunderstood and convinced that the pot was calling the kettle black. Political and other leaders often exploit such defence mechanisms and, as a result, lead their followers deeper and deeper into unconsciousness and more and more split off from energy, imagery and impulses that the individual needs to integrate, if s/he is to individuate and responsibly exercise conscious choice. It is clear, then, that the pastor, as a figure of leadership in the community, can consciously seek to raise the consciousness of his congregation, both collectively and individually; or, from a position of his own insecurity in relation to parts of himself that threaten him, he can lead his congregation in the condemnation of those sectors of society that represent outside what is unacceptable to himself on the inside.

Gareth:

Gareth was fifteen and something of an all-rounder—an able student, a skilled athlete and a competent musician. The girls pined for him from afar, for although he could certainly be warm and humorous, in female company he tended to become aloof and disdainful. Some two years earlier he had had his first homosexual encounter with an older boy at school, and since then a voracious sexual appetite had found some physical satisfaction in a promiscuity that was emotionally barren and often endangering. It was with a mixture of relief and suspicion that he entered into sexual relations with his pastor, Kevin, with whom he had frequent contact. Gareth would finish school and go round to the vicarage where tea and some time in bed preluded his piano practice in the church hall and postponed the inevitable return home to his impoverished, depressed and possessive mother. As Gareth relaxed into a more monogamous arrangement with his pastor, the latter became more and more frantic about his infatuation with the boy, which had become obsessive.

The pastor began by growing a beard. This was followed

by a conscious effort to 'delouse' himself, as he put it, of his tendency to be rather 'camp'. He became suspicious of the youth leader and his suspicions began to find voice in his sermons, which alluded from time to time to idealistic notions of how the adults are and must be responsible for the demise and potential of today's youth. He found himself cleft in two. In public, he harangued the gay community, made it clear to prospective gay parishioners that they were not welcome, and threw himself into the courtship of a pious virgin, who held that sex was only for procreation. In private, he became more pursuant of Gareth, and, when parted from him, fell into the loss of soul that is experienced when two people who are in love are separated from each other.

The pastor married and eventually had three children. Gareth left home and went to university. In the holidays and for many years afterwards, the two men would meet occasionally for sex and a meal together. Gareth, empowered by the knowledge of his lover's secret life, succeeded ultimately in persuading him into counselling; before then, the pastor used the structure of his particular communion to climb to a position where his public and private lives could be kept as far apart as possible, but where his inner cleavage forever threatened his sanity and his family.

What was happening inside the pastor? In a broad sense, he tried consciously and unconsciously to ward off an aspect of himself (his homosexuality) that threatened his equilibrium as a person and as a pastor, and was unacceptable to both, not to mention his elders and betters in the church. Threatened by possession by his anima, which left him feeling and behaving in an effeminate way, he unknowingly compensated by growing a beard, which he hoped would re-establish him as a man and lend him an air of virility (a strengthening of the persona). His 'delousing' operation represented a further attempt at denial of unwanted behaviour. As this got pushed further into unconsciousness, it then tended to be seen in projection on to the youth leader, whose role brought him into contact with adolescent boys. The denial and projection taking place within himself then became institutionalised and enacted in his church, which he tried to keep as a 'good' place with all the unacceptable homosexual impulses kept outside, which was then felt to be where the 'bad' was located.

But it is clear from the example that the pastor was driven—he was not in control of his behaviour. The reason for this is that he was overwhelmed by a complex, which means that the amount of will disposable to him was severely depleted and that his power to make conscious choices was limited. As Jung quite humorously put it, 'Everyone knows nowadays that people "have complexes"; what is not so well known . . . is that complexes can have us' (CW8 para 200).

The feeling-toned complex and the archetype are two of the basic tenets of analytical psychology. On the basis of Jung's research on complexes, Freud embraced the term into psychoanalysis, preferring it to the word 'conflict', and glad to have experimental validation of his theory of repression.

Jung defined a complex as the

> image of a certain psychic situation which is strongly accentuated emotionally and is, moreover, incompatible with the habitual mode of consciousness. The image has a powerful, inner coherence, it has its own wholeness and, in addition, a relatively high degree of autonomy, so that it is subject to the control of the conscious mind to only a limited extent, and therefore behaves like an animated foreign body in the sphere of consciousness. (CW8 para 201)

Of our pastor we might hypothesise that he was very bound up with his mother, over-involved and over-identified with her. He had a strong mother-complex, in which his mother formed the nucleus of the complex. This nucleus acted like a magnet and drew towards it all the feeling-toned memories of and associations to the mother–son relationship, and their relationship with other members of the family. Gareth, on the other hand, may have had a father-complex, in which he was driven by a compulsive search for the masculinity (represented by the penis in his sexual encounters) which his absent father was unable to embody and to support as it emerged in Gareth. The pastor had had a difficult experience with his mother, just as Gareth had had with his father.

Complexes arise in three ways. First, they may be the result of traumatic events in early childhood which are often but not always repeated. (An example would be abandonment.) Secondly, refusal to suffer through a painful situation in the present may result in the discarding of the threatening feeling into the unconscious, where it may form or join a complex. Thirdly, there are other complexes,

> that have never been in consciousness before and therefore could never have been arbitrarily repressed. They grow out of the unconscious mind and invade the conscious mind with their weird and unassailable convictions and impulses. (CW11 para 22)

Jung was alluding here to an intelligent man, who suffered with an imaginary cancer. This man would imploringly assure his listeners that he was suffering from an intestinal cancer, while in the next breath despondently declare that he knew his cancer to be a figment of his imagination.

On the whole, complexes are the results of repression and are to be found in the personal unconscious of the individual. They are experienced bodily and their presence is always indicated by bodily sensations. Palpitations, sweating, blushing, stammering, constriction (often in the throat), 'butterflies'—all these and many more indicate to the person and to the beholder that a complex has been activated. The imagery attached to a complex often appears in dreams, and usually consists of two or more people interacting; for example, an overfeeding mother and a retching child; a punishing father and a cringing child; two parents happily in bed together and an excluded child.

The ego can relate to the complex in several ways. It can try to integrate the affects contained in the imagery and struggle for its meaning (e.g. the rage of the father and the fear of the child, and what that relationship might mean). This usually leads to the person feeling more energised and enriched and having more choice about his behaviour. Or, the ego can see an element of the complex in other people all the time (so that all women become overfeeding mothers). Thirdly, he can become possessed by the complex, and, in such a state, can unwittingly endanger the psyches of those with whom he comes into close contact. In such a state, the ego is no longer at the centre of consciousness, but has been taken over by a 'shadow government' (CW16 para 196). The more a man tries to repudiate the punishing father in himself, the more likely it is that such a figure will appear in dreams, later in other people outside himself and finally take over the person, so that he will become a tyrannical punitive person towards everyone in his social field. People will say, 'He's not himself, what on earth has got into him?', and they will feel inclined to give him a wide berth, rightly sensing not physical danger, so much as some sort of psychic infection. Lastly, the ego can use its range of defences against the complex, keeping it at bay in the unconscious where it might mysteriously codify itself into an illness.

These examples emphasise the darker aspect of the complex, which in fact has both positive and negative sides to it, as Jung pointed out:

> Complexes obviously represent a kind of inferiority in the broadest sense—a statement I must at once qualify by saying that to have complexes does not necessarily indicate inferiority. It only means that something discordant, unassimilated and antagonistic exists, perhaps as an obstacle, but also as an incentive to greater effort, and so, perhaps, to new possibilities of achievement . . . [Complexes] should not be missing, for otherwise psychic life would come to a fatal standstill. (CW6 para 925)

Just as the personal unconscious is the home of the complex and its associated imagery, so is the collective unconscious the home of the archetype and archetypal imagery. As we have seen, most complexes arise from personal experience, but they are fed and buoyed up by imagery generated by the archetype. Such imagery evokes in the beholder feelings of awe, fascination, reverence. The experience has a numinous quality, quite akin, I think, to the amazement, awe and fascination of the toddler who suddenly collapses on to his bottom, picks up a leaf, and seems to fall in love with it, as if it is the most wonderful thing he has seen in his life.

But it is the quality of the feeling rather than the quality of the thing that is important. Furthermore, the imagery often initiates direction in a person's development (such as sexual behaviour in adolescence) or brings about a change in direction (such as the deepening of a religious attitude in mid-life and beyond). The imagery also draws out of the person the instinctual, behavioural response, but it also invites the person to explore the meaning of such a response. In this way, the spiritual and material poles of the archetypal image get into relationship with one another. To be stuck in platonic relations with other people, however loftily spiritual, would be as meaningless and possibly as boring as to be stuck on the tramlines of promiscuity. The one is to be addicted to a search for meaning; the other is to be driven by instinctuality stripped of any meaning.

Archetypal imagery has a dual nature. The archetypal image of the Great Mother can be split between the good, nurturing, life-supporting, releasing mother; and the bad, depriving, death-dealing, clinging mother. It is the real mother who mediates for the infant the archetypal image of the mother. Failure to do so will glue the infant to one end of the axis in a way that will hinder his development. In fact, as we will see later, stuckness at the positive or negative end of the axis will mobilise defences of an almost unassailable nature.

If a baby is left to cry too long and too often in the first three or four months of life because, let us say, his mother is depressed and isolated and, therefore, unable to empathise with and meet his needs, then he will be left with an unmediated image of an abandoning, cruel, witchlike mother, who has an all-or-nothing quality about her, and who will be projected on to subsequent women and probably all other people as well. Such others may well be idealised as a defence against the terrors of the earlier deprivation; but either way, the 'other' will not be related to as a human figure, only as a god/demon, Sophia/Circe figure.

Just as the complex can possess the ego, so the archetypal image can overwhelm the ego and lead to serious psychic disequilibrium. Often this takes the form of identification with the archetypal image.

Simon:

Simon had just celebrated his thirty-second birthday. It was an early Easter, and he had left his apartment on Maundy Thursday morning dressed *only* in a fur coat, as protection against the lightly falling snow, its pockets rattling with the clatter of credit cards. It was mid-afternoon when the police picked him up after a tip-off from one of the shopkeepers along London's Oxford Street. Simon gave them his vicar's number. The vicar arrived, and was horrified to hear that Simon thought that he had 'blown' £3,000 that day on clothes that, he said, 'I'm going to give to the poor before I die'. The vicar called his wife, an efficient and practical woman, who took Simon back to the vicarage, while the vicar returned all the purchases to their rightful stores, all the while mindful of preparations that needed to be made for the important evening service. He returned to the vicarage and called Simon's GP, who sectioned him and admitted him to hospital. This was not before the vicar had accompanied Simon back to his flat (to collect clothes) and had been accosted by neighbours, who complained of the terrible banging that issued forth from Simon's flat the previous night. On investigation, the vicar discovered a huge crucifix in Simon's bathroom. Simon had intended to be crucified on Good Friday, and had spent the previous night constructing his frame of death.

In Simon's case, we can discern an identification with the archetypal image of a Saviour—an image that is universal, has depth, autonomy and meaning. It is not at all personal. Simon lives this out through a night. Something happens (we don't know what) so that by morning he has become identified with the archetypal image of the Trickster, and manages, despite his bizarre garb, to trick people (who are used to shoplifters, con-men, etc.) into spending an amount of money beyond his means. In addition, he shows no concern for himself, is as high as a kite, and is looking forward to his agonising death on the cross the following day. We cannot be certain, but we can surmise that his horrendous death is a punishment in fantasy for his hubris, and that neither his self-importance nor his self-denigration (both exaggerated) had any relation to each other. There was no possibility of a middle way.

A word about the archetype. It is a 'system of readiness for action' (CW9(i) para 199). It is a form without content. Think of a bell. There is a form without any content—a system of readiness for action. Something comes along from the environment; it is a clapper, and it strikes the bell. The bell springs into action and produces a ring, which sounds out into the environment and affects both the environment and the bell. Had the bell been struck by a sledgehammer it would have cracked or broken; had it been dusted with cotton-wool, no sound would have issued forth. The bell affects the environment; but the environment potentiates the bell.

The collective unconscious contains the inherited pre-dispositions of man to respond to all the typical and universal situations that occur through the life-cycle—birth, bonding, separating, marrying, procreating, letting go, dying. And many, many more. There are as many archetypes as there are possible human situations. But it might not have escaped the reader that the situations I have chosen to list are ones that mark major transitions in life. A transition is a change, and any change makes us anxious.

The feeling of anxiety leads us back to defences, since it may now be apparent that the imagery and the behaviour generated by the complex or the archetype can be profoundly disturbing to the extent that the ego, the executive part of the personality, has to take defensive action against inflation or possession.

> Just as the body reacts purposively to injuries or infections or any abnormal conditions, so the psychic functions react to unnatural or dangerous disturbances with purposive defence mechanisms. (CW8 para 488)

There are many anxieties that assail us in the course of development. We will now turn to these and to the defences that we need to possess, modify or relinquish if we are to mature as individuals.

Anxiety and Defences in Infancy

There are people whose very early relationship with the mother seems to contain a 'basic catastrophe'. This might take the form of the baby taking-in milk without any love attached to it; or it might be that the mother died very early on, or was very depressed after the birth; or the birth of twins may have made good-enough mothering impossible; or the father may have contracted a serious illness just as the child was born, thus leaving mother with insufficient holding by him to enable her to bond and care for the child. Whatever the reason, people suffering from this 'basic catastrophe' seem at an early age to have erected an impermeable barrier between what is felt to be the self and everything that is not the self. Such a barrier consists of 'defences of the self' (Fordham, 1974), and effectively seals off the self from everyone and everything when it feels threatened. Erecting the barrier is in essence a retreat from the risks of inter-personal relatedness to the relative safety of a feeling of self-absorption or self-sufficiency.

In his book *The Child*, Neumann describes vividly how, when the nucleus of the personality is inundated with bad experiences, the ego becomes a 'distress ego', and the world, the mother, the Thou, bear the imprint of doom (Neumann, 1973, p. 74). The deep imagery attached to this distress ego is of hell, where hunger, pain, cold, desolation, helplessness and loneliness preponderate. The central symbol is hunger, the wish to gnaw and devour. Since such a weak ego can easily be overwhelmed by the unconscious, it shuts off. The feelings of unloved-ness, forsakenness and inferiority are covered over by a rigid, aggressive and negativistic personality that is forever despairing and isolated. Anyone who manages to get close to such a damaged person will encounter almost unendurable anger and rage as well as a longing, almost impossible to fulfil.

Brian:

As a summer break approached, Brian told his counsellor a dream, which quite dramatically led to a feeling of intense closeness between them. While on the one hand pleased at this development, the counsellor was nevertheless wary, since he had had long experience of Brian moving closer and then withdrawing as the longing for dependence was suddenly cancelled out by a terror of abandonment. Brian left that session saying that he had had some mothering from the counsellor, and was clearly feeling grateful.

When they next met, the counsellor was not surprised to hear that Brian had run two long races over the weekend (despite not feeling well) and had collapsed at the finishing line. The counsellor suggested that Brian was trying to steel himself for the break. Brian dismissed this idea, but went on to describe a new anti-tank missile that left the shell of the tank intact but totally destroyed the crew and the interior. The counsellor persisted, and suggested that perhaps Brian was frightened that he might experience the summer break as a traumatic missile that would leave him shattered inside, just like the early abandonment by his mother had done. Although great care had been taken to prepare Brian for the break, it was not sufficient to prevent him from denying the upsurge of awful feelings, which he subsequently acted out during the holiday. He resigned impetuously from his job, turned his own holiday into a survival course, and managed to do more damage than usual to machinery and gadgets at home.

He had reproduced a life in ruins, where everything bore the imprint of doom. The tank image is a remarkable description of a subjective state in which an inner personality, felt to be shattered and vulnerable, is contained in and held together by a coat of armour that defends it against the ravages of the outer world.

The tank-like defensive structure of Brian's personality has a very different feel to it from the compliant exterior of Marion (see Chapter 2). Compliance is the hallmark of the false self, the purpose of which is to hide and protect the true self. This latter was impinged upon unbearably in infancy in such a way that the infant was required to give meaning to the mother's feelings and behaviour rather than the other way round.

Verity:

Verity was the only survivor of three children; her brother and sister were respectively stillborn and died shortly after birth. Both parents were themselves very deprived, the mother being orphaned when she was three, and the father suffering a great deal at the hand of his parents. To these lonely souls, already plagued by multiple loss, was born this precious daughter who, from an early age, actually perceived that it was her role in life to make her parents happy, mainly by complying with their implicit and explicit expectations of her. After a successful career as a film producer, she married happily and had children. When these were well established at school, she went into voluntary work. By now, she was a compulsive care giver, prone to somatic illnesses from time to time and inexplicable periods of feeling depressed.

One day, one of her clients threatened to commit suicide. Despite knowing that this client had the support of a GP and social worker, the back-up of a psychiatric hospital and residence in a hostel, Verity offered to phone her every day over the next two weeks. On the second day she forgot, only remembering the next day and being overwhelmed by guilt.

The compulsive care she was giving to her clients, her friends and her family, a care that was highly tuned to their needs and founded on a life of accurately observing and interpreting signals of need from others, was now being sabotaged by her own need for some time to herself, among other things. Failure to listen to such warnings often forces the body into rescuing its owner from exhaustion by manufacturing physical symptoms. The hidden, needy true self, apparently despised by the parents and certainly by Verity, was seeking an opportunity to come out of hiding, and waiting for conditions to be favourable. Once bitten, twice shy.

The defences of the self and the false self are two modes of protection against anxiety of fairly catastrophic proportions —

namely, that the inner fairly drastic defences can come into operation at this time of life; there is not space to deal with this subject here.

We turn now to the so-called primitive defences, primitive in the sense that they are the earliest defences to be mobilised by the ego.

Primitive Defences

Splitting

This is a process whereby the ego divides both itself and the other person (family, group, organisation, etc.) into two parts, one of which is experienced as good and the other as bad. Its purpose is to protect the good from feared contamination or destruction by the bad, and to minimise the confusion arising from having loving and hating feelings towards another person or oneself. Splitting is indispensable because it forms the basis of discrimination, selective attention and repression (Segal, 1973). When carried too far, it leads to a profound and sometimes irreparable cleavage in the personality. A person with such a deep split who is being assessed by a training committee or being interviewed by a panel for a job will often produce a split in the committee and make decision-making almost impossible.

Hugh:

Hugh's Post Ordination Training (POT) consisted of two consecutive small groups of fellow curates and deaconesses, meeting over three ten-week terms. The first group was a seminar in which the *modus operandi* was the discussion of a paper on pastoral care; the second group was a forum for sharing and comparing problems arising in work. The first group was led by a clergyman, and the second by a female psychiatric social worker.

Towards the end of the year, Hugh's vicar asked how his POT was going. Hugh, to his own surprise, replied that he thought the seminar leader was pompous, arrogant, often detached, and required the members to do too much reading.

On the other hand, the social worker was supportive, understanding, facilitating, wise, etc. Hugh reflected on this unbalanced picture and realised that by splitting the training in this way he was avoiding an anxiety about the impending loss of the group and the leaders, and a fear that the good things he had received from the training would be wiped out by his bad feelings.

Denial

This is the disclaiming of an internal feeling of impulse, or of an external situation. It is often accompanied by a feeling of omnipotence, giving the illusion of being in total control of emotions.

Examples:

(1) For some months after her mother's death, seven-year-old Jennifer referred to her mother as if she were still alive. The loss was denied for most of the time, but used to burst through and take her by storm unexpectedly. Someone of seven does not possess a sufficiently strong ego to cope with the tidal wave of feelings that such a loss would evoke.

(2) I recall noticing a nun striding out across a three-lane dual carriageway, apparently oblivious of any danger and probably trusting in some form of inner or outer guardian. She was omnipotently denying a situation of external danger.

This second example illustrates how much easier it is to perceive the operation of these defences in other people than in ourselves. The mechanism that enables us to see in others what we cannot see in ourselves is projection.

Projection

Feelings, impulses, and undesired aspects of the personality that create anxiety can all be projected on to another person (group, family, etc.). Positive capacities tend also to be projected when they are felt to be under attack from the rest of the personality. A projection can be followed by relief; that feeling then gives way to one of depletion. Projection is part of a process in which I split myself into good and bad parts; then I relegate what I do not like to my shadow. Then is the time for myself to work on the personal and collective sources of the projection and reclaim that part of myself. The recipient of a projection often acts as a hook for it in terms of their personal qualities or behaviour. A feeling of greediness, forming part of the shadow, may be projected on to someone else who actually is greedy, but possibly does not have a problem with that feeling. I project that on to someone else, who will have characteristics that make him a good 'hook' for the projection. Although the shadow is usually encountered in someone of the same sex, it can also be met in partnerships and marriages. Furthermore, projection of the contrasexual image (anima/animus) forms the basis for heterosexual relations. However, excessive projection leaves the projector depleted of attributes, qualities, capacities and their associated energy—all of which he needs for effective functioning. The absence of projection means that the individual is absorbed in navel-gazing and not relating. Such a person may find it hard to empathise with other people. Empathy has its seeds in projective identification.

Projective identification

This refers to a process in which unwanted aspects of the self are evacuated in to another; the other then experiences a pressure to think, feel or behave in a way that dovetails the projection. The other feels 'possessed' by an invasive foreign body, identifies with the projection, and feels controlled by it.

Projective identification is an extremely difficult concept because it reeks of mystification. It is not observable; but the experience of being on the receiving end is undeniable and usually unpleasant, sometimes to the point of physical illness or moments of 'madness'. In work with clients who have suffered extensive early damage, projective identification is often the major source of information about what the client is actually feeling, but cannot experience at that moment. The purposes of projective identification are to communicate what can be communicated in no other way; to avoid separation from the 'good' person; to control the 'bad', persecuting person. The process of projective identification brings with it the twin anxieties of a fear of retaliation and of a concern that the projected parts are now imprisoned in the recipient of the projection.

Subjectively, the recipient of the projection will feel 'all right' until he comes into contact with the projector. Then he will suddenly feel invaded by a feeling or impulse that has nothing to do with him, and of which the projector seems totally unconscious. The task is for the recipient to process the projection in such a way that the projector can take it back in a less toxic form. How the recipient processes the projection may be more important than what he might choose to say about it to the projector.

Lawrence:

Lawrence, the hospital chaplain, had been asked to visit Mary, a middle-aged mother and wife, who was about to have yet another major orthopaedic operation. Mary had spent a large part of their time together telling Lawrence about her many hospitalisations as a child; of the physical pain she had suffered; the helplessness of spending months in plaster; the terror of lying on her back listening to doctors talking about and over her. Most of this was reported in a very matter-of-fact way that made Lawrence feel uneasy.

Towards the end of the hour, Lawrence suddenly found himself visualising a painting he had seen at the Royal Academy summer show depicting just this very scene of a patient lying in bed surrounded by doctors. The painting depicted the helplessness, the terror and the unrelatedness between the healer and the wounded. We could surmise that, because Lawrence had allowed himself through the painting to have the experience of feeling abandoned and helpless, he could receive and metabolise Mary's anxiety. Lawrence became aware of terrible butterflies and an acute anxiety. This led to an overwhelming feeling of sadness and abandonment. Sifting through himself, he could find nothing in his personal or professional life at that moment that could evoke such feelings. He concluded that the imminent termination of the interview was generating an anxiety in Mary about being left (by her parents) with inhuman carers, who would subject her to considerable pain with no real guarantee of improved physical mobility at the end of it. Lawrence felt an enormous pressure to stay with Mary, as well as a feeling of being filled with a sense of desolation of which she was unaware. Before terminating the interview, he promised to visit her regularly while she was in hospital, so conveying to her his under-standing of her need and her fear.

This illustrates how the very act of containing the projection may enable the feeling-tone of the projection to be withdrawn, because the unbearable feeling has been transformed through understanding and thinking into a psychic.reality that can be faced and experienced.

Identification, idealisation and omnipotence

I have linked these three together because they are often encountered as a trinity. Identification does not mean finding an identity. It means assuming someone else's identity and virtually becoming what one fantasises that person to be. It therefore denies separateness and separation. The person identified with is often idealised and fiercely defended against attack from others; it is 'the others' who usually pick up the denied negative feelings about the idealised person. Ideal-isation often swings into its opposite, denigration, particularly after disillusionment. Omnipotence defends against helpless-ness, but it also precludes learning. A person using these defences can imitate but cannot internalise.

Andrea:

Andrea was in her late twenties when a new deaconess arrived in the parish. Andrea latched on to her and gradually 'climbed her way inside her' so that she began to dress, speak and behave like the deaconess. The latter's comments at the Bible study group were avidly seized upon and repeated later, out of context and undigested, but apparently coming from within herself. The deaconess's 'forgetting' to turn up at the local Chinese for a meal with Andrea was the event that shattered the illusion and brought forth a torrent of abuse and an unforgiving posture, characteristically present with this trinity of defences.

In this example, there is an interaction, which is an unconscious process. Thus, when the deaconess 'forgets' to go to the restaurant, she is playing her part in the unconscious scenario. She unconsciously does what presumably she felt it tactless to say ('I don't want to meet you'); or she wasn't aware of what she felt; or she felt very uneasy in the presence of such idealisation because it played into her need to be good. Again, she might have unconsciously picked up Andrea's envy of her, and feared an envious attack.

There are other defences that come into operation when a person feels severely threatened, in danger of abandonment, or of falling to bits. But we will move now into the ego defences, which operate when aspects of someone, rather than the whole person, feel under threat.

Ego Defences

In 1936 one of Freud's daughters, Anna, wrote a book called *The Ego and the Mechanisms of Defence*. It was the first systematic study of the ego's defences. In it, Anna Freud lists ten defences, to which we will add some others.

Regression

To regress is to withdraw from a seemingly insoluble conflict or a situation of intolerable frustration. In regressing, the person returns to an earlier developmental level in order to avoid the anxiety generated by the present. An example familiar to most people is that of the child who, shortly after the arrival of a sibling, returns to behaviour and ways of relating that he has left behind. A child out of nappies might suddenly start wetting himself. Regression can have a downward spiralling effect. Someone who has regressed from all the conflicts of a triangular situation to the illusory safety of a twosome might then find himself having to defend against the loss of the other, and might do this by eating or drinking too much.

Repression

This is the means by which something that is unacceptable to the conscious attitude is relegated to the unconscious. There it will attach itself to a complex and seek reintegration into consciousness, sometimes in the form of a symptom. A daughter looking after a dementing mother requiring full-time care might be almost beside herself with anger and want to strike her mother. Such an impulse might be unacceptable to her conscience and thus be repressed. However, the next morning she might wake up and have real difficulty in moving her right arm. Such a paralysis would represent a compromise between her wish to strike (or go on strike) and the punishment for having such an impulse.

Reaction formation

This consists of an attitude, feeling or behaviour that is completely contrary to an unacceptable feeling or impulse. In the example above, the daughter's death wishes towards her mother may be unacceptable. Through a reaction-formation she might find herself precipitated into being extraordinarily caring and considerate. An impoverished pastor tempted to embezzle church funds might find himself being over-generous to every tramp who knocked on his door.

Isolation

This means the severance of a feeling from an idea or a feeling from an experience. Each of the two elements is isolated from the other with the result that no associative links can be made. An experience common to everyone is that of having a feeling (sadness, for example) and having no idea of why that feeling has arisen. The so-called 'anniversary reaction' is another example. Here, the bereaved person feels filled with grief, but the grief has become isolated from the death of the loved one. Often it is a friend who can re-link the feeling with the event of the loss.

Undoing

This is a defence often grouped with reaction-formation and isolation; all three are found in obsessional neuroses. Freud (1926b, p. 227) described undoing as 'negative magic'. In 'The Rat-Man', Freud (1909, p. 31) describes how the patient removed a stone from the road along which his lady love was to travel in her carriage. To protect another passer-by, he moved the stone again, thereby endangering again his lady-love.

Introjection

Whereas introverts tend to project from their inner world in order to bring the outer world to life, extraverts tend to introject the outer world to do the same for their inner world. Like projection, introjection is a normal developmental process. It becomes a defence when the ego is afraid of being overwhelmed by separation anxiety or loss. The pain of the feared or actual loss is mitigated by the sufferer taking in more and more of the other person. Just before Michael, a pastor, retired, he happened to need to rummage around in his secretary's desk. There he stumbled upon a whole bundle of memos and notes he had sent her about tasks needing to be done and a collection of bits and pieces he recalled throwing away. He left everything untouched, but understood his find as an outward sign of an inner process of introjection preceding his departure.

Turning against the self

This is the defence most often used by those contemplating, attempting or committing suicide. The purpose of the defence is to protect the other from uncontainable destructive impulses, almost invariably triggered off by a feared, imaginary or actual abandonment. In its less extreme forms, it is the defence responsible for periods of mild or not so mild depression, in which anger is turned in on the self rather than expressed to the offending other.

Clients who present as depressed are relieved if they are asked directly about feelings of wanting to harm or kill themselves. Not asking such a question is often a defence of the pastor against the unthinkable thought of the client committing suicide. An unpublished study undertaken at a London hospital showed that 78 per cent of people admitted after a suicide attempt had seen their GP within the previous seventy-two hours, and many had obtained medication which abetted them in their attempt, so relieving the GP of anxiety. This is not to criticise GPs; it is to point out that each professional needs defences in order to do the job, but some might be over-defended. More of this in Chapter 6.

Reversal

If you are unable to *hear* the other person, it is often difficult to be certain whether the other is laughing or crying. The two are very close to each other. In times of anxiety, the one often appears as the other. News of a death can be received with laughter, which, in turn, can cause terrible offence. There is no conscious intention to laugh. The laughter is a reversal of the more normal tears and suggests that the ego is threatened by the grief.

Displacement

A father who is refused sex one night by his wife is sharp the next morning with his son. His anger is displaced from his wife on to his son. Some firms now have a room housing punch-bags on which staff can displace their feelings about the job, senior staff, etc.

Passive to active

In her last counselling session, a client announced that she was going to leave early. Her formative years had been peppered with painful separations, and her leaving the session early was a way not only of dealing with her anxiety, but also of letting the counsellor know what it was like to be left—a sort of revenge.

Identification with the aggressor

This is a defence usually employed in relation to figures of authority who create anxiety through the threat of punishment. It contains the mechanism of turning passive into active. Some prisoners in harsh regimes identify with their harsh warders to ward off the fear of what might happen to them and give their fellow inmates a rough time.

Rationalisation

This is the use of reason to justify particular behaviour and to obscure the deeper motivation for it.

Dramatisation

This is a form of manic defence in which experiences that have proved meaningless or unfulfilling are imbued with dramatic affect and exaggerated. When the narrator is dramatising, the listener tends to feel irritated and disbelieving.

Reparation

Reparation is the defence used at the stage of concern, when the bad and the good mother, formerly split, are realised as one and the same person. Reparation is made out of guilt over the imagined destructive attacks made on the mother. This defence has been explored in Chapter 1.

Manic defences

These manifest behaviourally in over-work, spending sprees, alcohol/food binges, hyperactivity, ceaseless internal or external chatter, promiscuity (particularly of a reckless kind), dangerous driving, compulsive artistic production, etc. They defend against loss and abandonment or against futility and emptiness. The person in the grip of manic defences emits feelings of triumph, control and contempt, and persons in their environment may feel reduced to being things rather than people.

Repetition-compulsion

This is the process whereby an individual places himself again and again in painful and distressing situations, all the time thinking that these situations are brought about by circumstances to which he contributes nothing. It is essentially a defence against remembering the original painful situation.

Tristram:

Tristram was a young man who, as a boy, had been sexually fondled by his widowed mother. On each occasion, she would inexplicably (to him) suddenly erupt in a rage and turf him out of bed. Pleasure and excitement were followed by rejection, and a tantalising relationship was constructed. As a student, and later as a young man, he kept finding himself in situations with women in which he would allow himself to be excited by them and then, on his failure to perform, find himself humiliatingly rejected. In the course of counselling, he managed eventually to 'remember' the original wound to his self-esteem, and so could begin to work on developing new understandings and new behaviour.

Religiosity

Religiosity appears in the guise of excessive piety and an over-scrupulous religious attitude. The religiose person is often deeply dependent on the good opinion of others and is in constant dread of any appearance of shadow elements, against which s/he defends by being sickeningly sanctimonious. Tele-evangelists in the United States have fallen prey to excesses of religiosity, so that news of embezzlement or sexual adventure has had a very shocking effect on their followers. Sometimes religiosity conceals or keeps at a manageable level identification with saints or religious leaders. In such cases, the defence is often best left alone as the following example shows.

Jonah:

Jonah lived in a bed-sit and looked like a tramp. He washed

infrequently and looked as if he seldom ate. From Sunday to Wednesday he attended every possible service at the local Catholic church, but was never seen during the other three days of the week (with the exception of Holy Week). His knowledge of the liturgy and the liturgical calendar was legendary, and he was an ardent but frustrated supporter of the Tridentine Mass, long since phased out. He often served at Mass and other ceremonies; when in the congregation he quietly spoke the priest's words, and, during High Mass, would sometimes turn to the elevated choirloft and conduct the choir. He was accepted and tolerated by clergy and laity alike, but remained friendless and isolated.

One day a new priest arrived at the presbytery. He soon noticed Jonah and asked his colleagues about him. They told him what they knew, including the fact that they knew that his name was not Jonah, but that was the name he insisted on being called; any attempts to find out his real name put Jonah in a state of panic. The new priest was quick to put two and two together and realise that Jonah really did think he was Jonah, and hence 'disappeared into the whale's belly' for three days of the week, being reborn on Sunday.

The priest had been told in seminary to be a firm representative of reality to people who were mentally disordered. Ignoring the advice of the priest-in-charge, the younger man took it upon himself to challenge Jonah in the sacristy after Mass, hoping in this way to strengthen Jonah's ego. Standing with his back to the door, the priest asked Jonah for his true identity. Jonah became agitated and panicky, and perspired heavily. He broke into prayer in Latin, and, when this failed to silence his inquisitor, developed a delusion that the priest was the devil, and attacked him. A parishioner heard the commotion and called the priest-in-charge, who took it upon himself over the next few weeks following Jonah's discharge from hospital to re-establish trust between him and the church.

To understand what happened between Jonah and the new priest, it is necessary now to explore their relationship from the vertex of transference.

FIVE

Distorting the Space Between

We read, but also we are read by others. Interferences in these readings. Forcing someone to read himself as we read him (slavery). Forcing others to read us as we read ourselves (conquest). A mechanical process. More often than not a dialogue between deaf people. (Simone Weil)

The space between people is rapidly filled with projections. Both pastor and client project on to each other. These projections distort the space between them, thus making it difficult for them to relate to each other. Such distortion is called transference and is mirrored by counter-transference. In this chapter we shall be seeking to understand these phenomena.

The exchange between the pastor and Jonah illustrates several points. As long as Jonah's inner space was left intact, he was able to lead a life that was meaningful to him and had no harmful effects on others. As long as the space between Jonah and the church (by which I mean clergy and laity) was left intact, Jonah's psychic equilibrium was maintained. Jonah's identification with the Old Testament figure was contained and tolerated by everyone. Nobody knew whether or not Jonah thought of his fellow parishioners as the people of Nineveh and the clergy as fellow prophets. It really did not seem to matter. But it was generally known that most people thought of Jonah as a religious maniac. Only his grandmother, having pondered the matter long in her heart, understood in a vague sort of way that his behaviour had something to do with his father having drowned in a boating accident in the

Lake District. Jonah had seen the accident, but had been unable to do anything to save his father.

From Jonah's side, the space between himself and his fellow humans allowed him to survive in the cocoon of his delusion until the young pastor imploded into it and transformed it from something benign into something very persecutory. The pastor had been consciously well intentioned. Unconsciously, he was having feelings towards someone in the present that originated in his past relationship with his own father, who had been prone to feelings of unreality and disorientation. For his father he had been a relatively successful ambassador from reality despite outbreaks of frustration and impatience. It was the pastor's frustration with Jonah that had filled the space between with menace so that it was then experienced by Jonah as inquisitional, and had reminded him of the intrusive questioning to which he had been submitted at the inquest into his father's death.

It may now be clear that for both men there were 'interferences in these readings'. Each was unconsciously and involuntarily experiencing the other as if he was someone else — a significant figure from the past. In other words, each was transferring on to the other psychic contents that did not belong to the other. It may be helpful to move on to a definition of transference.

Definition:

It is the experiencing of feelings, drives, attitudes, fantasies and defences towards a person in the present which do not befit that person but are a repetition of reactions originating in regard to significant persons in early childhood, unconsciously displaced onto figures in the present. (Greenson, 1965, p. 155)

Although this definition is restricted to a two-person relationship, it is important to note that Jung stated that,

The transference itself is a perfectly natural phenomenon which does not by any means happen only in the consulting room — it can be seen everywhere. (CW16 para 420)

Thus, transference occurs between one individual and

another, between an individual and a group, or between an individual and an institution. Jung envisaged it as:

> a specific form of the more general process of projection . . .
> a general psychological mechanism that carries over
> subjective contents of any kind into the object . . . is never a
> voluntary act . . . is of an emotional and compulsory nature
> . . . forms a link, a sort of dynamic relationship between the
> subject and the object. (CW18 paras 312–17)

Jung's definition allows for the projection of impersonal as well as personal contents, and therefore makes space for the projection of archetypal figures such as the Wise Old Man, the anima and the shadow.

Transference can be positive or negative. In its positive form, it consists of feelings of love, admiration, fondness, liking, concern, devotion, yearning, tenderness, respect. In its negative form, it appears as anger, hatred, hostility, mistrust, abhorrence, loathing, envy, bitterness, contempt, annoyance. Its hallmark is its impropriety; the feeling is not appropriate to the situation. It is too intense. Furthermore, the recipient of the projection feels (with the exception of the delusional transference) that s/he is being related to 'as if' s/he is someone else. This means that the transference is essentially symbolic in that it is

> the best possible formulation of a relatively unknown thing,
> which for that reason cannot be more clearly or character-
> istically represented. (CW6 para 815)

It is vitally important for the pastor to understand this. Without such understanding, these projections will be taken personally and will result in the pastor feeling inflated or deflated, depending on the positive or negative quality of the projection. The less stable his self-esteem, the more prone he will be to being buffeted by projections, not only from individuals but also from groups. Some of these projections can be very burdensome, particularly when they are at odds with the pastor's self-image or at variance with the way in which his family or friends experience him. Essentially, they have to be worn, uncomfortably, like an ill-fitting cassock or suit, or like sackcloth and ashes, until such time as the transference becomes more conscious—that is, the projection withdrawn, not its contents, something to which we will return.

For Jung saw the transference as a bridge to reality, a liminal space, in much the same way as the narthex is a liminal space, between the entrance of the church and the nave; a space that divided the uninitiated from the initiated. In Christian terms this might be likened to limbo; in psychological terms, I am addressing what Winnicott called 'transitional space', that space which exists between what is me and what is not me, and is the space within which symbols can emerge, and which is the basis of culture and creativity. This is the space in which the capacity to play develops. It is the imaginal realm in which there is no room for the deadening effects of repression nor for the impulsive enactment of desire; between the two there lies the painful intensity of feeling, the striving for detachment and the struggle to interiorise that which can be felt to be outside oneself.

Transference invites reflection. That which is experienced as a powerful emotional link with another, fundamentally known as not an other but as a part of myself, can facilitate the capacity to think about a feeling or a quality that fascinates because it animates. The projector, though unconscious of his act, none the less knows in his bowels that he has evacuated contents either loathed or precious. Jung reminds us:

The intensity of the transference relationship is always equivalent to the importance of its contents to the subject. If it is a particularly intense transference, we can be sure that the contents of the projection, once they are extracted and made conscious, will prove to be just as important to the patient as the transference was. When a transference collapses it does not vanish into the air; its intensity, or a corresponding amount of energy, will appear in another place, for instance in another relationship, or in some other important psychological form. For the intensity of the transference is an intense emotion which is really the property of the patient. If the transference is dissolved, all that projected energy falls back into the subject, and he is then in possession of the treasure which formerly, in the transference, had been wasted. (CW18 para 327)

In counselling, therapy or analysis, helping the client to rediscover 'the treasure . . . formerly wasted' is usually an implicit, if not explicit, goal. The pastor is in a rather different position. He is seen as a figure(head) in the community, who is expected to be always available. For many people, he represents a presence, and this presence has a largely feminine and possibly maternal feeling to it. The church, the pastor's dwelling place, and the pastor himself, carry projections that, for the faithful, are positive and belong to the positive aspect of the feminine archetype. Such qualities would include: the capacity to offer containment, giving, transforming, providing wisdom and inspiration, giving birth and rebirth (Neumann, 1955). Although the pastor is 'known' to have a job, he tends to be seen not as someone engaged in doing something so much as someone devoted to being. In fact, the more he does, the more he dispels and even evades the very projections that the community need him to carry. For the non-church attender, the pastor may also have a symbolic role, his presence acting as a constant reminder of an interior life perilously neglected.

Pastor and psychotherapist, then, by virtue of their roles both evoke transference feelings in others. The difference between them lies in their response to these feelings. For the psychotherapist, transference is the 'fulcrum' of the work, to borrow Rosemary Gordon's term (Gordon, 1968). Jung stated, 'The transference to the analyst builds a bridge across which the patient can get away from his family into reality' (CW4 para 428).

The psychotherapist responds to the transference not only by tolerating it. He spots it, unpacks it, interprets it and works through the process again and again with his patient. The pastor, on the other hand, may well spot transference feelings, but it is not his job to interpret them unless he is working specifically in a counselling role.

We can now begin to differentiate various types of transference.

Archetypal

This consists of the projection of impersonal contents, such as the Wise Old Man, which have a fairly overpowering effect. Fordham says that such projections 'are parts of the self that need to be integrated. They are also progressive and contain material through which individuation can take place' (Fordham, 1978, p. 84).

I consider that pastors are, by virtue of their role, particularly likely to evoke archetypal transference. This further emphasises the need for the pastor to carry rather than to collude with or evade these projections. How he does this will be explored later. But the archetypal transference can be culturally mediated before it appears in a more personal form.

A needy parishioner complains to his pastor about maltreatment at the Welfare Benefits Office. He has projected on to the Welfare State the image of the Depriving Great Mother. The parishioner was born at the height of Truby King's reign, and so was fed every four hours by a personal mother naturally influenced by cultural trends of the time. Archetypal, cultural and personal aspects of the self all interweave in that example.

In discussing the archetypal transference Jung writes:

It goes without saying that the projection of these impersonal images . . . has to be withdrawn. But you merely dissolve the *act* of projection; you should not, and really cannot dissolve its contents. . . . The fact that they are impersonal contents is just the reason for projecting them; one feels they do not belong to one's subjective mind, they must be located somewhere outside one's own ego, and, for lack of a suitable form, a human object is made their receptacle. So you have to be exceedingly careful in handling impersonal projections. It would, for instance, be a great mistake to say . . . : 'You see, you simply project the saviour image into me. What nonsense to expect a saviour and to make me responsible.' If you meet such an expectation, take it seriously; it is by no means nonsense. The whole world has a saviour expectation; you find it everywhere. (CW18 para 369)

Once again, in the same lecture, Jung warns against the dangers of being infected by such projections. The danger of infection is probably greater the closer the projection is to the role of the recipient. In other words, a pastor might be at special risk from the projection of a saviour image.

Personal

This can be broken down into smaller types of transference relating which might include:

Part/whole person relating.
Habitual relating.
Past-pattern relating.
Split relating.
Erotic ways of relating.

Part/whole person relating

Maureen:

Sister Maureen was in the second year of her social-work training when she went on placement to a day centre for drug addicts. Previous placements had included a counselling centre, a children's home and a social-work department in a hospital. In all those settings, she had not only learned a great deal, but she had found that she could relate to her clients, and that both she and they seemed to benefit in various ways from the relationship. Her placements had gone well.

After only two weeks at the day centre, however, she became demoralised and began to doubt her capacity to function effectively as a counsellor/social worker. She requested an early meeting with her tutor, at which she hoped to ask for a transfer. Her tutor was able to help her to understand that her feelings of demoralisation came from being treated by one particular addict as part of a person. This addict was forever trying to wheedle money out of Sister Maureen, money she was sure he would use to buy supplies.

She had no feeling of being related to as a whole person. Rather, she was seen as a breast to be ruthlessly exploited and discarded when its usefulness was over. What was missing in the addict's approach was any sense of concern for Sister Maureen as a person, because he did not see her as a whole person. She was only part of a person, and so felt that she was being treated as a thing.

Habitual relating

Thomas:

Thomas was an oboist in his forties. He was illegitimate and had been left in a nursery for the first three years of his life. His mother married and he went to live with her, but in appalling conditions that exacerbated the early deprivation. When he was twelve, he was taken into care, having been sexually abused and beaten by his stepfather. He was later transferred to a special school, where he became religious and developed a love of music. But his behaviour, despite his intentions, got worse and he was threatened with admission to a psychiatric hospital. He ran away, did labouring jobs and earned enough money to obtain musical tuition. He got himself through music college and had established himself as a successful and sought-after musician. But he was deeply troubled by his fantasies and his impulses. He plucked up courage, picked up the phone, and rang his pastor. The call came when the pastor was in the midst of a family crisis. He was unable to respond to Thomas's request for an appointment that day, and forgot to take Thomas's number. The next day Thomas phoned again; the pastor was out, leaving his wife to weather the abuse that once again issued forth from Thomas. In the end, the pastor made contact and arranged an appointment.

This is an example of someone who habitually reacts to situations of frustration or disappointment with the sort of rage that breaks off communication and reconfirms him in the idea that nobody is available when he is in need. This is a habitual transference stemming from his early experiences of being in an institution. It also represents a transference to the institution; any kind of institution, including the Church or an aspect of it, is likely to induce this response, especially when there is any hint of neglect, any possibility of being let down.

Past pattern relating

David and Geraldine:

David and Geraldine came to consult their pastor, Ken, about plans for their marriage ceremony. David was quite a successful press photographer and Geraldine ran her own hairdressing business. Ken was struck by the way in which Geraldine took command of the situation and outlined 'their' requirements. But as he listened he became more and more aware of a sort of passive aggressiveness issuing forth from David towards himself. It took the form of blocking or disagreeing with all Ken's suggestions. Ken found himself addressing more and more of his comments and queries to Geraldine and feeling increasingly angry with this obstructive parishioner. In the course of their subsequent meetings, it transpired that David had been sacked from his job because of a personality clash with his male boss. It was Geraldine who casually said that he would be better off working for himself on a freelance basis, because he always ran into trouble with bosses; it was probably something to do with the antagonism between him and his father.

In this latter example, Geraldine came to the rescue and unwittingly explained to Ken the antagonism that seemed to exist between himself and David. Ken had been turned into another negative father figure, despite his attempts to show interest and be helpful.

Reflection about these sorts of interactions with a supervisor or in a support group can sometimes help to unhitch the pastor from the projections being made on to him, and help him to realise that he is being seen as someone else. Another example comes to mind.

Sandra:

Sandra was a university student who gave an evening a week

to the church youth club. Her warmth, her attention to her appearance, and her practically creative gifts particularly drew the girls to her. Often, as she danced or cooked or helped the girls in various activities, she would see out of the corner of her eye a rather beautiful adolescent girl, usually sitting on her own, sometimes cocooned by a personal stereo, and always looking in an aloof and cold way at the world around her. Sandra tried to make contact, but the girl would slope off, dismissing Sandra with a pleasantry.

At church, she noticed that sometimes the girl was with her father, sometimes not. She also noticed that the father seemed unintegrated into the congregation. She asked the pastor about the family and discovered that the mother had died of an illness some six years ago. In discussing the matter with the youth leader, Sandra came to see that this girl could not bear to get close to another older female in case she lost her too, like her mother. Since Sandra was to leave university soon, she decided to make no further overtures to the girl, thinking that she did not want to foster an attachment that would then have to be broken.

There are other attachments that have been broken and left people spiritually or religiously adrift. I am thinking of attachments to various images of God, to priests or nuns, or to 'the Church'. During childhood it is common for people to have personified images of God. 'He' is thought of as a person, certainly powerful, often very old and wise. 'He' is prayed to with requests to help win tomorrow's football match or to stop Mother noticing that most of the chocolate biscuits have been devoured. These prayers become more sophisticated with the passage of time, and other dimensions of spiritual life may or may not engage the developing individual.

Often during late adolescence a person will rebelliously and healthily break away from his parents, but also from all sorts of other parent imagos. These may include God, actual priests, a once-nurturing convent school, and the wider body of 'Mother' Church. Embroiled in and lost sight of in the healthy drive towards independence and emancipation from tradition is what we referred to in Chapter 2 as the spiritual instinct. After withdrawing the projections from a personified God, etc., the individual finds himself far from at-one-ment. A sense of incompletion, a vague restlessness, feelings of futility or purposelessness are some of the tell-tale signs.

Beth:

Beth had gone away to school in a convent at the age of nine. She had become fervently religious, even somewhat pious, and when she went to the senior school she felt she had a vocation. She was set on joining the order until a close friend was unjustly expelled. Her faith sustained her for a while, but she was gradually assailed by doubts and slowly but surely broke away from her religion and left the school after her O-levels. For years she would have nothing to do with religion, and sometimes even aggressively asserted her atheism. Life had gone well for her, but she always felt slightly dissatisfied. One day, she was browsing in a bookshop and turned distastefully away from an edition of Julian of Norwich. But somehow, the book beckoned her and she started to read. Familiar, half-forgotten passages moved her and she bought the book. She experienced what she described as 'a feeling of coming home', at the same time feeling that her image, notion and experience of 'God' had undergone a long, slow and mostly unconscious transformation. She had discovered a division in herself, often felt as something exterior.

Split relating

Dominic:

Dominic was chaplain to a residential therapeutic community for very disturbed people in their early twenties. He went there once a week, and for some months felt rather apart from the life of the community—politely tolerated. He was delighted one day when one of the residents, Michael, asked to see him on his own. This young man poured forth a horrendous history, which almost moved Dominic to tears. A strong bond seemed to have been forged between them. Every week, Michael would make a bee-line for his new-found sympathiser. He would 'confess' to various petty crimes, present himself as maltreated by the world, and give Dominic the impression that he was his only friend in the world. Into their conversations crept mild criticisms of the director of the community: he was often away; he really did not understand in the way that Dominic did; he had his favourites, mainly the women; he was blind to the physical discomfort of the place; he was ruthless towards people who did not pay their rent on time, etc.

Dominic began to look around with new eyes, and found himself agreeing with his protégé. The place was dilapidated; the director often had women in his office; the turnover of residents must be the result of ruthless policies. Dominic approached one of the staff 'confidentially'. The latter insisted on Dominic raising the whole issue at a staff meeting, a process that would inevitably integrate Dominic further into the community. With great trepidation, Dominic attended and shared with the staff the history and content of his relationship with Michael. The director thanked him, welcomed his presence, and helped the staff to explore the situation.

In fact, Michael had approached several of the male staff in this manner, claiming to each that he was the special person to him. The consistent 'baddy' was the director, to whom Michael could express no negative feelings for fear of retaliation. All those feelings were split off and reported to other male members of staff, creating a therapeutic vacuum in the relationship between Michael and the director.

Other examples of split transferences might include nursing staff, where one shift is seen as good and the other as bad; parish staff, where the curate is good and the vicar bad; church wardens; archdeacons, area deans; prioriesses, novice mistresses; bishops, spiritual directors; organists, choir-masters; a husband, a wife; a chairman, a vice-chairman, etc. Essentially, good feelings are felt and expressed towards one person (group, institution) and bad feelings towards another. The purpose of such a split is to protect the good from the bad; the effect is, on the whole, to make both relationships vacuous.

Erotic ways of relating

Pastors of both sexes, like teachers, therapists, pop stars and stylites are fated to be scourged or delighted by people falling madly in love with them. This happening is joked about in chapter houses, common rooms, analytic congresses, green rooms; it is even reported to be the origin of semaphore, since the stylites needed a method of communication from pillar to pillar across the desert, whereby they could share tactics for getting rid of excessively devotional laity. But the jokes betray an anxiety.

An erotic transference occurs when a person develops intensely sexual and erotic feelings and impulses towards another person; the feelings are interwoven with all sorts of fantasies. Feelings, impulses and fantasies combine to produce behaviour that can be very difficult for the pastor to manage, and can evoke feelings of guilt and longing in the pastor, and, sometimes, loathing. The feelings in the client are usually derivatives of unfulfilled longings in relation to a parent or sibling of the opposite or the same sex. They often, though not always, have little to do with the actual person of the pastor. Needless to say, a pastor whose own inter-personal life is in disarray or disquiet is especially vulnerable to erotic transference, and, if it occurs, should seek personal help immediately.

Veronica:

Veronica was the daughter of Scottish pioneers in South America. Well heeled by mining ventures, they had sent her to public school in England. She had obtained a scholarship to Oxford, had read theology, and gone on to take orders as a deaconess. A brilliant career in this role followed before she took a permanent position in a parish. She married and had one son. Her husband was a dedicated man and father; but her rather ascetic appearance lent her an air of neglect. Her occasional sermons were erudite and inspired. In them, she hinted at a knowledge of the psychological as well as a love of music, literature and painting. She began to notice from the pulpit the wild eyes of a Bohemian-looking man locked on to her in a state of rapture. Veronica's previously fluid delivery became jerky and uncertain. She became fascinated by those eyes; every time she dared to look, there they were, beckoning, adoring, alluring. She was horrified, even mortified, by her reaction, and decided to use in her next sermon part of a series on types of love, the last verse of Rilke's 'Turning Point':

> Work of the eyes is done now
> go and do heart work
> on all the images imprisoned within you; for you
> overpowered them: but even now you don't know them.
> Learn, inner man, to look on your own inner woman,
> the one attained from a thousand
> natures, the merely attained but
> not yet beloved form!
> (*The Selected Poetry of Raines Maria Rilke.*
> London, Picador, 1987)

She hoped that this might 'symbolise' the experience for him. When the phone rang one Sunday evening, the distraught man at the other end impressed her no more than many others had done. She offered him an appointment, which she regretted ever after, and put the matter to the back of her mind for the time being. The rest of the story is long and complicated and need not concern us, apart from the ending. This distressing and distressed man, whom she immediately recognised, wreaked havoc in Veronica's marriage, in the parish and in its environment. Veronica finally took out an injunction forbidding him to enter the church precincts and to have any further contact with her.

The parishioner had developed an intense erotic transference to her, the power of which had eroded some of her personal and professional boundaries and rendered her unable to think her way clearly through the situation. She had unconsciously fostered the transference by being available on the phone and for interview, and out of panic had denied what was there to be seen. Another case might drive the point home.

Eric:

Eric was a single man in his early thirties, who beavered away quietly on his own in a suburban parish. He lived in a small terraced house as a bachelor but also as a lay brother of a monastic community. His home, furnished only with essentials, left his parishioners with a mixture of admiration for his austere lifestyle and, particularly among the women, a strong wish to look after him and soften his self-imposed discipline. In bearing he was erect; in appearance lean and wiry. Nothing about him ever seemed out of place, but a habit of nervously shifting his eyes belied an exterior calm.

In his work, he placed great emphasis on worship and devoted much of his time to counselling, in which he had trained to quite a high level. The bishop was aware of Eric's good reputation, but could not rid himself of a mild feeling of discomfort. What actually was this man up to? He seemed so difficult to get to know. The bishop also found himself feeling very controlled by Eric during interviews with him, and found that probing resulted in Eric pruning his answers until they were almost monosyllabic.

Over two or three years, the bishop noticed that Eric never asked for anything for himself, although at times his façade faded and he looked quite worn out. Eventually, the bishop took the bull by the horns and told Eric that he was anxious to get some support for him; he introduced the idea of a pastoral support group, where Eric could share his work experiences and possibly help others who were similarly burdened. Eric reluctantly agreed, feeling that he had to conform in order to retain the bishop's agreement for him to practise in his area.

He joined an existing group, and very quickly became the leader's assistant, contributing insights, offering ideas and solutions, but always participating from a distance. Then he gradually began to introduce his work, in particular his counselling of a forty-year-old woman who lived in tragic circumstances. She was a dazzling redhead, a former actress, of beauty, intelligence and charm who, as far as Eric knew, had surrendered her career to the obligations of looking after her dementing widowed father, a retired GP. Eric presented his work like an exotic hamper; there was nothing anyone could offer; one could only look at it enviously and be left speechless.

The group leader remained puzzled, but eventually intimated that he had never been in a group that was so consistently silent about a member's work; he ventured the idea that the members seemed helpless about breaking through the disarming way in which the work was presented because possibly they sensed, rather as he did, something vulnerable in Eric. The members reflected in quietude. Then a young woman in the group began to ask questions tentatively. Why had this woman come to see Eric? How often did he see her? Where did he see her?

As Eric began to retreat into a corner, members' faces revealed a lively interest. Well, actually he had started by seeing her in his study, but he began to feel a bit uncomfortable. Uncomfortable? You mean the room wasn't comfortable? Yes, sort of . . . well, not that so much. What was it then? Er . . . it started one day when she came in wearing a very strong perfume. (The men in the group perked up.) I couldn't get the smell out of the room after she had gone. Was it nice? Well, some people would think so. Did you think so?

It transpired that Eric had panicked at this first manifestation of erotic feelings towards him, but at the same time he had felt unable to mention this to the group. Counselling sessions had not only become more frequent, twice a week, but the bewitching Yvonne was telephoning in the evening and, as if that was not enough, was blackmailing him into protracting sessions through tears and threats of suicide. Continuing to beaver on in his usual way, he had suggested meeting at her house, hoping for some protection from the father's presence and imagining that he could control the time boundaries more easily.

He arrived for the first session at her house, and was greeted by Yvonne wearing her bathrobe. He was introduced to the dementing father, who occupied the ground floor, and then ushered upstairs to Yvonne's boudoir. Once there, she lazed seductively on her bed, enticing him with wafts of the now familiar perfume. The room was rather dingy and unkempt. Overflowing ashtrays lay abandoned all over the place, and clothes were scattered around. Eric was over-whelmed. The room and Yvonne incarnated everything he abhorred — sensuality, lust, alcohol, smoke, surrender to the pleasures of the body. Yet, to his horror, he found he could not extricate himself. The domiciliary visits continued, and the scenes of seduction took on a life of their own. Truly, he was enthralled. So was the group! This omnipotent, omniscient man, formerly without much trace of a shadow, had been completely submerged by the erotic fantasies of a woman who throughout her life had searched in vain for love, a search she was now directing at Eric.

It took the group some three years of work to help Eric modify his ascetic and self-sufficient defence so that he could feel more human and more accepted. The presentation of his work with Yvonne was a landmark in his development. It was, he said later, the first time in his working life when he began to glimpse, then look at and finally acknowledge, his mistakes in a way that enabled him to learn.

Quite naturally, Veronica, like Eric, had become caught up in a complex interflow of feelings. The intensity of feelings in both the man and the woman constitute what is known as counter-transference:

> The emotions of patients are always slightly contagious, and they are very contagious when the contents which the patient projects into the analyst are identical with the analyst's own unconscious contents. Then they both fall into the dark hole of unconsciousness and get into the condition of participation. This is the phenomenon which Freud has described as the counter-transference. It consists of mutually projecting into each other and being fastened together by mutual unconsciousness . . . all orientation is lost. (CW18 para 322)

Many readers will know from their own experience that what Jung elsewhere refers to as 'psychic infection' can evoke feelings of shame, embarrassment, delight, longing, guilt and confusion, all of which can be brushed aside by a wave of self-condemnation. Such feelings are difficult to share with colleagues, particularly ones senior and on whom promotion is sometimes dependent; they are equally difficult to share with partners since they often provoke a jealous attack rather than a deepening of understanding. There is a real danger that the pastor will become imprisoned in secrecy.

What, then, can be done?

The first step is acceptance of the role that the other is asking the pastor to discharge. This is what the psychoanalyst Joseph Sandler has called 'free-floating role responsiveness' (Sandler, 1976). It is a readiness to accept whatever role is being asked of the pastor without necessarily *enacting* it. For instance, a whingeing masochistic parishioner may be locked in an internal prison of suffering; he may project the image of the rescuer on to the pastor. To enact such a role would probably alleviate suffering in the short term, but would not deal with the internal problem, so the situation would be repeated. Other roles might include those of: saint, prophet, lover, disciplinarian, moral judge, champion of the disadvantaged, brother, mother, teacher—all these and many more in their positive and negative aspects. The principle is that the projection is accepted; the pastor and pastoral counsellor do not try to dodge it, even though it may be extremely uncomfortable (e.g. a harsh moral judge) or extremely flattering (e.g. saviour).

The second step is acceptance of those feelings that are a response to being perceived in whatever role, however unwelcome these feelings might be:

> Condemnation does not liberate, it oppresses. I am the oppressor of the person I condemn, not his friend and fellow-sufferer. I do not in the least mean to say that we must never pass judgement when we desire to help and improve. But if the doctor wishes to help a human being he must be able to accept him as he is. And he can do this in reality only when he has already seen and accepted himself as he is. (CW11 para 519)

Behind Jung's admonition to befriend oneself—something easier said than done but often promoted by personal therapy —is the idea that these very feelings, which can be so difficult to contain, act as 'a highly important organ of information' (CW16 para 163).

The third step, then, is to work at understanding these feelings and to see how they affect the mutual involvement of pastor and client. When the pastor feels completely stuck in relation to a situation or frighteningly caught up in feelings to do with a relationship with a client, it is helpful to ask two questions:

(1) What is the client saying, doing or unconsciously communicating to affect the pastor in this way?
(2) what, in the pastor's inner world, past experience or present situation is so tuned into the client that the pastor cannot see the wood for the trees?

The first question belongs to a supervisory setting, the second to the private work of self-exploration, sometimes in a therapeutic context.

To illustrate the usefulness of processing counter-transference feelings, I have drawn on an area that is familiar to many pastors, whose job involves them in visiting or working in hospitals. It is the area of hospital practice, and has been written about in an invaluable paper by the psychoanalyst Emmanuel Lewis (Lewis, 1979). The many harrowing feelings that emerge in pastor and doctor alike in the course of their work and unconsciously influence their actions, sometimes adversely, provide a common meeting point in which to deepen understanding.

We can note that pastors, like doctors, often find themselves limited by personal and institutional resources, as well as by the personal limitations of their clients, often surviving in adverse social conditions. Lewis's thesis is that unconscious collusion between doctor and patient generates feelings of hopelessness and helplessness and gives rise to what he calls the Pontius Pilate Syndrome.

A girl of nine was brought to a casualty department because she seemed to be having some sort of fit. The houseman confirmed that and prescribed appropriate medication. The paediatrician was called in and he decided to keep the girl in hospital, mainly because of the anxiety that the girl's hysterical condition had generated. The girl came from a family beleaguered by problems. The mother had been sterilised some years before this incident and had not slept with the father since then. She had been thoroughly investigated at another hospital for her problems with obesity. Of her five children, one was severely subnormal and hospitalised but was known to the subnormality consultant, who was considered sensitive and caring by his colleagues.

Doctors and nurses met the next day with Lewis, who was acting consultatively to the team. Everyone was very keen to help the hysterical girl and the whole family, and so there was general amazement when Lewis pointed out that the whole family was in the care of a GP and involved in two other hospitals where they had been subjected to therapeutic zeal. He suggested that it might be better if the GP were informed of the situation so that he could co-ordinate the fragmented care, which this unhappy family was in danger of receiving; also, that the hospital take no further action. It seems he had to press his view very hard against a united and shared wish to 'do' something for this girl and her family.

Lewis suggested that, like Pontius Pilate, the team had to learn to do nothing and hand back the situation to the appropriate place. Then Lewis realised that he had got that wrong. Pilate had done something, in that he had made a decision—and then washed his hands. Pilate was confronted with a situation that he did not understand and that made him feel helpless. Having searched around for an answer to his dilemma, Pilate eventually decided to tell Jesus that he could find no fault with him, but would none the less have him scourged—a totally inappropriate course of action. Pilate was then threatened by accusations that he was no friend of Caesar if he did not have Jesus killed. He condemned Jesus and then washed his hands. Lewis goes on to say that, in the case described, he felt identified with Pilate's wife, who warned Pilate to steer clear of Jesus because of a dream she had had about him.

Pilate was trapped between Jesus' determination to be punished (through death) in order to redeem others and the possibility of himself incurring the wrath of Caesar, an authority figure. Such a situation naturally induces terrible feelings of helplessness. These feelings are experienced frequently by people in the caring professions, and they tend to be dealt with by surrendering to impulsive or carefully considered action. But, if the client does have an unconscious need for punishment, for example, then the danger is that the pastor might act punitively by repeatedly 'forgetting'—for example, to write a letter of referral. The client is punished, but the pastor then feels consciously or unconsciously guilty and might himself seek disapprobation from his seniors or angry punitive responses from his clients. It is easy to see how both parties can get swept further and further into a state of mutual unconsciousness.

Helplessness is one difficult feeling in the counter-transference. Another is boredom. Masud Khan tells us that Winnicott was invited shortly before his death to talk with a group of young Anglican priests. They wanted to know how to know when to refer someone for psychiatric treatment and when to make themselves available as listeners to people who could talk their way through difficulties. Winnicott replied,

> If a person comes and talks to you and, listening to him, you feel he is boring, then he is sick, and needs psychiatric treatment. But if he sustains your interest, no matter how grave his distress or conflict, then you can help him alright. (Winnicott, 1986, p. 1)

Parishioners, clients and patients often report anxieties that they are boring their counsellors or therapists. These anxieties stem in part from the need to go over the same ground again and again in order to deepen understanding or to work through some newly gained insight or attitude. Sometimes the counsellor is being unconsciously tested; sometimes the wish to bore into the counsellor is only thinly disguised. Boredom in the listener can signal to the client that the latter is not emotionally present, for a variety of reasons. The counter-transference response in this case is often to feel terribly drowsy, uncontrollably so, to the extent that surreptitiously pulling one's hair, pinching oneself, breathing deeply are all totally ineffective. With failure to address this emotional desert, the only cure I know consists of splashing the face with cold water—the colder the better! But one cannot do that during a session. Better, then, to tackle it head on by addressing the client's fear of his aggressive impulses expressed through his anaesthetising the emotional field.

Lastly, I want to say something about hate. This is an extremely powerful affect and one that in my experience sends shivers of horror down pastors' spines. It seems incongruous with the role of pastor because it is often thought of as destructive and very hurtful to the other person. Hate can be approached from its opposite, the monastic dis-ease of 'accidie', a condition in which the importunate monk would be overtaken by sloth and torpor, and sometimes regress or want to regress. Accidie lacks energy; hate is the feeling that provides us with the energy to separate from parents, to terminate interviews on time, to take holidays. It is as clean and clear-seeing as rage is diffuse and blind. It is the feeling that Christ used when he drove the money lenders out of the temple. On a more everyday level, it is a feeling well known to mothers (and helping professionals), and much more dangerous if denied. Winnicott (1947, p. 201) suggests that sentimentality is the product of repressed hate. He gives some reasons for mothers hating their babies:

The baby is an interference with her private life.

He treats her as scum, an unpaid servant, a slave.

His excited love is cupboard love, so that having got what he wants he throws her away like orange peel.

At first he does not know at all what she does or what she sacrifices for him. Especially he cannot allow for her hate.

He is suspicious, refuses her good food, and makes her doubt herself, but eats well with his aunt.

After an awful morning with him, she goes out, and he smiles at a stranger who says 'Isn't he sweet?'

In the same paper, Winnicott describes how knowledge of his own hatred enabled him to set very clear limits for a disturbed boy he and his wife had taken in to live with them. When the boy's behaviour became intolerable, Winnicott would put him outside the front door. When the boy was ready to come in, he could ring a special bell. Both could hate each other in safety.

That boy may have been a child version of the schizoid adults studied and treated by the Scottish and solitary psychoanalyst Ronald Fairbairn. He described (Fairbairn,

1940, pp. 46–7) the sort of individual whose love for his mother was felt to be destructive and not accepted. Such a person 'may quarrel with people, be objectionable, be rude. In so doing, he not only substitutes hate for love in his relationships . . ., but also induces them to hate, instead of loving him.' Fairbairn, interestingly, saw this sort of hate as 'moral', in so far as 'if loving involves destroying, it is better to destroy by hate, which is overtly destructive and bad, than to destroy by love, which is by rights creative and good' (Fairbairn, 1940).

Don:

Don was a pastor with a withered hand who had taken a year's sabbatical to complete some research on clergy marriages. Away from his Cornish roots, he felt somewhat isolated in London and joined a pastoral support group.

The male and female leaders of the group came one day to supervision exasperated. After only a few weeks of being in the group, Don had managed to alienate not only the members but also the leaders. He attacked their *modus operandi*, the normative functioning of the group; he was full of answers to issues and questions that invited exploration rather than dogmatic certainty. The leaders felt that he had a chip on his shoulder and that he was so vulnerable that they could not confront him. They hated him as much as the members appeared to, and talked about him as a 'group wrecker', someone who cut across and destroyed the communicative web that had been woven over the years. They wanted to exclude him, but they felt sorry for him. The questions in supervision were: (1) What function did he perform for the group? (2) How could he be unhooked from this role? (3) What was the purpose of him getting everyone to hate him? (4) How could the leaders use the hate generated in themselves and in the group?

These are the sorts of questions that a pastor might encounter, and to which we now turn in the next chapter.

SIX

Understanding the Space Between

In the most powerful moments of dialogic, where in truth 'deep calls unto deep', it becomes unmistakably clear that it is not the wand of the individual or of the social, but of a third which draws the circle round the happening. On the far side of the subjective, on this side of the objective, on the narrow ridge where I and Thou meet, there is the realm of 'between'. (Martin Buber)

Christ was a group worker. He spent his working life with twelve other people, collaborating with them as a team, and discharging a leadership role firmly entrenched in the Rabbinic tradition but also dependent on his charisma. From time to time, he accentuated his leadership by withdrawing into the wilderness to reorient himself for his own spiritual reasons. And then, like most pastors, he returned into everyday life where he was required to function in small and large groups. He seems to have been aware of the mindlessness and the tendency to polarise that exist in crowds, and it was perhaps his knowledge of crowd processes that enabled him to foresee with certainty his betrayal and his death as a scapegoat. As I said, his *modus operandi* was essentially that of the group worker: 'For where two or three are gathered in my name, there am I in the midst of them' (Matt. 18.20). What he had begun was entrusted to his group of followers, a group that gradually spawned the Christian community.

Community is not only an entity or a structure like a monastery. It is also a process that has to do with exchanging what is held in common. And what is held in common is the content, perhaps belief or religious experience. In Buddhism, community (*sangha*) is one of the Three Refuges, the other two being the Buddha and the teaching (*dharma*). Community, then, as structure, process and content is a phenomenon that we can find in most of the major religions. Whitehead seems to see it as a sort of matrix of religious practice: 'The world is a scene of solitariness in community. The topic of religion is individuality in community' (Whitehead, 1926).

For most people, the notion of community is a much later one than that of group. The first group experience is the family. It is the initial training ground where the developing individual experiments with sharing and possessing; with feelings of rivalry, jealousy and exclusion; with role different-iation, different styles of leadership and relationships with a variety of authority figures (mother, father, grandparent, elder sibling, etc.); with the pleasure and frustration of co-operating over tasks; with the dilemma of forging, maintaining and then being allowed to change identity, role and individuality, etc. Then, even allowing for nursery schools or playgroups, the child is catapulted into the institutional life of school.

From then until his demise in hospital or nursing home he will spend a vast amount of his time in groups, organisations or institutions of one kind or another. It is puzzling, then, that we are often relatively unconscious of how we participate in groups and of how they affect us. This chapter aims to provide the pastor with a perspective on groups and institutions within which s/he may see more clearly the processes at work in various professional settings, and so feel a little more at home in the 'realm of "between"'.

As Samuels has reminded us, Jung was active politically and discharged a leadership role in the politics of depth psychology (Samuels, 1985). However, his writings are full of warnings against the dangers of the collective and of mass psychology,

> the bigger the group, the more the individuals composing it function as a collective entity, which is so powerful that it can reduce individual consciousness to the point of extinction. (CW10 para 891)

Jung was undoubtedly influenced by the devastation of two world wars and by the considerable number of patients who had adapted to the social mores of the times at the cost of their individuality. While his negative feelings about groups and masses shine clearly through his writings, there are passages that have a different flavour to them. They tend explicitly or implicitly to link four concepts together: individuation, community, relationship, and self. To these four, I would add Foulkes's concept of the matrix as a linking idea (Foulkes, 1948). But before that, let us return to Jung:

> Individuation is at-one-ment with oneself and at the same time with humanity, since oneself is part of humanity. Once the individual is thus secured in himself, there is some guarantee that the organised accumulation of individuals . . . will result in the formation of a conscious community. (CW16 para 227)

And again,

> Individuation has two principal aspects: in the first place it is an internal and subjective process of integration, and in the second it is an equally indispensable process of objective relationship. Neither can exist without the other, although sometimes the one and sometimes the other predominates. (CW16 para 448)

In both passages, Jung hints at a process of extending over time, but one in which we are left (as I will leave the reader) to grapple with the chicken and egg question: which came first, society or the individual? But one of the important points in the first passage is Jung's knowledge or intuition that an individual secure in himself has the capacity to relate in a conscious (i.e. knowing something with others) community. This has enormous implications for large groups and for what de Maré has called the 'humanising of society' (de Maré, 1987), something based on the concept of the ancient Greek theatre, which enables face-to-face, contained contact facilitating people to be political (i.e. part of the city state). This has implications for synods, church assemblies, chapter meetings and large ecumenical encounters.

It seems unnecessary, therefore, to be paralysed by the dichotomy of the individual and the collective, or, in more pathological terms, the isolated and the institutionalised individual. But as Simmel has pointed out (Simmel, 1950), there is an enormous tension, particularly in contemporary city life, between the development of individuality, enhanced by increasing social complexity and role differentiation, and oppression of individuality through the process of fragmentation. It is possible for an individual to discharge many roles, and to keep these discrete from one another. While this way of life may bestow a feeling of freedom, it may also deny a need for intimacy out of which genuine freedom can grow. He concluded that membership was at one and the same time needed for the development of the self and dreaded for the constraints it imposed.

Between isolation and engulfment there is what Winnicott calls a

> third area, that of play, which expands into creative living and into the whole cultural life of man. This third area has been contrasted with inner or personal psychic reality and with the actual world in which the individual lives, which can be objectively perceived. I have located this important area of experience in the potential space between the individual and the environment . . . this potential space is a highly variable factor . . . [it] depends on experience which leads to trust. (Winnicott, 1967a, p. 121)

This 'third area' corresponds, I think, to the 'third way' between the isolated and the institutionalised individual. It lies eminently in the small, median or large group, as well as in the institution. Later, we will discuss what sort of interplay between personality, structure and process within groups and institutions and their relation to the community at large foster the development of individuals and maintain this 'third area'. The third area lies between the mother and the baby; the self (as an organiser of development, expressed in images of wholeness and as an archetype that unpacks during the process of growth) and the ego, to which the self is superordinate; the group (as a gestalt greater than the sum of its parts) and the individual; the matrix of communication and relationship in a group and the single utterance of a member. Jung expresses all these as follows,

> for the mother is also the matrix, the hollow form, the vessel that carries and nourishes, and it thus stands psychologically for the foundations of consciousness. (CW16 para 344)

The 'third area' is the one in which the symbol is formed, in which meaning is discovered through play. To work and to love in life are not enough; play is essential, and in adult life this is transformed into common experience shared by members of groups engaged in cultural and religious activities. Bion divided groups into two kinds: 'work' groups and 'basic assumption' groups (Bion, 1959). Conflict arises at the interface of the two. A work group refers to a group of people, be it a committee or a Bible study group or a pastoral support group, who have a specific task to perform or objective to meet. To this end, a degree of conscious collaboration is needed in conjunction with the capacity to think, plan, and to test reality. The individual develops through participation, and the group gains from the individual's contributions. A mutual system of growth is created, and the group both enriches and is enriched by its environment, to which it relates as an open system.

In contrast, the basic assumption group is totally pre-occupied with all sorts of terrors and anxieties, which undermine its capacity to work. Individuals operate on primary process thinking, the function of which is to relieve tension at all costs and to ignore the demands of reality. In primary process thinking, time and space are ignored; wish-fulfilment overrides reality testing; images are fused; the pleasure principle is in command. The result is an impoverished group that produces nothing, fails to relate to the outside world and leaves its members gorged on futility. The basic assumption group behaves 'as if' its members implicitly share and are bound by a particular assumption. The energy generated by the basic assumption is used to defend the group from fantasised threats to its survival. The defence mechanisms used are projective identification, splitting, idealisation and denial. It will be seen that each of the basic assumptions is concerned with a search for a leader to extricate the group from the primitive anxieties that are infecting its members.

There are three basic assumptions: dependency, pairing, and fight/flight.

Dependency

An observer of a group functioning on the basic assumption of dependency would conclude that 'the group is met in order to be sustained by a leader on whom it depends for nourishment, material and spiritual, and protection' (Bion, 1959). The leader of such a group is made to feel that he is all powerful and endowed with all knowledge. The members appear to be unable to think, are largely passive, and are prepared to wait for ages for the leader to solve the problem. It eventually dawns on the members that the leader either is refusing to provide a solution or is unable to do so. When this occurs, the members search around for someone else and, Bion maintains, elect the maddest person in the group. This person is doomed to fail, and the group then tries to seduce back into role the deposed leader. The whole situation becomes highly charged and can sometimes be resolved only by recourse to a higher authority.

Pairing

In this basic assumption, the group members seem to be congealed in a glue of hope. The atmosphere is one of hopeful expectation that, through the fantasised sexual union of two of the members (who can be of either sex), a Messiah (or an unborn thought) will be created who will lead the group to the promised land. Paradoxically, it is important that the Messianic leader never emerges, for the members know, unconsciously, that they will be let down and that the leader will not be able to rescue them from all the destructive feelings swirling around, including despair. In Jungian terms, pairing is an archetypal manifestation of unconscious enactment of the coniunctio (see Glossary).

Fight/flight

Despair lurks in this basic assumption group whose members are hell-bent on finding a leader who will create and maintain an enemy 'out there', some sort of scapegoat, in order to fend off the awful realisation that the actual enemy is within. The leader is expected to act like someone in charge of a small military unit. Decisiveness and action are sought of the leader by the members. Once this persecutory state has passed, the leader is then totally ignored and finds himself as constrained by the group as is every other member. Nobody can be themselves.

Bion maintained that certain structures in society carry these basic assumptions for society-at-large. The Church carries dependency, the aristocracy carries pairing, and the armed forces carry fight/flight. Each in its own way is expected to deal with fear, despair and suspicion.

Pastors working in groups of various kinds will have experienced both the work group mentality and the basic assumption groups, and will know of the oscillations that can take place within a group meeting and over a series of meetings. It is unlikely, however, that pastors will see unalloyed forms of Bion's basic assumption groups. This is because Bion seems to have failed to take into account the effect of his presence and personality on the group. He always addressed the group as a whole, never any of the individuals in it, and this produced states of extreme frustration in which it was inevitable that the members would embark on frantic searches for another kind of leader. By addressing the group as a whole, Bion failed to acknowledge the separateness of the individuals within it and therefore induced regression, leaving himself as the sole and mostly silent owner of the capacity to think.

His approach is very different from the group analytic approach of Foulkes who, throughout his writings, emphasises the 'unconscious instinctive understanding of each other' and the availability of the powerful resource of the open system of the group to the individual who is locked in the closed system of his problem:

> The group can only grow by what it can share and only share what it can communicate and only 'communicate' by what it has in common, e.g. in language, that is on the basis of the community at large. In that sense group [work]

means applying 'common sense'—the sense of the community—to a problem by letting all those openly participate in its attempted solution who are in fact involved in it. (Foulkes, 1948)

This open participation is not as easy as it may sound. Many people feel threatened by the thought of exposing themselves to a group situation, and pastors are often expected to lead, conduct, and chair groups with diverse tasks and of various sizes. We can consider groups under three intertwined aspects: structure, process and content.

Structure

This consists of the purpose, the membership, the location and time of the group (both in the sense of its life and in the duration of its meetings). As a general principle, it is the leader of the group who holds primary responsibility for the structure, and who exercises leadership by creating and maintaining firm boundaries around the issues of Why? Who? Where? and When? The leader also gives thought to the physical structure of the group situation. For example, a circle of eight comfortable armchairs might be appropriate for a pastoral support group, but less appropriate for a finance committee whose members might need a table for their papers and notepads.

The task of the group is held in the minds of all the members, but, as Bion has pointed out, the members can engage in anti-task activities. I recall being on a committee in a psychotherapy unit in which we all spent the entire one and a half hours bickering over the minutes of the previous meeting because we were all so overwhelmed by the anxiety about the clinical situation in the day hospital, which was the only item on the agenda. In that sort of situation, the leader, if he can withstand the projections and pressures from the group, has a choice over whether to be authoritarian, democratic or *laissez-faire*. The more he tends towards the *laissez-faire* end of the spectrum, the more he will collude with anti-task activity. When the members seem to have dropped the task from their minds, it falls to the leader to hold on to it tenaciously and at least to confront the group with what it is doing.

All groups have membership boundaries that range from being very firm to very loose. To introduce a new member to a pastoral support group, for example, would require several weeks' notice to the existing members and a lot of discussion about the imaginary new member and his effect on the group. On the other hand, a pastor running a coffee bar for the over sixties may make it clear that anyone in that age group is welcome. The more closed the group, the greater will be the impact of any changes in membership. Care over the entry of a new member is balanced by care over the exit of a member or of the leader himself. Loss of the leader has a strong impact on a group because of the transference projections he carries. We will return to this in Chapter 8.

Groups are also bounded by time and space. The time boundary signifies in part the value the members give to the group. Attendance for the agreed time and life of the group contains a message of love; lateness or unexplained absence contains a message of hate. A group can often be 'led' by an absent member, whose absence implies that he has better things to do. Committees that meet for a specific time (e.g. two hours) tend to be more productive than those that are open-ended. Silent retreats would be intolerable for most people unless they had a definite ending. Time is often used by people to test out the authority of the leader of a group and can be an arena in which power struggles and battles for control can take place. A young pastor was troubled for some weeks by a lonely but intrusive young male parishioner who kept arriving for an evening meeting some fifteen minutes early, just as the pastor was finishing his evening meal or washing up. The pastor would let the young man in, feel bound to entertain him until the beginning of the meeting, and then find him hanging around at the end after the others had gone. Being sympathetic, the pastor tolerated this for some weeks before being driven to confront the parishioner and to insist that he came and went at the same time as the other members of the group.

We have already seen how change makes us feel anxious. Groups become very territorial; a group identifies with the room in which it meets or the order of rooms in which it meets (e.g. a circulating house group). In principle, the more intimate the group, the more important it is to keep the setting as stable as possible so as to minimise anxiety. A pastoral support group, where considerable personal disclosure is the main currency, would need a very stable setting, which would promote a sense of trust and safety. Discussion groups with adolescents would need similar stability. On the other hand, a group planning a summer fête might be happy to hold each meeting at a different person's house. The interior of a church holds enormous meaning for parishioners. Pastors are sometimes surprised and sometimes annoyed by parishioners who 'complain' when changes are made to the shapes and spaces within a church. Changes in location of the altar, in seating arrangements, in lighting, etc. are sometimes introduced by new incumbents or by established ones who get swept along by the fashion of the times. Such changes need consultation and preparation, particularly since they often prelude deeper changes in the ritual and liturgy, which profoundly affect meaning, fantasy and religious experience.

Process

This refers to the dynamics of the group, the interactions and the processes of communication that naturally occur once the structure has been established. The web of communication may be primarily verbal, as in a committee or a pastoral support group, or it may be primarily non-verbal, as in an activity group. And there is the whole range of what lies in between. Groups seem to go through stages of development that are fairly predictable. Tuckman has suggested that there are two aspects to group development: task activity and group structure (Tuckman, 1965); within each he listed four developmental phases. The four phases of task activity are (1) orientation to the task, (2) emotional response to the task demands, (3) open exchange of relevant interpretations, and (4) the emergence of solutions. In phase (1), members define the task and decide on tactics. In phase (2), there is an emotional response to the demands of the task, including some resistance. Phase (3) is encountered when members openly exchange information and opinions. Phase (4) sees the work proceeding well as solutions emerge.

When Tuckman talks of group structure I prefer the term process. The group goes through four phases: (1) testing and dependence (sometimes called forming); (2) intra-group conflict (storming); (3) development of group cohesion (norming); (4) functional role-relatedness (performing). This schema is useful in providing the pastor with some way in which to understand the developmental level of any particular group and in more accurately gauging his expectations of a group. The Jungian analyst Mary Williams (Williams, 1948) envisaged the progress of a group as a development from jungle life, via warring nomadic tribes to a settlement in a secure stockade!

Louis Zinkin has formulated the notion of 'individuation of the group', a process that enhances the individuation of each member in it:

> My thesis is that it is the individuation of the group, rather than of the individual, which enables the individual to experience a sense of belonging to a greater whole; that this can be regarded as the development of a group-self [which] in turn provides the group members with some notion of a larger, transcendent self, ultimately a sense of 'all there is' . . . and that this is a religious experience. (Zinkin, 1989, p. 213)

Process also refers to such phenomena as pairing, sub-grouping, the formation of cliques and scapegoating. This latter often occurs when a group cannot openly attack its leader and so chooses one of its weakest members upon whom the failure of the group can be blamed. Process includes the ascription and acceptance of roles ('She always comes up with bright ideas'; 'He is usually silent', etc.). To their fury, sometimes people get stuck in roles and often, on reflection, find themselves in the same sort of role as they had in their family of origin.

The processes of communication can be intra-personal, inter-personal or trans-personal, and these latter two can be facilitated by the projection of personal shadow material as well as archetypal figures enshrining disavowed aspects of the self such as the hero(ine), the Old Wise Man, the Great Mother, the seductive anima, the child.

Content

This is determined by structure and process and refers to the meaning that the pattern of relationships and the result of interaction have for each participant. The meaning is totally personal and individual since, whatever the nature of the group, it is the individual who experiences it. Groups, like anything else, can be positive or negative; they can be destructive and cruel to individuals or to other groups; or they can facilitate growth and creative thinking. Although writing about group psychotherapy, Yalom cites ten curative factors which I think can be applied to any group situation:

(1) imparting of information;
(2) instillation of hope;
(3) universality;
(4) altruism;
(5) corrective recapitulation of the primary family group;
(6) development of socialising techniques;
(7) imitative behaviour;
(8) inter-personal learning;
(9) group cohesiveness;
(10) catharsis. (Yalom, 1970, p. 78)

While in small groups it is often easier to think than to feel, in large groups the reverse is true. Pastors spend more time than many other people in large groups — deanery meetings, synods, assemblies, etc. — and are sometimes surprised by their own anxiety levels in those groups. Large groups exhibit all the dynamics of small groups, but there are significant differences. In a large group, the speaker addresses the whole group, not an individual in it. Much of the important communication is silent, and responses are hard to judge. There is often a loss of ego boundaries experienced subjectively as an inability to think. If voluntary, this can be pleasurable; if involuntary, it can be very alarming and distressing. There is a loss of inner–outer distinction and this makes analysis of the situation even more difficult. Intelligence is swamped by a terrific flow of energy which, if the group is feeling persecuted, can lead to mob hatred, panic or repressive institutionalisation. Many large groups do not meet regularly and consistently enough to allow for the development of dialogue, thought and culture. Pat de Maré has been pioneering in the field of large-group dynamics for some years. He sees the large group as an opportunity for the individual to discover what it means to be a citizen. But this cannot be done on the basis of occasional or irregular meeting or weekend marathons. Such situations simply produce frustration that is never transformed. Similar states of frustration occur in organisations, to which we now turn.

Since the Second World War, systems theory has had a profound influence on a widely divergent range of disciplines. The rapid advances in technology, computer science and engineering have been both the cause and the effect of the ever-expanding application of systems theory. One such field of application has been organisational theory. But so as not to get carried away by the illusion that systems theory is a twentieth-century invention, I shall quote an eighteenth-century clergyman, who defines a system in this way:

> Any particular thing is a one or a whole, made up of several parts; but yet, that the several parts even considered as a whole do not complete the whole, unless, in the notion of a whole, you include the relations and respects which those parts have to each other. Every work, both of Nature and of art, is a system . . . it is for some use or purpose out of and beyond itself. (Butler, c. 1736)

Von Bertalanffy (1968), generally accepted as a leading exponent of modern systems theory, defined a system as 'an order of parts and processes standing in dynamic interaction'. A system has order because its parts and elements are at one and the same time differentiated and integrated, and are constantly interacting with each other. A system results from its parts having a mutual influence upon one another which then changes them both. Each system is made up of smaller wholes, called 'sub-systems', and is usually part of a larger system called a supra-system—for example, a parish, a deanery, a diocese, the Church of England, the universal Anglican Community. From this example, it is clear that sub-systems stand in a hierarchical relation to one another, while at the same time forming a continuum, such as cell to society, parishioner to the body of the Church.

A system can be closed or open. One might conceive of a hermitage as a closed system and a parish as an open system; the one is static, the other living and dynamic. A system also has a purpose or a goal, and an open system's activity is regulated by the 'feedback' it receives from its environment. The system is open because its boundaries are not fixed, but permeable so that there is a constant exchange between the system and its environment of energy/matter, people/ information. A system is also autonomous because it contains within itself the capacity to control the permeability of its boundaries. If stability is threatened, the boundary can be made more firm. For example, the threat posed by women seeking ordination may result in some branches or sects of the church devising tactics to exclude women. As a living system engages in controlling its boundaries over time, it develops a steady state by constantly adjusting the perme-ability of the boundary. This means that the system is both stable while it undergoes various transformation, but at the same time it contains tension which enables itself to be transformative, creative and autonomous. Revolutionary change in a system is usually catastrophic and leads into the process of enantiodromia, a running into the opposite, by which all participants are endangered. Prior to this, in-formation gets reduced to noise, like a intense crackle on a telephone line; or the lack of information gives birth to rumour and gossip.

Figure 6.1 is a diagrammatic representation of an open system of a parish. The open-system quality is signified by the broken line around the circumference; the continuous line represents closure of the boundary, which would lead to eventual randomness within and eventual death. Outside the circle is the environment which provides material provision for the parish, people and feedback. It is also the place to which the parish exports the effects of its work, and information to the public at large and to the hierarchy about its activities.

At the top of the circle is the pastor. His three primary tasks are (1) to control the boundary (e.g. he might refuse to baptise a child or to marry a couple); (2) to plan the spiritual and social activities of the parish; (3) to balance and optimise people, structures and roles, activities, technologies and supports. He is also accountable to an authority higher than

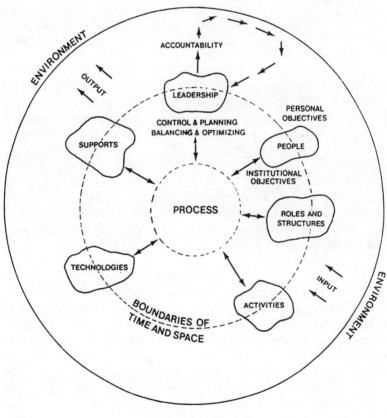

Figure 6.1

himself and has to reconcile the avowed aims of his work with the overall policy laid down by his managers. Failure to identify adequately with that policy will ultimately lead to his resignation, dismissal or his founding of a splinter group.

Like the pastor, each of the people, the parishioners, will come to the parish with personal objectives, such as spiritual growth, which have to interdigitate with the objectives of the parish. A parishioner seeking help with contemplative prayer may not flourish in a very fundamentalist set-up. Again, like the pastor, each parishioner will come with life experience, a certain type of personality, and certain skills, which the parish may or may not recognise and utilise.

The pastor, his staff and the parishioners engage in a dynamic process of creating a structure of ascribed and acquired roles in order to perform the activities of the parish. The structure will include committees and sub-committees, task groups and social gatherings. Within all these, certain people will have ascribed roles (the pastor dispenses communion, the organist is responsible for music) and others will have acquired roles (someone may offer to take on fund-raising; another to represent the parish at a conference). Optimally, acquired roles will relate to an individual's potential and skills.

Some activities may need technology, either in terms of plant and machinery (e.g. a word processor for the production of the parish magazine) or in terms of skill (e.g. an architect to design the parish hall).

Then there is the element of support. The pastor will need the support of his hierarchy (both in terms of supportive management and of provision of salary, etc.), his staff and his parishioners. He might also need support for himself outside the parish and the hierarchy, a space in which he can reflect on his work with a supervisor or a pastoral support group. He in turn will be looked to for support to people in their various roles, and, at times, to dismiss them from them. His own personality, authority disposition and splitting skills will very largely determine how he discharges his role. He might, for instance, function primarily on a one-to-one basis; or he might minimise one-to-one contact and find it easier to delegate wherever possible to various groups (sub-systems) in the parish. The one is led from in front, the other from behind, and there can clearly be flexibility depending on the stability of the parish. The more anxious he becomes, the more likely he is to want to take more and more control of the parts and processes of the system.

Such anxiety may stem from where he places himself and others on a hierarchy of needs. A viable system would be one in which the participants felt adequately sheltered, clothed and fed, had a sense of belonging to the parish, in which their self-esteem was enhanced, leading to a greater sense of independence and the chance to move towards wholeness, individuation and a realisation of potential. Other yardsticks might include: the balance between centripetal and centrifugal forces, between being and doing; the location of a space in the system in which opposites can be constellated, held and transcended. This use of difference can be very difficult in, for example, a psychiatric unit where the polarisation between the organic and psychotherapeutic approaches might turn into a ritualised, non-productive dance.

Another source of anxiety may paradoxically reside in the way the social system is structured as a defence against anxiety generated by the job. Imagine a highly deprived, problem-ridden inner-city area with racial hostility, a high rate of mental illness, child abuse and unemployment. In the midst of it there is a social services office situated on the first floor of a modern office block overlooking a mainline station. Clients come upstairs, have to ring a bell to gain admission, and then wait to be seen in one of two windowless, smoky and smelly interview rooms by an intake worker.

The intake team work in an open-plan office, with phones constantly ringing, bits of paper flying around in the breeze caused by fans; the windows cannot be opened because of the noise from the trains. Sickness, absenteeism and staff turnover are high. The young, mostly newly-trained members of the team are faced daily with disturbed and disturbing clients. They have to take important decisions about removal of children into care, compulsory admission to psychiatric hospital, etc. The stress is enormous.

There is a group of clients, many of whom see the intake team as the enemy, a team of child kidnappers and imprisoners of the mentally ill. There is a team of social workers, who went into a 'helping profession' only to find themselves attacked verbally and physically and forced into installing security devices on the door, which both protect them from the inimical clients, but also imprison them.

To cope with the anxiety generated by the task, the department insists on a myriad of forms being completed about each client contact (so that worker and department are accountable to the social services committee and to the public) and provides the team with a procedural manual, consisting of a number of flow charts that embrace all possible situations. Through these devices, the client becomes more and more depersonalised, and the worker gets more and more frantic as the amount of paperwork to be done reduces client contact time. At the same time, the worker, faced daily with disturbing impulses and behaviour, infantile in origin, projects these on to the client population in the hope of mastering outside something that is inside himself. We all do this in play, for example. But if the symbolic attitude, the 'as if' quality of play, is lost and the worker's inner fantasy becomes equated with the client's situation, then there are major problems. The defences designed to reduce anxiety and colluded with by the worker break down, and the worker regresses. Elliot Jaques puts it like this: 'Individuals externalise those impulses and internal objects that would otherwise give rise to psychotic anxieties, and pool them in the life of the social institutions in which they associate' (Jaques, 1955).

How might this apply to pastors? Bruce Reed defines the purpose of the church as 'facilitating and managing regression to dependence on God through Christ in such a way that the worshippers in reverting to the intra-dependent mode, are involved in a change which provides the basis for development, growth and creativity, both individually and corporately' (Reed, 1976). Reed is describing a process of oscillation between regression to dependence on some person/object/idea outside oneself and progression to dependence on something that has become internal. What anxieties might assail those who try to perform this task?

In the management of regression to dependence, it can

happen that the needy, dependent, greedy and hungry aspects of the pastor get split off and projected on to the parishioner. The image that comes to mind is that of the wolf, the shadow of the pastor. The anxiety then arises that the pastor will have to become totally available and self-sufficient and, as a result, terribly isolated in the sense of not being able to get his own dependency needs met. The parishioners collude with this by projecting so many of their strengths on to their pastor. At the same time, the pastor experiences his hierarchy as another voracious wolf, forever prowling around asking for more money for the diocesan coffers. The hierarchy also colludes by giving out overt or covert messages that to ask for help is a sign of weakness. This stems from the increasing isolation of pastors who travel up the hierarchy and project their own weakness into their subordinates.

The management of progression to intra-dependence creates an anxiety that the pastor will become redundant and will be abandoned and rejected by his parishioners. If everyone becomes so intra-dependent, what hope is there for survival of the Church, particularly with attendance figures down to 5 per cent of the population? Once again, the pastor is faced with the anxiety of isolation. But in this case, there is also the loss of status, which, in the management of regression to dependence, is boosted, at least for the time being. Socio-culturally, these anxieties may be fuelled by an upsurge of sects and religions that foster dependence.

Many pastors are made anxious about the nature of the task. What actually are they supposed to be doing? Finding it difficult to manage the oscillation between extra- and intra-dependence, some pastors find a way out of the dilemma by engaging in social action. The Church then becomes a competitor with other sectors of society. The search for recognition and status gets channelled into quasi-political activity, further confusing boundaries between home and work, the spiritual and the temporal, and the social isolation is redressed by pseudo-intimacy.

Some pastors own up to a fear of madness. The pastor discharges so many roles during the course of a day that he can be left feeling very fragmented, with parts of himself discretely deposited around the parish but not in dialogue with one another. Faced with both the joyful and tragic aspects of *rites de passage*, often flooded with confidences that are burdensome to carry, buffeted around by projections from society, hierarchy, parishioners and family, there is a real anxiety that he will lose the feeling of being in touch with the centre of himself and with the centre that is beyond himself.

This chapter on groups and institutions would be incomplete were it not to contain something about the place of women in the Church. Correspondence columns in the press testify to an almost collective schism on this issue between head and heart, with many people rationally supporting women's fight for entry into the priesthood and emotionally feeling uneasy about it. What I think is at stake is woman's search for the Divine in herself, for the inner goddess emancipated from patriarchal values and projections that have silenced women in the Church for 2,000 years. This search is beautifully portrayed in Grimm's fairy tale 'The girl without hands', a story that describes the unfolding of the individuation process of woman through various transformative agents.

A rather naïve and unconscious girl, still tied to her parents and living dependently on them, is handed over to the Devil by her impoverished father who is seduced by promises of vast wealth. In return for riches, her father promises the Devil whatever is behind his mill. He is unaware at that moment that his daughter is sweeping behind the mill. When the miller's wife wakes up her husband to this fact, it is too late to break the contract with the Devil. This 'pious' girl lives sinlessly for three years, and then, on the day appointed for the Devil's arrival, washes herself and protects herself with a magic circle. She was not yet ready to leave and begin her journey. The Devil is furious and demands that the miller bars his daughter from water, which protects her against his diabolical intent. (*Diabolos* means 'he who throws things across and muddles them up', i.e. who promotes consciousness, akin to Lucifer, bringer of light.) The Devil returns only to find that the maiden has wept on her hands, and again she remains untouchable. The miller is ordered to chop off his daughter's hands or lose his own life. He does so, but the maiden once again weeps over her hands, and the Devil's third and final attempt to make off with her is thwarted. She finally refuses her father's offer to look after her for the rest of her life and leaves home. She arrives at a royal garden, surrounded by water, which prevents her entry, until an angel parts the water for her. She enters the garden and eats just one beautiful pear. Her meal is witnessed by the gardener, who informs the King. The next night, King, gardener and a priest who was to speak to 'the spirit' keep watch and see the maiden approach the tree and eat just one pear, using only her mouth. Her faith in the compassion of others is rewarded when the King promises not to forsake her. He marries her and has silver hands made for her. The King leaves for a journey, and his wife bears him a child. A series of letters between the King's mother and the King are intercepted and rewritten by the Devil. The King is deceived into thinking that his wife has produced a monster and his mother is deceived into thinking that he wants his wife and child killed. The mother takes pity on her daughter-in-law and grandchild and sends them away, keeping the tongue and eyes of a hind as proof of death for the King. The Queen leaves with her child on her back, and eventually comes to a great forest, in which there is a house where 'all dwell free'. Here she spends seven years, and 'because of her piety' her hands grow again. Meanwhile, the King returns, wakes up to the facts, and searches for seven years for his wife, whom he at last finds in the forest. Husband, wife and the child, called 'Sorrowful', are reunited and live happily ever after.

There is much that could be said about this story, but I will confine myself to a few comments. The father seems unable to make a go of it in the world. He also has on his hands a girl who cannot or will not grow up. She is schooled in household matters, but little else. However, she has faith and piety. The mother is both more conscious of the father's shadow, his greed, but stands by while her husband sells his daughter to the Devil, a Hermes-like figure, god of crossroads and thresholds. The daughter is invited to become conscious but uses water, often a symbol of the unconscious, to remain at home, in childhood. Once her hands, which after all enable her to feed and to look after herself, are cut off she leaves home. She arrives in the King's garden, aided and abetted by an angel, a messenger, and is temporarily transformed by a more positive male figure, the King, who provides her with artificial independence in the form of silver hands. (As an aside, it is interesting to notice that three men keep watch in the garden; it is the spiritual man who speaks to the spirit in the maiden, and enables her to enter the household.) Abandoned once more by a man, who himself has to go on his own journey, she is left to the wiles of the Devil and finally has to leave her haven. She spends seven years in 'the dark night of the soul', the house in the forest, where her hands grow. This state of indwelling, a place where all can live freely, enables her to find her own strength and independence, the Divine within, and she is able to enter upon a different sort of coniunctio with the King. Masculine and feminine, each having travelled their own journey, are in balance with one another.

Jung saw the dogma of the Assumption as

> the most important religious event since the Reformation . . . it leaves Protestantism with the odium of being nothing but a man's religion which allows not metaphysical representation of woman. . . . The feminine, like the masculine, demands an equally personal representation. (CW11 paras 752–3)

Mythological and religious themes converge here. It is to the Trinity that the feminine principle is added, thus producing the quaternity. The contentious issues over the place of women in the Church are not ones that I can tackle theologically. But I do wish to point out that the social and cultural mores of our times are such that woman has now a different opportunity to discover her own authority, the feminine within, her own way of being and doing, which neither has to ape nor compete with the masculine. She is in the process of becoming emancipated from the illusion that womanhood is motherhood and from the search for an elusive, if not illusory, image of woman which has somehow got lost over the millennia. I can see no justification from a psychological point of view for excluding women from the forum of the Church, where this struggle for meaning and role is being enacted, both on a personal, individual basis, and through social and political action. The two interact. Perhaps it is no coincidence that until recently the voice of women was spoken through the mystics—Julian of Norwich, Teresa of Avila, etc.; the word 'mystic' comes from the greek word *muo*, meaning 'I am silent'. For how long?

To return to the concept of role *vis-à-vis* the pastor: in my own mind, I think rather simplistically of a continuum: administrator–minister–pastor–priest/ess–religious, secular to sacred. The administrator is concerned with the daily ticking-over of the parish—buildings, funds, reports, statistics, bureaucracy, and has the role of manager. The minister is one who serves or assists another. The minister lies somewhere between the administrator and the pastor, the latter of whom is concerned, like a shepherd, with the overall well-being of his congregation. The pastor actively engages with people's needs and with the secular world, often acting as a bridge from the world of the profane to the world of the sacred. While the pastor is turned towards the congregation, the priest, who is ordained, consecrated and empowered to dispense the sacraments, is turned towards God and acts as a bridge between the God out there and the God within.

Of the clergy (pastor/priest), Monica Furlong writes:

> I am clear what I want . . . I want them to be people who can by their own happiness and contentment challenge my ideas about status, about success, about money, and so to teach me how to live more independently of such drugs. I want them to be people who can dare, as I do not dare, and as few of my contemporaries dare, to refuse to work flat out, to refuse to compete with me in strenuousness. I want them to be people . . . who can face the emptiness and possible depression which often attack people when they do not keep the surface of their mind occupied. I want them to be people who have faced this kind of loneliness and discovered how fruitful it is, as I want them to be people who have faced the problems of prayer. I want them to be people who can sit still without feeling guilty, and from whom I can learn some kind of tranquillity in a society which has almost lost the art. (Furlong, 1966)

It is to the lifelong contemplation of the God within that the religious is drawn in a monastic setting, to which all the concepts introduced in this chapter can be applied.

> Monasteries make the whole of life an extended musical drama. This drama is one in which the monks take part with their entire lives: it is built around their deepest religious mysteries, and it mysteriously releases the soul. . . . The drama brings about nothing except for the individual soul. . . . This has to be experienced, not explained, but those whose whole life it is are often satisfied. They know the full force of a river that most of us have never entered and few of us have ever observed. (Levi, 1987, p. 21)

Many readers and some ex-religious may find Peter Levi's description rather idealistic, but none the less the monastic setting may still be unsurpassable as one that simultaneously holds the greatest potential and the greatest obstacles to discovering and relating to the soul.

SEVEN

Relating to Inner Space

———

This is at bottom the only courage that is demanded of us: to have courage for the most strange, the most singular and the most inexplicable that we may encounter. That mankind has in this sense been cowardly has done life endless harm; the experiences that are called 'visions', the whole so-called 'spirit-world', death, all those things that are so closely akin to us, have by daily parrying been so crowded out by life that the senses with which we could have grasped them are atrophied. To say nothing of God. (Rainer Maria Rilke)

In this life, we have the opportunity to relate to various kinds of otherness, and the depth to which we relate to one kind invariably affects the way we relate to the Other. The more I am open to myself and what inhabits my inner space, the less likely I am to distort the space between myself and the outer Other, or to blur the image. Similarly, deep relationship with the contents of my inner space enables me to reach the depths of the Other outside myself, and this mutual reaching for depth creates the richness of the relationship. The Other in myself may be fantasy, image, symbol, physical symptom. Each or all of these may, however, be experienced by me as an Other of a particular kind, one that seems to transcend me and is not personal to me. This experience of something transcendental and trans-personal is often referred to as religious.

In this chapter, I wish to move towards answering the question: What does Jungian psychology have to say about these experiences of the Other on the level of the personal and the trans-personal?

The necessity for exploring this question is twofold. First, the pastoral worker will be approached by people suffering from feelings of futility, meaninglessness, alienation, puzzle-ment about their suffering, fear of death, etc.; as well as people who have had visions, religious experiences and even, occasionally, by people who claim that their houses are inhabited by poltergeists (vicarages are renowned for this phenomenon!). All these people, in their different ways, lie on a spectrum between those who have lost or never had a religious experience and those who have been overwhelmed by such an experience.

Secondly, one of the central concepts of Jung's psychology — individuation — emerged from Jung's study of religions and their symbols:

> the psyche is transformed or developed by the relationship of the ego to the contents of the unconscious. In individual cases, that transformation can be read from dreams and phantasies. In collective life it has left its deposit principally in the various religious systems and their changing symbols. Through the study of these collective transformation processes and through understanding of alchemical symbol-ism I arrived at the central concept of my psychology: the process of individuation. (*MD&R*, p. 200)

He suggests that when this process is blocked, the person is in an abnormal frame of mind and that some other psychological function is exaggerated through the admixture of the energy which should normally be in a religious experience. So that, for instance, an enormous amount of thinking as part of a greedy quest for the conquest of knowledge might take place at the expense of sensual or religious experience. Below is a case in point.

Hermione:

Hermione was in her late fifties and approaching her retirement when she approached her pastor complaining of feelings of futility so severe that at the end of a day she often just sat in her room staring into space. She was the only child of elderly parents, who had kept her in bed for much of her early childhood convinced that she was ill. She was kept at home and taught by her parents until she was nine. She lived in the big house of the village, and was discouraged from playing with other children. She grew up with a precocious intellect, and, after a spell at boarding school which was probably her salvation, she went on to university, eventually graduating with the bonus of a husband, who was distantly related to her.

Her father's death a little later saddened her deeply, but also released her from an internal prison of prohibition and anxiety. She and her husband shared a deep faith, which sustained them both in their voluntary work. Their first child was stillborn because of blood-matching problems. The couple then had a daughter, and later adopted another girl and a boy. Meanwhile, Hermione's mother had taken to her bed after her husband's death and was to stay there for the remaining forty years of her life, alive but dead, and inducing terrible guilt in Hermione who could do nothing to make her better.

The family grew up happily until the adopted daughter had a furious row with her father, culminating in her leaving the room with the hateful message 'Drop dead'. Two days later he had died of a heart attack. The girl became a drug addict and tyrannised the family for some years. Hermione's faith was dwindling. Robbed of her husband and then of everything precious in the house to pay for her daughter's drug supplies, she none the less struggled on, working full time, caring for the children, running a house, and rescuing her daughter several times from near-death situations. Loneliness drove her into years of study, the accumulation of knowledge, and a frantic pace of life. She lived through the young people that thronged her house, but could not find new inner life for herself. Stillness, silence, being alone, all frightened her.

Then in the space of three weeks her mother, the old family gardener and one of her oldest friends all died. The children had all left home and retirement loomed large.

Futility closed in on her, nibbling away at all that was still enjoyable and joining forces with an envy of other people's happiness that spoiled what she had created for herself. It was in this context of an unfocused sense of something being wrong, rather than her having done something wrong, that she told her pastor an interesting story.

Feeling lonely one evening, she had taken herself off to an

Indian quarter of the city in which she lived. Waves of
nostalgia had broken over her as she wandered through the
streets, savouring smells familiar from her travels. She
wandered into a Sikh temple, where she found people engaged
quietly in religious observance. Later, she went for a curry in
a small cafe and got into conversation with the proprietor,
who picked up her interest in spiritual matters. As they
talked, he confessed his puzzlement over Western church-
going. 'People go to church to find stillness in the heart', he
said to her. 'You cannot find stillness and peace if you come
away feeling guilty because of the sermon. And so much
standing up and sitting down, and singing and kissing.' They
laughed. But he had reminded her of something she had
lost – a stillness, which could create an emptiness into which
something could flow. As she drove back, an image came of
the blind, the lame and the paralysed, who waited patiently
by the pool at Bethsaida. The cure could not come out of
patience, hopefulness or will power, although all these were
needed. Before anyone could be cured, the water had to be
disturbed by an angel who broke up the image releasing the
water from stagnation and allowing the possibility of
transformation. But, paradoxically, the water had to be free
of the wind for the image to occur, and be transmitted.

In talking with her pastor, Hermione began to see that the
frantic pace of her outer life was echoed in the incessant
chatter that went on in her head, and that the combination of
the two left little space for the other to emerge from within.
This led her to set aside a quiet time each day, during which
she would reflect on her dreams, or contemplate or draw an
image from within that she would then try to understand as
she witnessed it unfolding with a life of its own. This brought
new meaning to her life and gave her process of individuation
a new impetus. Reflecting on and relating to these inner
others was, for Hermione, religious in much the same way as
Jung meant:

> Practical consideration of these [archetypal] processes is
> the essence of religion, in so far as religion can be
> approached from a psychological point of view. (*MD&R*,
> p. 324)

Here, before going further into trying to answer the question I posed at the beginning of the chapter, I want to draw some sort of boundary between the theological and the psychological, for it is important not to muddle them up, although both have the soul as their central concern.

Jung defined religion as 'the careful and scrupulous observation of the numinosum . . . a dynamic agency or effect not caused by an arbitrary act of the will' (CW11 para 6). This has much in common with William James, for whom religion consisted of 'the feelings, acts and experiences of individual men in their solitude, so far as they apprehend themselves to stand in relation to whatever they may consider the divine' (James, 1902).

Within the context of these definitions, Christian theology gives prime importance to a God believed to be an objective reality beyond men, whereas psychology views God as a subjective reality of man's inner life. Neither excludes the other, but there are clashes. Whereas theology might posit the notion of the will, psychology might retort with the notion of unconscious motivation. The will is seen psychologically as an instrument of the conscious mind containing both a potentiality as well as a danger. It has a potentiality because it is a source of freedom and of independence; it is a danger because it is a constant cause of one-sidedness, which can lead to a lack of relatedness and a dangerous build-up of the opposite in the unconscious (e.g. the type of person who employs a military approach to life on the outside, where all feeling seems to be killed off in the service of reaching the objective, but is plagued by terrifying dreams on the inside).

Theology can presuppose an objectively given order believed to be known, whereas psychology is empirical and subjective —belief is based on experience, and dogma can be seen as a defence against experience.

Theology might require of the believer the suppression of the shadow, a process that is conscious and that the psychologist might see as causing worry, conflict, suffering, but not necessarily neurosis. Repression, on the other hand, is an unconscious defence, and might lead to neurosis. It is in the lifting of repression that something new occurs. Jung puts it like this:

Psychoneurosis must be understood as the suffering of a human being who has not discovered what life means for him. . . . To the patient, it is nothing less than a revelation when, from the hidden depths of the psyche, something arises to confront him — something strange that is not 'I' and is therefore beyond the reach of personal caprice. He has gained access to the sources of psychic life, and this marks the beginning of the cure. (CW10, para 534)

Then there is the different understanding of religious rites. Some pre-psychological clergy, for instance, are insistent on the submissive attitude of lay people to religious rites. Jung notes that for the healthy person the rites of religion can act as a defence of the ego against inflation. But a weak ego may be stunted in its growth, so that for men we find an abandonment of themselves to Mother Church and an abnegation of their responsibilities, and for women we find a problem with the father and most particularly with authority.

I have outlined some of the boundary issues between theology and psychology. The one I wish to highlight is the psychologist's emphasis on experience. The psychologist cannot prove or disprove the existence of God. So-called proofs are mostly meaningless anyway. What he can demonstrate is the existence of an archetypal image of God, the image of the self, a supra-ordinate centre of existence. Along with the image is the experience of numinosity, the feeling that there is something larger than the me that I am aware of and outside other people's awareness of me. The assimilation of the image (which may be a mandala, for example) and its symbolic meaning is immensely enriching. Such imagery arises spontaneously and is only partly a result of man's adaptation to consciousness. Before consciousness, there is no discrimination or separation. As consciousness is achieved, there is a division between I–Thou and I–It, which produces a state of two-ness, of doubt (the latin word *dubium*, of two minds). This state is both external (baby–mother) and internal (conscious–unconscious). It is in the space between the two, conscious and unconscious, and out of the tension between the two that the image happens to us; we do not create it.

Jung's emphasis on experience was probably fired by his profound disappointment in his father's failure adequately to address the young Jung's religious questions. We can envisage Jung's religious development as spanning a huge arc between the ages of three and fifty-four. When three, he dreamed of being in an underground temple and seeing a huge phallus standing erect on a golden throne. He was terrified, but his mother called out to him, 'Yes, just look at him. That is the man-eater!' By the age of fifty-four he had arrived at 'the central point in my thinking and in my researches, namely the concept of the Self' (*MD&R*, p. 199). (Readers will forgive him for claiming more than one central point to his psychology!) This central point emerged from his collaboration with Wilhelm Reich on *The Secret of the Golden Flower*, a Chinese yogic text, in which the transformation of the hairy phallus of his early dream into the supra-ordinate self was symbolically portrayed.

Between the years 1916 and 1926, Jung was preoccupied with Gnosticism, which he saw as a bridge to a more living appreciation of the Christian tradition. The word Gnosis means knowing or knowledge. The Gnostic was and is someone with a deep conviction that the supreme achievement of life was the attainment of an absolute knowledge of the truth of existence, a knowledge that arises in the heart, intuitively and mysteriously, and is called the knowledge of the heart. At one level, its links with Zen Buddhism (in which Jung was also interested) are clear:

A special transmission outside the teachings;
Not standing on written words or letters.
Direct pointing to the human heart,
Seeing into its nature and becoming enlightened.
(Attributed to Bodhidharma, an Indian monk who is said to have brought the Zen School to China)

From Gnosticism, alchemy, the study of the religious symbolism of both East and West; from his self-analysis and his clinical work; from his own spiritual development, Jung formulated certain ideas about the spiritual instinct.

First, he saw it as a principle *sui generis* and as

indispensable; as a source of insight and as a power behind the process of individuation, which, as I have stated before, is not about becoming perfect but about becoming whole.

Secondly, between ego and self there is an exchange, the currency of which is the symbol as it is expressed in dreams, fantasies, visions and synchronistic phenomena.

Thirdly, the symbol arises when the individual needs to become more conscious or when the unconscious spontaneously wishes to reveal part of itself. The symbol is forward looking and often takes the person out of an impasse.

Fourthly, the process of individuation includes finding an appropriate persona, confrontation with the shadow, relating to the various archetypal figures that lead eventually to the emergence of images of wholeness, whose characteristic is the *coincidentia oppositorum*. These images are thought of as representations of the self. Diagrammatically, the process can be schematised as in Figure 7.1.

In his autobiography, Jung called it his 'Confrontation with the Unconscious', and he is in no doubt about what it entails: 'The progressive development and differentiation of consciousness . . . involves nothing less than a crucifixion of the ego' (CW9(ii) para 79). I think Jung is echoing Meister Eckhart, who instructs, 'Observe yourself, and wherever you find yourself, leave yourself: that is the very best way' (Eckhart, 1987).

For this progressive development of consciousness, Jung engaged in a process and developed a method. The process was threefold. It consisted of

(1) letting happen;
(2) considering and impregnating;
(3) confronting oneself with.

By 'letting happen' Jung meant the adoption of an attitude of openness and playfulness. He allowed into awareness anything that occurred to him, including his childhood pastime of playing with stones. What occurred to him we do not know, because he wrote it down in the 'Red Book', which remains unpublished. But we can empathise with the courage needed to maintain such an attitude if we allow ourselves to adopt the same attitude.

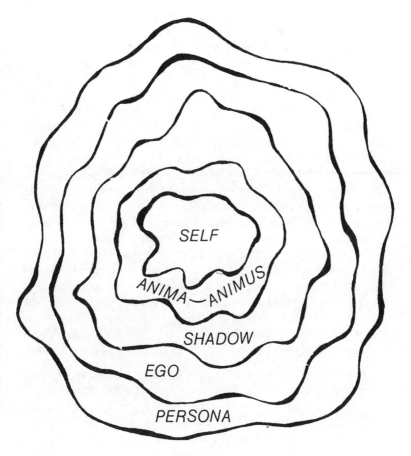

Figure 7.1

It quickly becomes apparent that the incessant procession
of chatter, thoughts, images, impulses and feelings that arise
contain elements that we would rather ignore. Furthermore,
we become aware of a danger—that of allowing ourselves to
give free rein to some of these impulses. By acting upon them,
we lose both the energy that is attached to them and that
quality of interiority which arises from the discipline of a
form. By 'form' I mean that which maintains a framework
within which an introspective process takes place.

We are reminded again of the *vas bene clausum*, to which I referred in Chapter 3. This might, for example, be an hour a day, in a certain posture on a meditation cushion; or it might be a specified time for play or prayer. It consists of a time, a place and an activity, the last of which might seem to the observer to be passive, but which is actually receptive. The similarity with the counselling framework is obvious. Once the form is established and maintained, often with great effort, it becomes possible to move on to the second stage, that of considering and impregnating.

Jung took to objectifying his stream of fantasies and images, fearful that, if he did not do so, he might develop a neurosis and be torn asunder by the feelings associated with them. Hence his need to write them down and to draw them. This is something he suggested to people quite frequently, having first advised them to discover their preferred mode of relating to the world. Visual people should draw, paint, model; verbal people should write; those most at home with sound should play or sing; the dancers should dance. All these activities were to help the person to become aware of something other within, and to put it outside where it could be considered, and given objective, externalised existence. He went on to say:

> To look at or concentrate upon an object conveys to it the quality of pregnancy. And if it is pregnant, it is alive, it produces, it multiplies. That is the case with any phantasy image. One concentrates on it, then finds difficulty in keeping it quiet; it gets restless, it shifts; something is added to it or it multiplies itself; one fills it with living power and it becomes pregnant. (Jung, 1976)

But there is still work to be done. The energy contained in the impregnated image or the person considering the image needs to be transformed into meaning. This is the ethical obligation contained in the process of confronting oneself. Consideration of the inner world, of the Other, becomes masturbatory unless it is transformed into an intercourse producing a search for purpose and meaning and, through meaning, an impact on the individual's life. There is a choice. One can grapple with the Other, the unconscious, and deepen the interior life, thus enriching inter-personal life; or one can turn away from the unconscious and perhaps lose the opportunity of finding meaning; or one can fall into its quicksands and risk possession. Mephistopheles, I think, would support the first choice:

> The greater part of the treasure is to be found
> Throughout your kingdom, untouched, underground;
> The natural resources of the nation
> Beyond both reckoning and imagination.
> But wise men will, when they have studied it,
> Place infinite trust in what is infinite. (Goethe)

These notes on the process take us back to Figure 7.1. Encountering the Other is not a linear process, but for didactic purposes I am going to begin with the persona and work inwards towards the self.

Persona

Jung says:

> The persona is a complicated system of relations between individual consciousness and society, fittingly enough a kind of mask, designed on the one hand to make a definite impression on others, and, on the other, to conceal the true nature of the individual . . . a parson must not only carry out his official functions objectively, but must at all times and in all circumstances play the role of parson in a flawless manner. (CW7 para 305)

Within this definition there lies a paradox—that between communication and deception. Cassock and dog-collar communicate to the rest of the world that their wearer discharges a certain role in society, whose members expect certain behaviour. But the mask of clothes also acts as a uniform, and so is potentially deceptive about the individual who disports it. Furthermore, the mask might even deceive the wearer himself. Jung amusingly describes how he once met someone who appeared to him to be saintlike. He was so intrigued that he stalked him for a few days, but found him culpable of nothing. Jung began to feel inferior and that he should improve himself. But on the fourth day, the man's wife consulted him. Jung concluded,

> any man who becomes one with his persona can cheerfully let all disturbances manifest themselves through his wife without her noticing it, though she pays for her self-sacrifice with a bad neurosis. (CW7 para 6)

From this example, it is clear that the mask can be defensively protective in the sense that the actor never comes to know himself. Alternatively, it can be positively protective in so far as it can convey boundary messages to do with time and place assigned to discharging a role and thus protecting the individual's private life.

Shadow

Jung says:

> The shadow is a moral problem that challenges the whole ego-personality, for no one can become conscious of the shadow without considerable moral effort. To become conscious of it involves recognising the dark aspects of the personality as present and real. This act is the *essential* [my italics] condition for any kind of self-knowledge, and it therefore, as a rule, meets with considerable resistance. (CW9/2 para 14)

Aspects of the personality that become dark, or shrouded in darkness, do so for two reasons. Either they are deemed unacceptable by the family environment and therefore repressed; or, being contrary to the conscious attitude, they become relegated to the unconscious. Stereotypically, boys do not cry and girls do not put up bookshelves. Because these behaviours are thought to be inappropriate to boyishness and girlishness, they tend to be spotted by the individual in someone of the same sex. These projections can occur in the external world or in dreams, where the dreaded aspect of oneself turns up uncomfortably. The more instinctual the behaviour that has been 'disowned', the more likely it is to appear in the form of an animal, whereas impulses to steal, for example, might be portrayed by a cat burglar dressed in black.

Individuals have their shadows. Groups often contain a member who carries the shadow of the group. This person cannot think; is always tetchy; is the one who weeps; is the one who loves. It is important to remember that the contents of the shadow are not necessarily bad. They are simply *experienced* as inferior and unacceptable. The shadow might contain the capacity to be intimate, because intimacy can be thought of as a weakness or sentimental or whatever. Societies also have their shadow. As Meier points out,

> In Genesis, we are encouraged to make use of everything present and to multiply. We certainly did so, right down to the atom bomb and the population explosion. We have abominably exaggerated this liberty to a point where we are about to extinguish ourselves by behaving as if we ourselves were the creators. (Meier, 1986)

Why does Jung talk about a moral effort? I think it is because confronting the shadow entails enduring the agony of shame. We look into the mirror and do not like what we see. It induces us to take flight and to hide, and it is often accompanied by very unpleasant bodily sensations. Guilt on the other hand often propels the offender into confession and into reparative behaviour which is seen or witnessed. Shame is closely linked to our sense of identity, to identification with our peers (what would they think?), and to the gap between our ideal self and our known self. The act of shaming another is also one of the most powerful psychological weapons available, often used against someone who is thought to be shameless (the wife who has an affair is called a whore). Whereas guilt is felt to be proportionate to the offence, shame is totally disproportionate. From my experience, shame is best dealt with by compassion and the sensitive use of humour. But these cannot be manufactured within the individual particularly when a contemptuous, shaming and humiliating parent has been introjected. Such a parent has seen his/her shadow in the child, and so a vicious circle has been constructed. There is no model of a compassionate response available.

In this context, a pastoral support group, for example, can be enormously powerful in detoxifying shame since the shameful revelation is frequently met with support, acceptance and continued warmth, and, sometimes, a similar revelation from another member, which reduces the awful isolation of shame. But shame has its positive aspects as well, as Sartre reminds us: 'I am ashamed of what I am. Shame therefore realises an intimate relation of myself to myself. Through shame I have discovered an aspect of my being' (Sartre, 1943). In other words, the shadow beckons us to become what we might have become.

Anima/Animus

Jung writes:

> Just as the anima becomes, through integration, the Eros of consciousness, so the animus becomes a Logos; and in the same way that the anima gives relationship and relatedness to a man's consciousness, the animus gives to woman's conciousness a capacity for reflection, deliberation and self-knowledge. (CW9/2 para 33)

In this section, I am digressing from classical Jung in so far as my position posits the existence of the anima and the animus in both men and women. But I do adhere to the notion that the anima/us is in a compensatory relationship to the persona. In other words, the ultra-macho man is inwardly very womanly. Whereas the shadow is usually encountered in projection on to someone of the same sex, the anima/us is seen in someone of the opposite sex. For the child, the parent of the opposite sex is the first carrier of the imagos of anima/us, and it is around the central core of the parental imago that all other imagos of the contrasexual archetypal image cluster, including respectively the concrete and more abstract one of Mother Earth and Father Time.

I am indebted in what follows to Robert Boyd (1989), who has constructed a paradigm in which the four stages of the anima/us can be specified in the context of the elementary and transformative character of each. Space allows only a summary sketch.

The anima is first met as a child of nature who, in her elementary character, can be giving or depriving and can be accepting or rejecting of relationship. Then she appears as a young sexual and sensuous woman who can join together to give depth to relationship or become ensnaring. Similarly, she can inspire (*la femme inspiratrice*) or vilify. Next she appears as the Mother who can be fruitful and facilitate creativity, but can also be smothering, and prevent further development. She can also appear as quite mad. Lastly, she appears once more as the Great Mother who is whole, wholesome and wise, but can also be falling to bits and quite inane.

The animus starts life full of energy, like Peter Pan, but can succumb to ennervation. His wish to explore can be counteracted by an unconscious inner restraint, whereby the acquisition of knowledge is at the expense of violating God the Father. The next on the inner stage is the hero who has to overthrow the father; his negative aspect is the enslavement of consciousness resulting in dependency on authority and minimal self-reliance. His wish to master skill and environment is counterbalanced by an evasion of challenge. In the third stage, he can make or destroy, invent or stagnate. In the last stage, the animus is concerned with separating in order to bring disparate parts into union. Negatively, he can attempt to break things up and prevent the making of links and patterns. He is either the Wise Old Man, the guru, the purveyor of wisdom, or he is the corrupt tele-evangelist who encourages the development of one aspect of the personality at the expense of others.

This thumbnail sketch of anima/us leads us to what Jung considered to be the role of the contrasexual archetypal image — that of mediator between conscious and unconscious, and the mediation is carried out by the less conscious sexual image.

The ego has by now grappled with the persona, shadow, anima/us on its way to the self.

Self

Jung says:

> It is only through the psyche that we can establish that
> God acts upon us, but we are unable to distinguish whether
> these actions emanate from God or from the unconscious
> . . . the God-image does not co-incide with the unconscious
> as such, but with a special content of it, namely the
> archetype of the Self. It is this archetype from which we
> can no longer distinguish the God-image empirically.
> (*MD&R*, p. 383)

Jung's writings on the self are extremely extensive, and his
use of the term is multiple. Essentially the term refers both to
the totality of the personality, and to a central patterning and
organising force which is beyond the conscious 'I'. It is this
central organising force that ineluctably moves the individual
towards individuation, integration and the feeling of wholeness, in which all the parts of the personality, conscious and
unconscious, fit and hold together for a while before the
whole process starts again on another loop of the spiral.

From the self emanate those symbols that bring about a
shift in attention, initiate a change of direction or attitude,
and produce an affect of awe felt to be numinous, and akin to
a religious experience. Anything can be a symbol of the self,
but stones, crystals and mandalas are frequently encountered.
Sometimes the symmetry of the mandala can be defensive,
offering a temporarily safe haven for the person in a state of
breakdown. The artist Louis Wain, for instance, painted cats
in an increasingly geometrical and fragmented way as his
psychotic illness ran its course over about eleven years.

For most people with a reasonably strong ego, attention to
dreams and fantasies constitutes a spiritual journey. Work
on these inner contents inevitably produces a change of
attitude from one in which 'I' and what 'I will' prevails to one
in which there is an acceptance of an integrating force beyond
the limitations of the ego. Jung writes of the self:

> a superior wisdom or will which must be dissolved through
> conscious assimilation of its contents . . . back to ourselves

as an actual living something poised between two world pictures (consciousness and unconsciousness) and their darkly discerned potencies. This 'something' is strange to us and yet so near, wholly ourselves and yet unknowable. . . . It claims all that and more, and having nothing in our hands that could fairly be opposed to these claims, it is surely wiser to listen to this voice. . . . I have called it the Self. . . . Sensing the Self as something irrational, as an indefinable existent to which the ego is neither opposed nor subjected, but merely attached, and about which it revolves very much as the earth around the sun — thus we come to the goal of individuation. The individuated ego senses itself as the object of an unknown and supra-ordinate subject. It seems to me that a psychological enquiry must come to a stop here. (CW7 paras 396–9)

Here now are two men who listened to 'this voice'. As so often happens, in both cases the self became active, so to speak, when the two men were at an impasse, the first largely because of external circumstances and the second because of internal blockages.

Between 1943 and 1945 Primo Levi was interned in Auschwitz. He had joined a partisan group in northern Italy and had been arrested. He was plunged straight into the unthinkable horrors of the concentration camp, where he was put to work as a chemist. He writes:

I must nevertheless admit that I experienced (and again only once) the temptation to yield, to seek refuge in prayer. This happened in the October of 1944, in the one moment in which I lucidly perceived the imminence of death: when, naked and compressed among my naked companions with my personal index card in hand, I was waiting to file past the 'commission' that with one glance would decide whether I should immediately go into the gas chamber or was instead strong enough to go on working. For one instant I felt the need for help and asylum; then, despite my anguish, equanimity prevailed: one does not change the rules of the game at the end of the match, nor when you are losing. A prayer under these conditions would have been not only absurd (what rights could I claim? and from whom?) but blasphemous, obscene, laden with the greatest impiety of which a non-believer is capable. I rejected that temptation: I know that otherwise were I to survive, I would have to be ashamed of it. (Levi, 1989, p. 118)

It is not possible to know what went through Levi's mind as he stood naked in the crowd. But clearly he was faced with life or death. Neither was a certainty. Was the momentary need to pray motivated by a wish for help with dying or for rescue from death? We cannot know. What seems likely, though, is that he suspended his will. The ego was faced with opposites—life or death. To have sided with one would have denied the other, and produced one-sidedness in consciousness. Instead, the ego seems to have taken up a position between the two, and at some point 'equanimity prevailed'. The strength of his ego enabled him to ride out the conflict, and the subsequent equanimity strengthened his ego. It seems to me that the equanimity was a manifestation of the self, in which the opposites were combined. In other words, it is not a question of this *or* that, but one of this *and* that producing a third, which combine the two. Perhaps this is what Meister Eckhart is getting at when he says, 'God is in all ways and equal in all ways for him who can take Him so' (Eckhart, 1987).

The second case is that of Thomas Merton, who, after an exuberant adolescence and early adulthood, entered a Trappist monastery, where he latterly lived as a hermit before his interest in Zen Buddhism took him to the East where he died. Before becoming a Trappist, he had battled with the idea of becoming a Franciscan friar, but had been told that the time between his conversion and his vocation was not long enough and that he should withdraw his application. He went through a period of spiritual turbulence and anxiety until one evening when:

I became aware of the wood, the trees, the dark hills, the wet night wind, and then, clearer than any of these obvious realities, in my imagination, I started to hear the great bell of Gethsemani ringing in the night. . . . The impression made me breathless, and I had to think twice to realise that it was only in my imagination that I was hearing the bell of the Trappist Abbey ringing in the dark. Yet, as I afterwards calculated, it was just about the time that the bell is rung every night for the *Salve Regina*, towards the end of Compline.

The bell seemed to be telling me where I belonged—as if it were calling me home. (Merton, 1948, pp. 364–5)

He hurried back to the friary in which he was teaching, desperate to talk to the one person whom he thought could help him. The light in the friar's room was out. Merton went to the friars' common room, where he found the only person in the room to be the one person he was seeking.

Once again, the decision to enter the Trappist monastery does not seem to have been the result of an act of will. To enter was the one thing Merton wanted; on the other hand, he was assailed with appalling doubts. By suffering through the tension between the opposites, the ego was strengthened to make a choice. Manifestations of the self are often experienced as a feeling of coming home. Both the sense of 'I' and the sense of self are enriched.

But this little vignette from Merton's life takes us to another concept of Jung's, namely synchronicity,

This principle suggests that there is an inter-connection or unity of causally unrelated events, and thus postulates a unitary aspect of being which can very well be described as the *unus mundus*. (CW14 para 663)

Synchronicity is 'the occurrence of a meaningful coincidence in time', or, 'the coincidence in time of two or more causally unrelated events which have the same or similar meaning' (CW8 para 827).

In Merton's case, an inner event (the imaginary bell) coincided with an outer event (the actual bell ringing at the Abbey), which produced another inner event (an inner certainty about going to the Abbey) which coincided with him finding the sought-after friar. The coincidence of these events is of little importance. What makes the events synchronistic is the meaning Merton found in them. It is also important to note that synchronicity tends to be experienced when the threshold of consciousness is lowered either because of the prevailing mental state or because of the shock induced by the meaningful coincidences themselves. Jung is also suggesting that the unitary nature of the self is mirrored in the universe by an integrating centre that is beyond the individual, but of which the individual is a part—the *unus mundus*—in which, it is said, a butterfly in the tropics creates a storm in the Himalayas. Everything affects everything else.

These meaningful coincidences often feel numinous, partly because of the impact of the meaning, but also because they evoke a sense of belonging to and being part of something greater than oneself.

There are three other processes, among many others, that foster the search for and discovery of meaning, and this feeling of being part of a whole. These are: meditation, dreaming and active imagination.

All the major religions of the world—Buddhism, Christianity, Hinduism, Islam, Judaism—employ meditation in one form or another. Its practice seems to have originated in India about 4,500 years ago, and from there it spread through the East making its way westwards on the backs of the various Christian traditions. As far as I know, almost all the 'schools' of meditation are agreed on posture. The person sits, either cross-legged on a cushion on the floor or on a chair. The back is unsupported and straight, and the head is squarely balanced on an upright neck. The eyes are lowered, the hands clasped, the mouth shut with the tongue pressed gently against the palate. The field of inquiry is the nature of mental functioning and the purpose is to gain insight into that.

There are basically two types of meditation, from which others have developed: one in which concentration is brought to bear on a single, emotionally neutral object; the other in which the mind is opened to all that enters it and the meditator observes everything that enters without being carried away by any particular content. Judgement is suspended as the contents of the personal and collective unconscious unfold before one. Meditation of this second type reaches down into the unconscious, and for this reason, as Wilber reminds us, it can be very dangerous:

> meditation, far from being a cure-all, can be extremely detrimental to borderline and narcissistic disorders (simply

because the person is desperately trying to create a strong and viable ego structure, and intensive meditation tends to dissolve what little structure the borderline has). (Wilber, 1983)

For brevity and simplicity, I am translating 'borderline' and 'narcissistic' as meaning respectively: people with a fragile sense of identity and reality; people suffering from disorders of self-esteem, at one moment feeling they are wonderful, and at the next feeling they are a nobody.

The benefits of meditation are well documented, as are its dangers. Thus, it is useful to do it under the supervision of an experienced guide who has already trodden the path and knows the dangers along it.

Meditation reaches down into the depths of the psyche from which dreams surface. Jung maintained that the dream showed the dreamer his inner truth and reality just as it is, rather than as he would like it to be. The relationship of dreams to conscious life is compensatory,

> because they contain ideas, feelings and thoughts whose absence from consciousness leaves a blank which is filled with fear instead of with understanding . . . they are the undisguised manifestations of unconscious creative activity. (CW17 para 185)

Attention to dreams forms part of the spiritual quest. Just as the pastor can, out of various possibilities, befriend a client or parishioner, so can he befriend and encourage those with whom he works to befriend dreams. The term 'befriend' in relation to dreams is borrowed by Hillman from existential therapy. Rather than rushing to interpret dreams, the dreamer can give space and time to his dreams, savouring the mood and feeling within them, and contemplating the elements of the dream, the dream figures, and the story that the dream tells. To rush in with interpretations of dreams can be as damaging as unsupervised meditation. But it is possible to reflect on dreams, to play with them and to think about the message they convey about the total life situation of the dreamer. What the pastoral counsellor thinks about someone else's dream is unimportant. What the dreamer makes of this language of the soul is all that counts.

For those who wish to befriend their dreams, Jung has some useful tips:

(1) Dreams run in series. It is possible to see a particular dream image gradually changing through a series. Ferocious wolves may be gradually transformed into friendly kangaroos. These transformations largely depend on the courage and honesty with which a dream is befriended, and on how it is befriended.

(2) Every part of the dream and all the actors in it can be thought of as referring to parts of the dreamer's self. This enables the dreamer to unhook the imagos of their own psyche from things and people in the outer world.

(3) Dreams can be befriended in the context of the dreamer's current situation. What is the dream saying to me about my life at this moment in time?

(4) Each element of a dream can be treated as a piece of sculpture. To experience a sculpture, it is necessary to walk around it, just as the interior of a church or cathedral is enhanced by circumambulating it.

A good example of someone who befriended his dreams is the late Harry Guntrip, a psychotherapist. Despite two analyses, Guntrip had a total amnesia until he was seventy of a trauma he had suffered at the age of three and a half. When he was thirty-seven, he became minister of a highly organised church in Leeds 'with a Sunday afternoon meeting of 1,000 men, an evening congregation of 800, and well organised educational, social and recreational activities'. For a while, he was aided by a colleague, but then this man left for the war. Guntrip collapsed with a mysterious exhaustion illness, from which he suffered episodically throughout his working life. After his second analyst, Winnicott, died, he had a long series of regressive dreams in which he not only recaptured the trauma of his younger brother's death, but he also re-saw 'the faceless, depersonalised mother, and the black depressed mother, who totally failed to relate to both of us' (Guntrip, 1975, p. 155).

This dream enabled him to feel sad for his mother who had been so damaged herself that she could not allow either of her two children to be themselves. It also enabled Guntrip to retire and to dismantle his manic defence of overwork and to write his deeply moving paper, which was published posthumously. Finally, the dream reveals itself in this example as a most potent healing (making whole) agent.

Guntrip's suffering and healing lead me back to the inherent dangers of the helping professions where personnel rely enormously in their everyday dealings with other people on empathy. This, as I have stressed from time to time throughout the book, renders them prone to psychic infection and contagion, and goes some way towards explaining why so many of us succumb to illness, addictions, exhaustion and, in some cases, suicide.

At the height of Jung's own illness, his confrontation with the unconscious, he developed a method of reducing these risks. It has come to be known as active imagination, and it has the potential to reduce psychic infection in both directions—into and out of the pastor.

Jung used to talk of active imagination as a process of dreaming with open eyes. First of all, the thoughts of ego-consciousness must be discarded in order to allow unconscious contents to make their entry. Then, fantasies, images or emotions appear. These are written down, drawn, painted, sculpted or modelled. The ego then reacts to the psychic contents, and, from the conclusions drawn, makes adjustments in outside life.

Fleur:

Fleur operated an open-door counselling service for young people in the crypt of a church. She was in her early forties, flamboyant, extraverted, and the kind of person who enthuses everyone about anything she or they are engaged in. She had a highly successful husband and five children, and she worked very hard. One day, she developed an abscess on her shoulder. She sat in her study at home and became aware of enormous tension in her shoulders. She began to feel she was being crushed. She drew a series of drawings and then spent the next few days contemplating these and found herself feeling sad. She reviewed her current situation, and came to the conclusion that she was doing too much. But the abscess cleared up and she continued with life. It was only when a second one appeared that she decided that she must give herself space. She took herself off to the country for a few weeks and used the time to restructure her life in such a way as to have more time for herself, her family and her inner life.

Like meditation, active imagination is not recommended for persons who are feeling fragile. The unconscious can be destructive if it is unleashed in the absence of respect for its enormous power. The unconscious can be overwhelming, can lead to inflation or possession, can precipitate people into impulsive, antisocial and destructive, or self-destructive, behaviour. But it can be equally dangerous if it is ignored. As in all life, a middle way seems to be the most life-enhancing.

But all the work, suffering, joy and richness that are the products of this inner journey are perhaps only a preamble to what Meister Eckhart describes:

> . . . the very best and noblest attainment in this life is to be silent and let God work and speak within. When the powers (i.e. of thought, imagination and sensation) have been completely withdrawn from all their words and images, then the Word is spoken. Therefore He (God) said: 'In the midst of the silence the secret word was spoken to me.' And so, the more completely you are able to draw in your powers to a unity and forget all those things and their images which you have absorbed, and the further you can get from creatures and their images, the nearer you are to this and the readier to receive it. (Eckhart, 1987)

There is a Zen story about a young monk who was devoted to his abbot. This monk lovingly planted two seeds, which he tended with care. They ripened and grew into two beautiful plants. Just before they were due to flower, the young monk took them as a gift to his abbot. He entered the abbot's room, bowed, and stretched forth his two hands in a gesture of giving. The abbot took one look and said 'Drop it'. The monk dropped the plant from his right hand and looked sadly at the smashed pot and plant on the floor. 'Drop that too', said the abbot. The monk dropped the plant from his left hand. 'Drop that as well', said the abbot. The young monk said, 'But I have nothing'. 'Drop it', roared the abbot. The young monk was enlightened.

EIGHT

Clinging, Severing and Separating

In order to arrive there,
To arrive where you are, to get from where you are not,
You must go by a way wherein there is no ecstasy.
In order to arrive at what you do not know
You must go by a way which is the way of ignorance.
In order to possess what you do not possess
You must go by the way of dispossession.
In order to arrive at what you are not
You must go through the way in which you are not.
(T. S. Eliot, 'East Coker', *Collected Poems 1902–62*, Faber 1963)

For more than thirty years, Jung was preoccupied with a study of alchemy, which culminated in the last book he wrote, *Mysterium Coniunctionis*, a vast labyrinthine text full of imagery that clusters around the individual's discovery of the self. It is a dense and difficult work, and beyond the scope of this chapter to summarise properly. In general, it describes the alchemical process, the opus, beginning with the initial state of chaos, and moving on through stages of darkness, dissolution and separation which must precede the final coniunctio of soul, spirit and body. The alchemical process is taken as an analogue of the individuation process, whereby the final goal in alchemy, the *lapis philosophorum*, is reflected in personal experience by the appearance of symbols of the self, which always beckon to greater potential wholeness.

As the alchemist worked with a mystical sister, so the baby develops within a mother–baby duo, a family, a culture and a society, each and all of which can act for him as a mystical sister. As we saw in Chapter 2, at each developmental level he is faced with opposites, and has to travel through darkness, dissolution and separation from the old before he can move on to the new. For him to individuate, he has at various points in his life to separate physically from his family. However, this will be of no avail unless he has also separated from rules and values that he has introjected from his parents, and from cultural and societal norms and values, so that he can act as an individual, and not as part of a mindless mass. At the same time, ideally, he retains roots in his culture, and grows into a different sort of relationship with his parents and family. He is neither too respectful nor too rebellious. He has available to him a whole range of feelings and can hold the tension of feeling attached yet separate.

Sometimes, however, things go wrong. At one end of the spectrum of attachment–separation, we encounter people who make 'anxious attachments' to others; they seem desperately needy, tend to cling to others, and in some cases feel that they do not exist when parted from other people. At the opposite end, we find people who seem cut-off, who seem to have severed their connections with their past, their family, and who seem unable to commit themselves to any person, group, cause, denomination, etc.

This chapter examines the process of separating, the pathological variants just mentioned, and some of the common defences against it. Clinging leads to the psychic death of the individual and to major difficulties in becoming a non-possessive parent and a free agent in society. Severing is an unilateral action; its aim is to sharpen boundaries, but it can result in isolation. Clinging and severing are a pair of opposites. In both cases, the compensatory nature of the unconscious pushes towards the opposite of the conscious attitude. The clinger will have a deep longing to break out of an oppressive prison; the severer will equally strongly be searching for a loving relationship. To achieve their desires, both have to separate, to undergo a process that is mutual, painful, full of uncertainty, but that eventually leads to psychic growth and to healing, or becoming whole.

For the pastor, the relevance of understanding these processes lies in his role as officiator at various *rites de passage*, such as baptism, marriage and death; in his everyday work, it occurs in the way he handles parishioners leaving, his own holiday breaks, his movements from job to job. His reactions to others separating from him or from his parish or the Church as a whole will, in large part, depend on how far he himself has individuated.

Victor:

Victor was planning to enter an enclosed, silent monastic order. He had agreed with the abbot of the monastery to test himself by living in a presbytery as part of a team ministry, and observing a religious life in the outside world before committing himself to the novitiate of the monastery.

The Abbot was shrewd.

Victor was illegitimate and fatherless for the first few years of his life. His mother carted him from one lodging house to another and she struggled to maintain them both by doing shift-work as a bus conductress. His contact with her seemed to him unpredictable, and he was left with various child-minders. Later, Victor's mother married a tempestuous man, who took advantage of his wife's evening shifts to commit buggery with Victor and beat him. Riddled with shame, guilt and hatred, Victor finally attacked his stepfather; at the age of sixteen, he left home. A few years later, dissatisfied with drifting from job to job, Victor settled into residential work with the handicapped. It was during this time that he developed strong attachments to senior male members of staff, but he was acutely sensitive, and, at the slightest expression of criticism on their part, he would ritually dress in a certain suit and take himself off on drinking binges.

The pattern emerged in the presbytery, but mushroomed when the priest in charge went on holiday or to take a retreat. Then Victor felt that his entire sense of identity had departed with the priest, and his clinging attachment was transferred to the magical, ever-present bottle; this restored the comforting illusion that loss and pain could be overcome by the primitive defence of splitting, the absent priest being the bad and the ever-present bottle the good. The binges were very dangerous, not just medically, but also because they resulted in highly self-destructive behaviour, for which Victor was eventually hospitalised.

There, then, was a premature, illegitimate baby, born to a fairly frantic mother. His early life experience seems to have afforded him little opportunity to develop object constancy, which is the capacity

> to create continuity out of memories, which leads to a dawning awareness of the inseparability (and relative unpredictability) of good and bad feelings within ourselves and in relation to objects. Thus a precariously balanced state of constancy is established in the relation between ourselves and our objects. (Plaut, 1975, p. 208)

('Objects' here refer to other people as the antitheses of 'subjects'.)

Victor's early years were full of fragmented experiences, constant partings, different carers, all working against his establishing any sort of roots in himself, his family or a home. From the relationship with his stepfather he took in a model of an aggressive and brutal sort of masculinity, in which love and aggression were hopelessly confused. But the stepfather gave a sense of stability and continuity of presence formerly unknown to Victor. He felt wanted, but in a way that made him feel shameful. No wonder, then, that he developed such an intensely ambivalent relationship with male authority figures. We might speculate that his desire to enter a silent, enclosed order sprang partly from repressed dependency needs for an ever-present mother, and partly from a search for a legitimised silence about his shameful secret. The setting would provide stability, continuity, infrequent separation (apart from the deaths of the elderly monks), and an externalised control over his terrifyingly destructive and self-destructive impulses.

In contrast, we might dwell on a person in whom the opposites of clinging and severing were constellated. She was looking for a middle way—that of separating.

Tessa:

Tessa was in her late twenties and the eldest of five children. As an infant, she had developed a serious skin complaint which made holding and feeding her an ordeal for baby and mother. Life was one long inconsolable itch. In later life,

Tessa noted that her mother could not stand any sign of weakness or illness in any of the children. On the whole, her father seemed regretful that he had had any children at all.

Tessa had managed to get away to university, but broke down before a second more successful attempt at separating. She worked below her ability in a job she had held since graduating, and she eschewed promotion in favour of familiarity and continuity. She had had boyfriends, but had broken off engagements, afraid of the separation from her parents and the commitment to the man. She met one of her ex-boyfriends three or four times a year, and the gaps would be filled by episodic long phone calls. She lived close to her parents and had much contact with them.

One evening, she arrived for a PCC meeting clearly distressed. The pastor managed to take her on one side before the meeting and asked what was troubling her. During the previous night there had been a strong gale. Tessa's eye had alighted all through the day on branches that had been torn from their trunks. She said: 'They're like children severed from their mothers'. The degree of her distress indicated that the image had touched upon deeply buried memories of being cut off from her own mother, who, of course, felt almost as helpless as her daughter to relieve the unbearable pain.

We might reconstruct that Tessa and her mother had been in an impossible situation. The pain of being physically handled by the mother had produced screaming in Tessa. It was, perhaps, her way of saying 'no'. The word 'no' is very important because it draws a boundary between the child and the parent both psychologically and physically. The baby who turns his head away from the breast is saying 'no'. And he has to learn to say that word without dire consequences. If saying 'no' means that the parent gets angry, feels too wounded, goes away, abandons the child, then the child is only left with the option of living *for* rather than *with* someone else. The physical expression of the word 'no' precedes the toddler's use of the words 'me' and 'mine'. It contains hate, which is the matrix of thought and the energy that dynamises separation, and it defines the child as a separate being. Only when he feels separate can he freely say 'yes' and let someone else in. As Christ said: 'Before Abraham was, I am'.

The second difficulty was that Tessa could not relinquish her mother because she felt there was nothing inside: Tessa was left empty, unsatiated. So a vicious circle was set up with Tessa feeling hungry but not being able to tolerate being held. She was saying 'yes' and 'no' at the same time. Over time, this has resulted in her finding it difficult to say either to anyone.

This is rather a specific example of someone who forms anxious attachments, in which separation-anxiety plays a prominent part. In a more general sense, how do these arise? Freud asked this question some time ago: '. . . when does separating from an object produce anxiety, when does it produce mourning and when does it produce, it may be, only pain?' (Freud, 1925).

In the United Kingdom, the psychoanalyst John Bowlby has devoted a large part of his working life to seeking to understand anxious attachments. Bowlby maintains that there is a strong link between a person's capacity to make what he calls 'affectional bonds' and his parents' ability to provide him with a secure base and the encouragement to explore from it (Bowlby, 1979). From his research, he concludes that people who make anxious attachments have experienced typical patterns of parenting, which include:

(1) one or both parents being persistently unresponsive to the child's care-eliciting behaviour and/or actively disparaging and rejecting him;
(2) discontinuities of parenting, occurring more or less frequently, including periods in hospital or institution;
(3) persistent threats by parents not to love a child, used as a means of controlling him;
(4) threats by parents to abandon the family, used either as a method of disciplining the child or as a way of coercing a spouse;
(5) threats by one parent either to desert or even to kill the other or else to commit suicide (each of them more common than might be supposed);
(6) inducing a child to feel guilty by claiming that his behaviour is, or will be, responsible for the parent's illness or death.

Almost in parenthesis, he adds an seventh pattern in which, more unusually, the mother exerts pressure on the child to act as an attachment figure for her, so turning upside down the usual emphasis in relationship.

These pathological patterns of parenting, in which threatened or real, emotional and/or physical abandonment abound, are not to be confused with internal archetypal imagery of the abandoned child. In the imagery of the collective unconscious, Jung saw the child as 'potential future'. The child archetype has a special phenomenology, an aspect of which is abandonment:

> Abandonment, exposure, danger, etc. are all elaborations of the 'child's' insignificant beginnings and of its mysterious and miraculous birth. This statement describes a certain psychic experience of a creative nature, whose object is the emergence of a new and as yet unknown content. . . . 'Child' means something evolving towards independence. This it cannot do without detaching itself from its origins: abandonment is therefore a necessary condition, not just a concomitant symptom. (CW9(i) paras 285–7)

Jane:

At the beginning of her counselling, Jane had a dream. She was back in the convent to which she had been sent as a little girl. One of the nuns had died, but she was excluded from the requiem. She felt utterly abandoned and bereft of her family. She went out into the garden, feeling wretched. Suddenly a child appeared and took her by the hand, showing her the various flowers and trees.

I will not go into the wealth of material to which this dream gave birth, the death of the mother, the exclusion from the family, the hope of renewal and rebirth imaged by the garden with its changing seasons, etc. What were important to her were the figures of the abandoned child and that of the child in the garden, a lost split-off part of herself who was to show her as yet undiscovered aspects. Strong affects of sadness, horror, guilt, the desire for revenge, and the intention to be less neglectful to the child were released in Jane. In the dream, neither child was hated by the other. Instead, the child figure showed compassion to the abandoned child, but a compassion that was selfless and detached. As Eliot says:

> The wounded surgeon plies the steel
> That questions the distempered part;
> Beneath the bleeding hands we feel
> The sharp compassion of the healer's art
> Resolving the enigma of the fever chart.
>
> (T. S. Eliot, 'East Coker')

The point I wish to make is that we take a great risk if we abandon the child within us. Its appearance is not always positively luminous; on the contrary, it often heralds in seemingly unbearable pain. But if it is pushed away, once again abandoned, then it is likely to gather a greater and greater charge in the unconscious, leaving us wide open to being taken over by the child, who, as Hillman points out, has been condemned to the orphanage, 'the breeding ground of renegade psychopathy' (Hillman, 1971).

One of the aims of pastoral care may be to enable the parishioner to bear along and nurse the inherent weakness and vulnerability of the inner child so that the parishioner's inner child's vision and imagination are released. Neither abandonment nor over-protectiveness can create the attitude that is expressed in the saying: 'Unless ye become like little children, ye cannot enter the kingdom of Heaven'.

Jane had her dream at a time when she felt abandoned by a mother figure, with whom she had had a terrible row. The break in the relationship left her full of loss. It is possibly in such a state of loss that the abandoned child image appears. Certainly Jung mentions remembering with great feeling, after his traumatic break with Freud, playing with sand and stones as a child of about eleven (Jung, 1961). He made a conscious decision to abandon himself to his inner child's wishes for certain periods of time, and returned to playing with sand and stones. He called this 'serious play' — serious, I think, because he took note of images and fantasies that arose during it. In fact, it is said that before embarking on a new book he would go down to the shore of the lake and do some 'serious play', so creating space for the inner, formerly forgotten, abandoned child.

I turn now to various pastoral situations in which the fear of loss or the experience of loss present themselves as the focus of work, along with some of the defences that are commonly used to avoid what seems unbearable. There is not scope to be encyclopaedic, so I have chosen situations that seem to me to be quite typical of the pastor's work-load. Often, the pastor's task in such situations is, using Frances Tustin's phrase, to transform the 'terribleness of "gone" to the feeling of "missing"' (Tustin, 1986), to nudge the bereaved from melancholic distraction into mourning, to change the hue of suffering from bodily symptom to psychic pain contained between pastor and client. I propose to present these situations under the headings 'Clinging', 'Severing' and 'Separating'.

Clinging

Unresolved loss

Andrew:

Andrew was referred to the hospital chaplain by the head of his department. He worked as an engineer, making and repairing surgical and medical equipment. His boss had noticed that he would suddenly burst into tears at work, and that the standard of his work had fallen. On his workbench stood a photo of his baby daughter who had died at the age of four months after a hole-in-the-heart operation. His colleagues would come to him and say, 'What a lovely baby'. He would angrily reply, 'Yes, but she is dead'.

Andrew was a tough, muscular man, a rugby player, with bushy black hair, and eyes reddened from crying. He splutteringly told his story.

'We were pushed into an operation queue. The operation lasted eighteen hours, and Tracey was opened up twice. Her chest filled with blood. The staff were rushing around. They seemed to be in a panic. I betrayed the baby's trust. The hospital reassured us. The family has fallen apart. Tracey cemented us together. [Andrew shows the pastor photos of Tracey and sobs rackingly for ten minutes.] I can't go home any more. There is nothing to talk about, no support. I cry alone in the cemetery or in Tracey's room. Caroline, my wife, holds all her feelings in. It's a relief to come to see you. I've been left so alone with my grief. I've got a physical pain in my chest. My wife sits around in her own sadness. I can't believe it. Everything seemed to have come together until the death of Tracey. My wife had a miscarriage four months ago. Tracey had an easy birth. What am I to do at Christmas? Tracey trusted me. Last Christmas she was a few weeks old; this one she would have been older and stronger. The bloody doctors did not know what they were doing. They took in a live baby and gave me back a dead one. We were never left alone with her, not allowed to hold her or to say goodbye to her. We've kept her room exactly as it was, and each night we creep out as if she was asleep in there. She liked green, and so everything is green. The line down the middle of the cot is disappearing (notice that this is twelve months later). Her room is a great comfort. My wife has still got one of Tracey's soiled nappies in a plastic bag. I should never have trusted the hospital. They are murderers. They've killed my baby.'

The pastor was almost overwhelmed by Andrew's grief, the rawness of it after a year. He noticed the guilt and the self-reproaches; the anger with the doctors and his wife; the identification with the lost child through the chest pains; the wish to replace the child quickly with another (that apparently had not been mourned); the expectation placed on Tracey that she would 'cement' the marriage; the possibility, later confirmed, that Caroline felt guilty about producing a defective child. While understanding that the loss of a child is one of the worst to overcome, he did not understand why Andrew's grief was still so enormous, and why the couple could not grieve together. Was the prolonged intense grief some form of secondary gain? Should Andrew be working in a department making and repairing instruments that would have had a part in Tracey's death?

He decided to see Andrew alone for a few sessions, with a plan to include Caroline at a later date. Andrew, who had been present for some of the operation, went over the event again and again, reliving the nightmare in much the same way as those who have suffered torture or other trauma. He later revealed that he had a stepson and felt very excluded from the relationship between the boy and his mother. Tracey had, therefore, been for him. Gradually, the guilt diminished and a quieter sadness surfaced.

The couple came for joint sessions in which it emerged that each was displacing on to the other anger with their previous spouses, anger of which each was afraid, particularly in Caroline's case, because her previous husband had been violent to her. The couple was suffering from compound loss — their previous marriages, Tracey, the miscarried baby, the vision they had had of their future together. To cling to Tracey's death glued them in the past and encapsulated for them both a great deal of anger and destructiveness, all projected on to the hospital. A by-product was Andrew's deteriorating work, which might have led to medical or surgical error and been the expression of unconscious revenge. Once their anger was expressed, the couple could begin to mourn together and gradually to build a new life.

Paddy:

Paddy was an Irishman who lived on a houseboat on his own and earned his living as a window-cleaner. He came from a large family and had been orphaned at an early age. The children were spread around various orphanages and for some years lost touch with one another. Paddy came over to London and found squalid lodgings, from where he began to look for work. In the orphanage he had become shy and withdrawn. In London, he took to wearing an old raincoat with the collar turned up, which gave those who met him the feeling that he wanted them to keep their distance. Only when working would he discard his coat and, once less covered, he would peer with fascination in and out of the windows of his customers, who liked him for his thorough work and quiet manner. But life was always the other side of glass. One Sunday, there was a notice in the porch of the church; the presbytery was advertising for a window-cleaner. Paddy got the job. From a wary start, this rootless and lonely man developed a trust in the parish priest, and the two men met every week over a pot of tea. The pastor helped Paddy to save and to budget. After a few years, Paddy had saved up for his dream—a houseboat, which he tended lovingly. Later, with encouragement, he returned to Ireland for short spells in search of his family. He found some of them, and then started going to a literacy scheme so that he could correspond with them. He remained a solitary man, but loved his boat, his work, his pastor, and, gradually, his reclaimed family.

Twenty years after Paddy's arrival in London, the pastor was due to retire. Paddy started to go to pieces. The man who had helped build his life and who had always been there was now to go. The pastor understood this and, in plenty of time, introduced him to his successor who, like Paddy, was Irish. The pastor left London for the country and he and Paddy corresponded.

Meanwhile, Paddy had started drinking tea with the new pastor. The meetings became quieter and quieter, and Paddy looked more and more uncomfortable. At last, he spoke out. The room was not the same; the furniture was different, the new man did not know him in the same way; his voice was different; the way he put things was rather puzzling; the tea always seemed a bit cold; the room smelled of tobacco, which was not fitting for a man of God. And so Paddy stopped going to the presbytery. Instead, he went down to the country once a month to see the original pastor to whom he had formed such a strong and loving attachment.

The early loss of both parents and siblings had plunged Paddy into misery and despair, out of which he had emerged with a strong degree of self-reliance and a sort of self-mothering symbolised by his coat. He related to people through glass, looking in on their lives and daily coping with feelings of envy, jealousy and exclusion. When at last he let his dependency needs out into the open, he was able to be nurtured by the pastor, who, so to speak, lent him the capacity to think, plan, organise and to achieve his ambition. With the departure of the pastor, the loan was withdrawn and Paddy nearly collapsed. We might have expected his dependency to be displaced on to some sort of addictive behaviour, but it wasn't. He could not shift from the feeling of 'gone' to that of 'missing'. Instead, he reverted to splitting, idealising the old pastor, and feeling highly critical of the new.

His case raises questions about how and when to terminate pastoral relationships. One of the goals of the work is to enable the parishioner or client to move from relative dependence on the pastor to independence. At the beginning of the work, therefore, it is often useful to ask the question, 'How little can I do?' rather than the more tempting question, 'How much can I do?' The former builds on the parishioner/client's strengths, the latter invites regression. This is especially in times of crisis, because learning and problem-solving are optimised when the defences of the person in crisis are lowered. In this situation the crisis-sufferer is not so beleaguered by hardened attitudes and habitual responses. Furthermore, s/he tends to narrow the focus of inquiry at a time when the objective outsider can maintain a larger perspective and help sufferers to extend their repertoire of responses.

When the task is accomplished, the work should be terminated. Ending is often difficult because of the feelings of loss, disappointment, anger and gratitude that come into the relationship. But if these are faced and acknowledged, both parties are strengthened and the separation is facilitated. Sometimes weaning is helpful, particularly for persons who feel they have no control over comings and goings.

Paddy is someone about whom one might feel there is a risk of suicide. After a brief period of misery and despair in the orphanage, Paddy had seemed indifferent to the loss of his family. But there must be a reason for that. It is now thought that the ego of the child is too embryonic to take the strain of doing the work of mourning; it therefore brings to bear on the loss means of self-protection that bypass the process. These means are either regression to an earlier stage of development, or, in the most extreme form, a complete absence of feeling. Later in life, when another major loss takes place, the affects of the first loss are also unleashed. The compounded feeling of abandonment is sometimes so agonising as to culminate in suicide.

Severing

Suicide is possibly the most extreme form of severing. Apart from road accidents, those who attempt suicide constitute the bulk of hospital admissions to casualty departments. The pastor is not uncommonly faced with working with people who have made suicide attempts or with the relatives and friends left behind after a person's self-destruction. Suicidal behaviour is very complex and needs to be understood. Like every other act, it has a meaning and a purpose, however remote these are from comprehension. Admission to hospital is often necessary, but brings in its wake an ambivalent response in some medical and nursing staff who feel bound to save the life of someone who has attempted to take it. The states of mind of both parties are, therefore, almost opposite. Often the patient is treated medically, kept in for observation, possibly seen by a psychiatrist, and then discharged. In a recent London study, 85 per cent of such admissions were quite clear, when interviewed, that they wanted to die. Of the other 15 per cent, some said they were trying to manipulate others, some that they did not care, and others that they could not remember what their intentions were. Many of the amnesic group subsequently died.

In the history of suicides, the incidence of rape, incest and child molestation is very high. In women, termination of pregnancy, sterilisation or hysterectomy often precede suicide or a suicide attempt. Many male homosexuals own up to having felt suicidal, and many lesbians admit to impulses towards self-mutilation. The affect that links suicide and perversion is intense aggression. So the questions invariably need to be asked: What or who was being murdered in the act? Who was the patient trying to protect by the act? In what ways may the patient have been trying to change the feelings of others towards him/her, even though posthumously in the case of successful suicide?

To the first question there are several possible answers, and, once again, I am not being comprehensive. In Chapters 2 and 4, I alluded to Winnicott's notion of the true and false self. The latter acts as a protector to the true self, which had to go into hiding when the infant realised that his role in life was to adapt to the maternal and family environment. Winnicott warns that suicide becomes a possibility when the true self comes out of hiding, because it will not risk a repetition of finding itself not acceptable. He also talks about the intellectual false self

> who feels 'phoney' the more he or she is successful. When such individuals destroy themselves in one way or another, instead of fulfilling promise, this invariably produces a sense of shock in those who have developed high hopes of the individual. (Winnicott, 1960, p. 144)

Kim:

Kim had just become a professor of philosophy at the age of thirty-five when she jumped to her death from the window of her fourteenth-storey office. She was the only child of successful academic parents, who had conceived her by mistake, and then continued to pursue their careers, giving her over to the care of nannies. Few of these stayed long, because of the expectations placed upon them. The parents devoted a couple of hours in the evening to their daughter, but found that they could not really get interested in her until she began to read at the age of three. From then on, they delighted in her every scholastic and academic achievement, and could most easily relate to her on the cerebral plane. She grew up to be a precocious child, more at home in the company of adults than children, and immersed herself in her studies. At a young age, she took up the clarinet and became technically highly proficient, but people said that her playing lacked feeling.

In her teens, her parents decided mutually to separate. She saw little of her father, who moved a long way away, and became an ear for her mother's disparaging monologues about him. Her view of men soured, and she grew up determined to avoid them, although her physical beauty drew them to her. Her parents' separation depressed her, but during her adolescence she became more aware of an inner deadness and of a distaste for her increasing success. She felt that nobody really saw her as she was, and she herself seemed to have forgotten who she was, if, indeed, she had ever known.

University conferred on her prizes and awards. She began to live with another woman, a fellow academic. Their relationship was sexual but passionless, and, like her parents, Kim was happiest when engaged in intellectual debate. Papers and a couple of books issued forth fairly effortlessly from her. They were well received, but their welcome among her colleagues only increased her sense of futility. Family, friends and colleagues admired her, but she secretly despised them all.

At a party thrown to celebrate her professorship, she impulsively sought out the college chaplain, a man of fine intellect combined with a warm heart, and one of the few men whom she respected. She asked if she could see him the next day. He was perplexed, because he knew her views on religion, which she had playfully challenged from time to time in the common room over coffee.

They met the next day. Kim, in a dazzling burst of articulation, described her state of mind to him. The neatness, logic and precision with which she expressed herself and the permanent suggestion of a smile as she spoke sent shivers down the chaplain's spine. He smelt a rat, and in listening to her history realised that the problem was so much deeper than her depression at becoming a professor. He was strong in his assertion that she needed a full analysis and gave her the name of an analyst, whom she phoned several times that day, leaving messages on the answering machine. By late that night her call had not been returned. She was found by students in the early hours of the morning.

Kim had survived by means of her mind. Like a firefly, it attracted the eyes of everyone who, at the same time, could not see what was in the surrounding darkness, because she could not see it herself. The brightness of her mind threw the rest of her personality into darkness. At the pinnacle of her career, she desperately wanted to rescue herself. Had she got into analysis she might have been reborn.

Few people involved in a regular therapeutic relationship commit suicide, unless they feel that the person helping has lost concern. But fate took a terrible turn. Kim's smiling depression, so often a forecast of suicidal feelings or behaviour, had not fooled the chaplain. He had pointed her in the right direction. But, at the last minute, she had been abandoned. Abandonment is a crucial issue in pre-suicidal behaviour, and one to which I will return later.

A second type of suicide can occur when a person confuses a part of himself with all of himself. In the suicidal fantasy, he wishes to kill off that part of himself that he hates for whatever reason.

Jessie:

Sixteen-year-old Jessie had slashed the wrist of her right hand and been admitted to the local hospital. The cut had been deep and life-endangering. Earlier in the evening, her mother had barged into her room only to find Jessie masturbating on her bed to the gentle rhythm of blues music.

'You disgust me,' she said, slamming the door as she walked out. Jessie had gone to the bathroom, taken one of her father's razor blades, run a hot bath, and savagely attacked herself. Bleeding, dripping and naked, she had staggered downstairs and her father had called an ambulance. Life at home for Jessie as the eldest of four children had not been easy. Her relationship with her mother was irksome and strife-ridden, particularly when her father, an airline pilot, was away. Mother's anger with her absent husband seemed to get displaced on to Jessie. The young girl had confided in the church youth club leader, Suzie, and it was she whom Jessie asked the hospital to phone in the middle of the night. Suzie came, and had to battle with the hostile parents to spend a few minutes with Jessie, whom she arranged to visit the next day.

Later in the week, Suzie reported her counselling session with Jessie to her pastoral support group. She described how the two of them had gone over in minute detail the events and feelings of the evening leading up to the self-destructive act. From the ecstasy of pleasure in masturbating to the fantasy of intercourse with her boyfriend accompanied by soulful music, Jessie had been plunged into horrendous feelings of guilt, shame and fury at her mother's intrusion. The look of hate and disgust in her mother's eyes had mortified her and she longed for the earth to swallow her up. The offending hand, representing an aspect of her enjoyable and yet guilt-ridden sexuality, had to be cut off. At the time, her hand, meaning her sexuality, had become all of herself rather than a part of herself, and it had to be destroyed.

Suzie worked for several weeks with Jessie, with the aim of trying to restore Jessie's enjoyment of her body and her sexuality. She helped Jessie to separate internally and externally from her mother who projected so much guilt on to Jessie, who, in turn, introjected it and became prone to depression. When Jessie, after leaving home, was finally able to discuss the episode with her mother, it transpired that the mother was repeating what her own mother had done to her as a child.

Thirdly, are the cases of those people whose anger in their depression gets turned against the self. The feeling of abandonment is reversed, so that the abandoned person leaves the abandoning person as abandoned and worthless as s/he feels.

Bernard:

Some years previously, Bernard had been treated for depression in a psychiatric hospital. There he had worked with an art therapist of Christian disposition, who had encouraged him in his desire to illustrate the Book of Job. An accountant by profession, Bernard had devoted much of his leisure time to art classes and had achieved a competence that allowed him to exhibit in a modest way. His visionary paintings seemed to capture the hearts and minds of a few followers of his amateur career, and he reinvested his profits from sales of his work in purchasing works of art with a religious content.

After discharge, he continued to attend the art therapy group while he rebuilt his professional and social life. Eighteen months later, a conscientiously prepared-for summer break came, and Jenny, his art therapist, went away for the month of August. He became very depressed and turned up one day with his uncle at the hospital asking to be admitted. Because, at the time, he was staying with his uncle, who lived in a catchment area other than that of the hospital, the duty psychiatrist refused admission and gave him the number of his uncle's local psychiatric unit. Bernard and his uncle made their way to the station to catch a train home. As the train came into the station, Bernard flung himself in its path and was killed.

Quite murderous anger towards the abandoning Jenny/hospital/mother was turned against the self, leaving the abandoning Jenny full of guilt, remorse and sadness, as well as great anger towards her own hospital, which had acted like an impersonal stone mother and had not taken into account the positive transference to the institution that Bernard had developed.

I have tried to indicate that much suicidal behaviour can be understood in terms of an attack on the whole self, a part of the self confused with the whole, or the other reversed into the self. The boundaries are not clear-cut and these areas often overlap. But there does seem to be a fairly typical pattern of behaviour that leads up to suicidal action.

Tom and Jerry cartoons may help us through this painful subject of unilateral severance through suicide. These cartoons are enjoyable and universally appreciated by children because the sado-masochistic relationship between cat and mouse is ritualised and contained. The children know the rules, just as Tom and Jerry do. Cat chases mouse; mouse provokes cat; each is terrified, tricked, captured, squashed, bamboozled, aggrieved, mocked, teased by the other. But there are rules, and everyone knows them. In the life of the pre-suicide, the same often exists between the person and the internalised parent. The sadistic parent is out for control rather than destruction of the child; the masochistic child is out for control over abandonment by the sadistic parent.

Suppose the rules suddenly change. The sadistic internal/external parent suddenly inflicts on the masochistic child an injury to his or her self-esteem — 'You disgust me' (an affect completely absent from Tom and Jerry cartoons). The victim has actually been violated. Practical joke becomes insult. At that moment, an acute sense of loss of love and self-esteem is felt. The victim feels abandoned by a person who is clearly intensely ambivalent. A mad confusional state of mind erupts in which love and aggression swirl around as in two rivers merging. There is maximum turbulence. In the pre-suicide's mind, this is experienced as madness. As Al Alvarez (1971) says, it is the unanswerable logic of a nightmare. It is in this state of mind that the suicidal act is performed. The ego at that moment is overwhelmed. The negative, archetypal, parental imago has taken possession of the ego, which is defenceless against the onslaught, and the act is perpetrated.

Before leaving this subject I wish to state that there are those whose apparent severance from this earthly plane is in fact a conscious choice, not a decision made in madness, based on concern for those left behind, and concern for their own quality of life in the face of unbearable pain—whether it be psychic or physical. Such are different from those among us who might identify with a kamikaze ideology: in these cases, the self is negated through the pursuit of glory (an ego preoccupation), masking an identification with the aggressor (negative parental imago) bringing about the destruction of the self.

There are other forms of severing with which the pastor is likely to learn to work. Parishioners leave the church unexpectedly; marriages break up; parish officials resign impetuously from their roles. An instance of severing frequently met in pastoral work is that of the client who suddenly breaks away from a befriending/counselling relationship.

James is a case in point.

James:

James, who was in his late forties, had an unconsummated marriage. He was a professional pastor, full of bonhomie, attractive, and relied on humour when in stressful situations. His father had been a fisherman before joining the army. His mother had been ill at his birth and had little capacity for love or care. James was the eldest of four children and made the most in his childhood of living in a remote house. The village church and its kindly pastor became a haven for him.

He entered the church and was quickly promoted to a role that was primarily pastoral. Here, he found himself in deep

water. One of the first cases he had to deal with was of a
pastor whose marriage had broken up. He found himself
straddling the twin horses of, on the one hand, needing to
exercise his authority in the matter, and, on the other hand,
wanting to help the pastor into counselling. All the time, his
own destructive marriage haunted him.

He eventually told his bishop of his own situation. The
bishop responded by relieving James of his role and of
insisting on him going into counselling. The former he felt as
a humiliation; the latter as a repeat of his authoritarian
skipper/army father.

His female counsellor was someone experienced and skilled
in dealing with the typical problems of pastors. She felt
naturally anxious that the motivation for counselling had
come from James's superior and not from within himself,
although this changed over the course of time. But counsellor
and client found it difficult to find a shared, common
language. He found her comments difficult to play with, and
was absolutely terrified of the implications of what he kept
telling her—namely, his dread of moving towards retirement
in a lifeless and barren marriage. Just as he and his wife
could not make babies, so he and his counsellor could not
generate ideas about his predicament, which would expand
his range of conscious choice. A turning point occurred when
he acknowledged that he was coming to her for himself and
not for his bishop. None the less, he could not face the
implications of what they were working on. After six months'
work, they agreed on a date to terminate the work.

The last session came and James did not arrive. The
counsellor was left feeling angry, hurt and abandoned. She
wrote a letter urging him to return for a final session, in
which they could bid farewell to each other, and round off the
review of the work, which had been under way over the last
four weeks. He did not reply.

This is another example of the defence of turning passive into
active. The feelings about the early abandonment by his
mother were reactivated unconsciously in the counselling
relationship. Rather than opening himself up to the feelings
of being left, he had to turn the relationship on its head and

give the potential abandoner the experience of being abandoned. He avoided the feelings of loss, anger and, perhaps, gratitude, which could have given a fiery charge to his chance of separating from his mother and his wife, and so of finding himself.

Separating

We live in an alarmingly self-destructive world. While the threat of self-destruction through nuclear devices begins to fade, we are immediately confronted by the paradox contained in the threat to our own planet through ecological arrogance and the discovery of new worlds, space years away, which, externally, although always internally, invite us to observe without interfering. It is, perhaps, the capacity to observe without interference that forms the essence of being separate.

I can see you, I can feel my way into you, but I am not you. An image, a thought, a feeling, lasts an extraordinarily short time. Even pain behaves like a chameleon, although we may long for its end.

> O the mind, mind has mountains; cliffs of fall
> Frightful, sheer, no-man-fathomed. Hold them cheap
> May who ne'er hung there. Nor does long our small
> Durance deal with that steep of deep. Here! creep,
> Wretch, under a comfort serves in a whirlwind: all
> Life death does end and each day dies with sleep.
> (Gerard Manley Hopkins)

The cliffs of fall occur many times through life: the achievement of the feeling that 'I am'; going to school; adolescence; leaving school/college; leaving jobs; death of parents; children leaving home; retirement; death.

How is one to die? And how can the pastor help those who are dying? Will the dying person cling, sever, or separate? What are the psychological factors that predispose towards a healing (making whole) death or an experience of death as yet another manifestation of persecutory anxiety?

Of one thing I am convinced from personal experience, but this may not accord with others' belief or lives. This is that there is a state of mind in which one is constantly dying. The alarm clock rings and I switch it off; that is gone; I stretch, that is gone; breakfast, work, morning coffee, etc., each can be left behind. The letting go allows the impact of the present. There are other states of mind—for example, feeling anxious—when one is locked into the future in a way similar to pathological mourning imprisoning the mourner in the past. But the moment-to-moment daily deaths can turn death from a happening into a process, that of constantly dying.

In the absence of conscious dying, the unconscious seems to take the lead. Jung noted:

> . . . a great many people whose unconscious psychic activity I was able to follow into the immediate presence of death. As a rule the approaching end was indicated by those symbols which, in normal life also, proclaim changes of psychological condition—rebirth symbols such as change of locality, journeys and the like. . . . Dying, therefore, has its onset long before the actual death. (CW8 para 809)

From her research on people in the process of dying, Rosemary Gordon found that the wish for life and the wish for death cohabit in the psyche, and that the balance of the two varies according to the psychological health of the individual and his or her nearness to death (Gordon, 1978). Her findings supported the hypothesis that the psyche prepares for death even when the individual is not conscious of its imminence. In an earlier paper, she puts forward the ideas that death is a boundary-less state which is unknown to us, but for which the psyche has symbols. Death as the goal of the homeostatic process is feared by the ego, the seat of consciousness which aids the process of separating and becoming separate.

While there is, then, an unconscious process of preparing for death, there is perhaps also a conscious process at work. Deutsch suggested that peaceful dying depended on three emotional conditions:

(1) the silencing of feelings of aggression towards others;
(2) the surrendering of emotional ties to people of this world;
(3) the disappearance of feelings of guilt. (Deutsch, 1965)

For these to occur, it is necessary for the dying person to

regress unembarrassedly to earlier states of development and ways of relating.

The *Divina Commedia* of Dante contains three images, which symbolise the inner journey of individuation. In the Inferno, there is the dark wood of unconsciousness; in the Paradiso there is the white rose, the mandala, representing the ideal of wholeness; and in between the two, in the Purgatorio, there rises the mountain. Of the mountain, von Franz says,

> [It] marks the place—the point in life—where the hero, after arduous effort becomes oriented and gains steadfastness and self-knowledge, values that develop through the effort to become conscious in the process of individuation. (von Franz, 1970, p. 94).

The hero myths are about the process of separation, separation of the ego from the unconscious, and separation of the child from the mother and family. The task of the hero(ine) is to separate from the world parents and so attain the treasure that, for the extravert, is an actual person (woman or man), while for the introvert it is the soul. For the hero, the dragon has to be slain in order that he may become independent. But for the heroine, as Covington (1989) has suggested, it is her time in the forest, a time of quiet rather than doing, that allows new attachments to occur which facilitate further separations.

Hilda:

Hilda had entered her convent at the age of eighteen to the delight of her parents. Only a few months had elapsed between her leaving school and then returning as a postulant to the nuns who had had her in their care since she was thirteen. After taking her final vows she worked in an administrative capacity before going to train as a teacher. Her years as a student were painful and she missed the interior stillness of the convent, its spiritual and liturgical rhythms and the companionship of her sisters. She returned qualified to her community, and, for many years, enjoyed her work and the respect and affection of her pupils. When Hilda was in her mid-thirties, her father died, and a little later her mother developed cancer and also died.

The peace of her life was broken, not so much by her bereavements as by an alarming sense of being released from something dimly perceived as oppressive. Doubts grew about her vocation and she felt tormented. Thinking this was an inevitable episode in her spiritual development, she surrendered to the maelstrom, but it did not abate. After several months, she consulted her Mother Superior, who, through her unobtrusiveness, enabled Hilda to reach the painful decision to leave the community that had been her home for so many years. The formalities took their time. The community was informed of Hilda's decision so that she could openly begin to say 'goodbye'. Her brother came to collect her early on the day of her departure. Both she and the nuns were in tears as the car drove slowly down the drive and she took a last long, loving and grateful look at a place and its people that her heart would not forget.

Conversation in the car was desultory. She felt awkward in her new clothes and bombarded by the noise of the motorway and the stimuli of the city of her destination. She stayed with her brother for a while, and then moved into her own little flat a few weeks before taking up a teaching job. Loneliness inhabited her and a sense of rootlessness made her restless. She joined a church, some of whose members welcomed her and others looked at her wryly, making her feel she was some sort of failure. But that passed. Her pastor eventually suggested that she should join a pastoral support group, and it was in that setting, a sort of transitional space, that she began to separate from her identity as a nun and to find herself anew.

Hilda had had to dwell in the forest before she could begin the arduous ascent of the mountain, which still continues.

Jung wrote:

Richness of mind consists in mental receptivity, not in the accumulation of possessions. What comes to us from outside, and, for that matter, everything that arises from within, can only be made our own if we are capable of an inner amplitude equal to that of the incoming content. Real increase of personality means consciousness of an enlargement that flows from inner sources. (CW9(i) para 215)

This leads us finally to some of the defences against separation, defences that reduce that inner amplitude of which Jung was writing. We could say that these defences cluster into three groups, not mutually exclusive: bodily, behavioural and psychic.

Some people react to separations by feeling that they do not exist in their bodies. It is as if their existence goes with the person who is leaving them. Others become hypochondriacally concerned and become obsessed with thoughts and fantasies about the insides of their bodies. Still others somatise so that what should be psychically painful is felt as a headache or backache, etc.

In the second group are people who rush into activity and behaviour, often of a self-destructive kind. Excesses of food and drink create an illusion of fullness where there is actually a feeling of emptiness. Wild sexual encounters give a sense of togetherness where actually there is loneliness and the feeling of abandonment. Workaholism dulls the pain of sadness and enhances a perhaps longed-for sense of self-sufficiency and satisfaction at work completed. Alternatively, the person to be left leaves first, thus turning passive into active.

Lastly, there are the more psychic defences such as splitting, mentioned in Chapter 4. We could also include denial, repression ('I forgot you were going on holiday'), rationalisation ('Of course you need a holiday; you work so hard') and intellectualisation ('The latest research findings on stress suggest that . . .').

The pastor, too, will have his own defences which will hinder or help his own process of separation as well as that of his parishioners or clients. At the beginning of his working life he may not value himself sufficiently to realise the impact of events like his holidays or his changing job on those who depend on him. But it is always very helpful for such people to know of breaks in continuity well in advance. The information in itself contains an implicit message that the event is psychologically and socially important, and sufficient warning leaves enough time for the pastor to be on the alert for signs of distress and defences against it.

But this care and concern for parishioners needs to be balanced by care and concern for the pastor's own feelings at leaving parishes, retiring, letting go of personal and professional relationships, and dying. Then there is hope that the awfulness of 'gone' can be transformed into the feeling of 'missing', and leave the abandoned person, parishioner or pastor, with the thought that:

> To go or stay is not really the question;
> Nor even to go forever, one can't allow here
> Death as a page its full relapse.
> In such a nook it would always be perhaps,
> Dying with no strings attached — who could do that?
> (Lawrence Durrell, *Vega and Other Poems*, Faber)

Glossary

—

Anima The feminine nature in the male unconscious; an inner attitude that is complementary to the character of the persona; the soul-image.

Animus The masculine nature in the feminine unconscious. Both anima and animus stand in compensatory relationship to the persona.

Archetype This is located in the collective unconscious; it is an innate structure which contains a readiness for action and is responsive to environmental feedback. It also generates archetypal imagery.

Archetypal Image Archetypes generate images that are awesome, fascinating, numinous and deep and call for assimilation by consciousness.

Complex This derives from the archetype and is located in the personal unconscious. It is a living unit of psychic life with its own core. It is autonomous, generates feelings and images, and determines behaviour.

Coniunctio An alchemical term referring to the process of joining together dissimilar substances, out of which union will come a third positive or negative element, which might, for example, be a new attitude.

Ego The executive part of the personality.

Enantiodromia The psychological law that states that everything runs into its unconscious opposite in the course of time.

Eros The principle of relatedness.

Individuation The lifelong process of struggling to become oneself.

Inflation A state in which the ego experiences itself as the centre of the personality with accompanying feelings of grandiosity. This state results from an invasion of unconscious contents or the effects of toxic substances.

Logos The principle of meaning.

Persona Characteristic roles and their associated behaviour and clothing (e.g. pastor, striving after saintliness, dog-collar and black suit or cassock).

Self '. . . is not only the centre but also the whole circumference which embraces both conscious and unconscious; it is the centre of this totality, just as the ego is the centre of the conscious mind' (CW12 para 444).

Shadow Part of the personality which is rejected, despised, disowned, considered inferior, and often projected on to someone of the same sex.

Symbol 'The best possible description or formulation of a relatively unknown fact, which is nonetheless known to exist or is postulated as existing' (CW6 para 814).

Symbolic Attitude The attitude taken by the observing consciousness to a symbol, whereby meaning is sought.

Transcendent Function A complex function, synthesising pairs of opposites into a symbol, thus enabling a transition from one attitude to another, a linking of inner and outer, or a change of pathways.

Unconscious:

Personal: The home of the complexes and all that is repressed.

Collective: The home of the archetypes and aspects of the psyche that are common to all mankind.

The unconscious stands in a compensatory relationship to consciousness.

Bibliography

Abelin, E. (1975) 'Some Further Observations and Comments on the Earliest Role of the Father', *International Journal of Psycho-Analysis* 56, pp. 293–302.

Alvarez, A. (1971) *The Savage God*. London, Penguin.

Bion, W. R. (1961) *Experiences in Groups*. London, Tavistock.

Bion, W. R. (1968) *Experiences in Groups*. London, Tavistock.

Bowlby, J. (1979) *The Making and Breaking of Affectional Bonds*. London, Tavistock.

Boyd, R. (1989) 'The Developmental Stages of the Anima and Animus in Small Groups', *Group Analysis* 22:2.

Butler, J. (c.1736) 'Fifteen Sermons', in J. Angus, ed., *The Analogy of Religion to the Constitution and Cause of Nature*. London, The Religious Tract Society.

Coate, M. A. (1989) *Clergy Stress: The Hidden Conflicts in Ministry*. London, SPCK.

Covington, C. (1989) 'In Search of the Heroine', *Journal of Analytical Psychology* 34:3.

de Maré, P. (1987) 'The History of Large Group Phenomena in Relation to Group Analytic Psychotherapy' (unpublished).

Deutsch, H. (1965) 'Absence of Grief', in *Neuroses and Character Types*. New York, International Universities Press.

Eadie, H. (1975) 'Clergy Stress', *Contact*, Summer.

Eckhart, M. (1987) 'The Talks of Instructions', in M. O'C Walshe, trans. and ed., *Sermons and Treatises*, vols 1 and 3. London, Element Books.

Edinger, E. (1986) *Encounter with the Self*. Toronto, Inner City Books.

Erikson, E. (1950) *Childhood and Society*, 2nd edn. New York, W. W. Norton.

Fairbairn, R. W. D. (1940) 'Schizoid Factors in the Personality', in *Psychoanalytic Studies in the Personality*. London, Routledge & Kegan Paul, 1952.

Fordham, M. (1974) 'Defences of the Self', *Journal of Analytical Psychology* 19:2.

Fordham, M. (1978) *Jungian Psychotherapy*. London, John Wiley & Sons.

Foulkes, M. (1948) *Introduction to Group Psychoanalytic Psychotherapy*. London, Heinemann.

Freud, S. (1909) 'Notes on a case of Obsessional Neurosis', London, Standard Edition 10; Penguin Freud Library 9.

Freud, A. (1936) *The Ego and Mechanisms of Defence*. London, Hogarth.

Freud, S. (1926a) *The Question of Lay Analysis*. London, Standard Edition 20; Pelican Freud Library 15.

Freud, S. (1926b) [1925] *Inhibitions, Symptoms and Anxiety*. London, Standard Edition 20; Pelican Freud Library 10, 1979.

Furlong, M. (1966) *The Parson's Role Today*. Paper given at the Wakefield Diocesan Clergy Conference.

Gordon, R. (1968) 'Transference as a Fulcrum of Analysis', *Journal of Analytical Psychology* 13:2.

Gordon, R. (1978) *Dying and Creating: a Search for Meaning*, Library of Analytical Psychology, vol. 2. London, Heinemann.

Gordon, R. (1987) 'Masochism: The Shadow Side of the Archetypal Need to Venerate and Worship', *Journal of Analytical Psychology* 32:3.

Greenson, R. R. (1965) *The Technique and Practice of Psychoanalysis*. London, Hogarth.

Guggenbühl-Craig, A. (1971) *Power in the Helping Professions*. Dallas, Spring Publications.

Guntrip, H. (1975) 'My Experience of Analysis with Fairbairn and Winnicott', *International Review of Psycho-Analysis*, 2, pp. 145–56.

Gutmann, D. (1977) *The Cross-Cultural Perspective: Notes towards a Comparative Psychology of Ageing*. New York, Van Nostrand.

Hillman, J. (1964) *Suicide and the Soul*. London, Hodder & Stoughton.

Hillman, J. (1967) *Insearch: Psychology and Religion.* London, Hodder & Stoughton; and New York, Charles Scribner's Sons.

Hillman, J. (1971) 'Abandoning the Child', in Hillman (1975).

Hillman, J. (1975) *Loose Ends: Primary Papers in Archetypal Psychology.* New York/Zurich, Spring Publications.

Hobson, R. (1985) *Forms of Feeling: The Heart of Psychotherapy.* London and New York, Tavistock.

Hobson, R., and Meares, R. F. (1977) 'The Persecutory Therapist', *British Journal of Medical Psychology*, 50.

Hobson, R. (1979) 'The Messianic Community', in R. D. Hinshelwood and N. Manning, eds, *Therapeutic Communities.* London, Routledge & Kegan Paul.

James, W. (1902) *The Varieties of Religious Experience.* The Penguin American Library.

Jaques, E. (1955) 'Social Systems as a Defence against Depressive and Persecutory Anxiety', in *New Directions in Psychoanalysis.* London, Tavistock.

Jaques, E. (1965) 'Death and the Mid-Life Crisis', *International Journal of Psycho-Analysis*, 46, pp. 502–14.

Jung, C. G. *The Collected Works* (referred to in the text as CW with volume and paragraph number, edited by Read, H., Fordham, M., Adler, G., and McGuire, W., translated in the main by Hull, R. London, Routledge & Kegan Paul; Princeton University Press).

Jung, C. G. (1961) Interview in *Good Housekeeping.*

Jung, C. G. (1963) *Memories, Dreams and Reflections.* London, Collins and Routledge & Kegan Paul.

Jung, C. G. (1976) *Vision Seminars.* Spring Publications.

Khan, M. (1979) 'From Masochism to Psychic Pain', in *Alienation in Perversion.* London, Hogarth.

Lambert, K. (1981) *Analysis, Repair and Individuation.* London, Academic Press.

Leach, E. (1976) *Culture and Communication.* Cambridge University Press.

Levi, Peter (1987) *The Frontiers of Paradise: a Study of Monks and Monasteries.* London, Collins Harvill.

Levi, Primo (1989) *The Drowned and the Saved.* London, Sphere Books.

Lewis, E. (1979) 'Counter-Transference Problems in Hospital Practice', *British Journal of Medical Psychology* 52.

Mahler, M. (1969) *On Human Symbiosis and the Vicissitudes of Individuation*. London, Hogarth.

Meier, C. A. (1986) *Soul and Body*. Santa Monica, Lapis Press.

Merton, T. (1948; SPCK edn 1990) *The Seven Storey Mountain*. New York, Harcourt Brace Jovanovich; London, SPCK.

Morley, R. (1984) *Intimate Strangers*. London, Family Welfare Association.

Neumann, E. (1955) *The Great Mother*. Princeton University Press.

Neumann, E. (1973) *The Child*. New York, Harper & Row.

Plaut, F. (1975) 'A Note on Object Constancy or Constant Object', *Journal of Analytical Psychology* 20:2.

Redfearn, J. (1985) *My Self, My Many Selves*. London, Academic Press.

Reed, B. (1976) 'The Task of the Church' (unpublished).

Samuels, A. (1985) *Jung and the Post-Jungians*. London, Routledge & Kegan Paul.

Sandler, J. (1976) 'Counter-transference and Role-responsiveness', *International Review of Psycho-Analysis* 3, pp. 43–7.

Sartre, J.-P. (1943) *Being and Nothingness*. New York, Philosophical Library.

Schafer, R. (1973) 'The Idea of Resistance', *International Journal of Psycho-Analysis* 54:3.

Segal, H. (1973) *Introduction to the Work of Melanie Klein*. London, Hogarth.

Simmel, G. (1950) in K. Wolff, *The Sociology of George Simmel*. New York, Free Press.

Tuckman, B. (1965) 'Developmental Sequences in Small Groups', *Psychology Bulletin*, 63.

Tustin, F. (1986) *Autistic Barriers in Neurotic Patients*. London, Karnac.

von Bertalanffy, L. (1968) *General Systems Theory*. New York, Braziller.

von Franz, M-L. (1970) *Introduction to the Psychology of Fairy Tales*. New York, Spring Publications.

Whitehead, A. N. (1926) *Religion in the Making*. Cambridge

University Press.

Wilber, K. (1983) *Up from Eden*. London, Routledge & Kegan Paul.

Williams, M. (1948) 'My Own Experience of Group Therapy', *British Journal of Psychology and Social Work*, 2.

Williams, M. (1966) 'Changing Attitudes to Death', *Human Relations* 19:4.

Winnicott, D. W. (1947) 'Hate in the Counter-Transference', in *Collected Papers: Through Paediatrics to Psycho-Analysis*. London, Hogarth.

Winnicott, D. W. (1958) 'The Capacity to be Alone', in *The Maturational Processes and the Facilitating Environment*. London, Hogarth.

Winnicott, D. W. (1960a) 'Ego Distortion in Terms of the True and False Self', in *Maturational Processes and the Facilitating Environment*. London, Hogarth.

Winnicott, D. W. (1960b) 'On Security', in *The Family and Individual Development*. London, Tavistock.

Winnicott, D. W. (1966) 'The Child and the Family'. Talk given to Nursery School Association of Great Britain and Northern Ireland, New College, Oxford.

Winnicott, D. W. (1967a) 'The Location of Cultural Experience', *International Journal of Psycho-Analysis* 48:3.

Winnicott, D. W. (1967b) 'Mirror-role of Mother and Family in Child Development', in *Playing and Reality*. London, Penguin.

Winnicott, D. W. (1968a) 'Contemporary Concepts of Adolescent Development and their Implications for Higher Education', in *Playing and Reality*. London, Penguin.

Winnicott, D. W. (1968b) 'Communication between Infant and Mother, Mother and Infant, Compared and Contrasted', in *What Is Psychoanalysis? The Institute of Psycho-Analysis*. London, Baillière, Tindall and Cassell.

Winnicott, D. W. (1986) *Holding and Interpreting*. London, Hogarth.

Yalom, I. D. (1970) *Theory and Practice of Group Psycho-therapy*. New York, Basic Books.

Zinkin, L. (1989) 'A Gnostic View of the Therapy Group', *Group Analysis*, 22:2.

Index

abandonment 197, 209-10
Abelin, E. 42-3
accidie 141
active imagination 189-90
adolescence 50-3
agape 29
Alvarez, A. 210
alchemy 72-4, 173, 191
anima 58-9, 98, 180-1
animus 58-9, 180-1
anthropology 74
anxious attachment 196-7
archetype 43, 99; defined 104;
  Job archetype 72
archetypal image: bipolarity 23;
  identification with 102-4; nature
  of 16, 101-2; of the feminine
  61, 124; split in 23
archetypal images: child 197;
  contrasexual 180-1; Chiron 23;
  Great Mother 102, 154, 181;
  Hero 154, 214; Old Wise Man
  13, 66, 125, 154, 181; Old Wise
  Woman 66; Saviour Hero 22,
  103, 125; Trickster 103;
  Wounded Healer 23
archetypal processes 170
Assumption, the 164

baby: and mother's hatred 141;
  mother-baby as prototype of
  ego-self 29
basic catastrophe 105
befriending 86, 137
Bion, W. 147-9
bisexuality 36
bitterness 72
Boyd, R. 180
Buddhism 143
Butler, J. 155

case examples: Adam 35-6;
  Aletheia 91-3; Alfred 68-70;
  Andrea 112-13; Andrew
  199-201; Angela 84-5; Archie
  77-8; Austin and
  Zebedee 93-5; Ben 41-2;
  Bernard 208-9; Beth 130;
  Brian 52-3, 105-7; David 81-2;
  David and Geraldine 128;
  Dominic 130-1; Don 142;
  Elizabeth 10-11; Emily 47-8;
  Eric 134-6; Fleur 189-90; Gareth
  97-9; Hermione 168-70; Hilda
  214-15; Hugh 108-9; James
  210-11; Jane 197; Jim 13-16;
  Jeremy 78-80; Jessie 207-8;
  Jonah 118-19; Justin 20; Kim
  205-7; Lawrence 111-12;
  Marion 42; Maureen 126-7;
  Melanie 45; Nick and Julie 57;
  Paddy 201-3; Peter 88;
  Philippa 24-6; Rufus 1;
  Sandra 128-9; Suzie 86-7;
  Tessa 194-5; Thomas 127;
  Tony 9; Tristram 118;
  Verity 107; Victor 193; Veronica
  132-3; Wendy 82-4
change: ch.3 *passim.*
Christ 141, 143
clinging 199-203
Coate, M. A. 86
coincidentia oppositorum 174
compensation, principle of 15
complex: defined 99-101;
  martyr 18
community 143-5, 149-50
confidentiality 76-80
conflict of opposites 55
coniunctio 61, 164; and gay
  couples 63; and groups 148

226